THE MANY FACETS OF TOUCH

Summary Publications in the Johnson & Johnson Baby
Products Company Pediatric Round Table Series:

THE MANY FACETS OF TOUCH

The Foundation of Experience: Its Importance
Through Life, With Initial Emphasis For
Infants and Young Children

**Chaired by
Kathryn F. Barnard, R.N., Ph.D.
T. Berry Brazelton, M.D.**

**Edited By
Catherine Caldwell Brown**

**Introduction By
T. Berry Brazelton, M.D.**

Sponsored by

Johnson & Johnson

BABY PRODUCTS COMPANY

Library of Congress Cataloging in Publication Data
Main entry under title:

The many facets of touch.

(Johnson & Johnson Baby Products Company pediatric
round table series; 10)

Bibliography: p.
1. Child development. 2. Touch—Psychological aspects. 3. Touch—Therapeutic use.
4. Infants (Premature)—Care and hygiene. 5. Sick—Psychology. I. Brown, Catherine
Caldwell. II. Series. [DNLM: 1. Touch—congresses. 2. Touch—in infancy & childhood—
congresses. 3. Nonverbal Communication—congresses. WR 102 M295 1983]

RJ131.M3133 1984   155.4'12   84-10030

ISBN 0-931562-12-0

*Toward a better understanding of the contribution
that touch will make for the human condition*

CONTENTS

PARTICIPANTS

Kathryn Barnard, R.N., Ph.D.
Professor of Nursing
University of Washington
CDMRC Residence Building
Office #212, Mail Code WJ10
Seattle, Washington 98195

M. Louise Biggar, Ph.D.
Box 185
Cheyney, Pennsylvania 19319

T. Berry Brazelton, M.D.
Chief, Child Development Unit
The Children's Hospital
  Medical Center
333 Longwood Avenue
Boston, Massachusetts 02115

Catherine Caldwell Brown, M.A.
Science Writer
105 Somerville Road
Ridgewood, New Jersey 07450

Marie-Thérèse Connell, M.A., R.N.
78 8th Avenue, Apt. 6G
Brooklyn, New York 11215

James T. Dettre
Director of Marketing Services
Johnson & Johnson Baby Products
  Company
Grandview Road
Skillman, New Jersey 08558

Marian C. Diamond, Ph.D.
Professor of Anatomy
Department of Physiology-Anatomy
University of California
Berkeley, California 94720

William C. Egan
Director of Marketing
Johnson & Johnson Baby Products
  Company
Grandview Road
Skillman, New Jersey 08558

Cathleen A. Fanslow, M.A., R.N.
Visiting Nurse Service of New York
107 East 70th Street
New York, New York 10021

Peter Gorski, M.D.
Director, Developmental and
  Behavioral Pediatrics
Mount Zion Hospital and
  Medical Center
Department of Pediatrics, Box 7921
San Francisco, California 94120

Allen W. Gottfried, Ph.D.
Associate Professor of Psychology
  and Pediatrics
Department of Psychology
California State University
Fullerton, California 92634

William T. Greenough, Ph.D.
Professor of Psychology and
  Anatomical Sciences
Department of Psychology
University of Illinois
603 East Daniel Street
  (829 Psychology)
Urbana-Champaign, Illinois 61820

Florence Helitzer
Science Writer
59 Harrison Street
Princeton, New Jersey 08540

James H. Johnson
Director of Hospital and
  Professional Programs
Johnson & Johnson Baby Products
  Company
Grandview Road
Skillman, New Jersey 08558

Anneliese F. Korner, Ph.D.
Professor of Psychiatry and the
  Behavioral Sciences
Stanford University School of
  Medicine
Department of Psychiatry and
  Behavioral Sciences
Stanford, California 94305

Seymour Levine, Ph.D.
Professor of Psychiatry
Stanford University School of
  Medicine TD114
Department of Psychiatry and
  Behavioral Sciences
Stanford, California 94305

Carla G. Lounsbury
Senior Administrator,
  Consumer Education
Johnson & Johnson Baby Products
  Company
Grandview Road
Skillman, New Jersey 08558

Jerold F. Lucey, M.D., FAAP
Professor of Pediatrics
Medical Center Hospital of Vermont
Editor-in-Chief, *Pediatrics*
Pediatrics Editorial Office
Mary Fletcher Hospital
Burlington, Vermont 05401

Elizabeth R. McAnarney, M.D.
Director, Division of Biosocial
  Pediatrics and Adolescent Medicine
The University of Rochester
  Medical Center
601 Elmwood Avenue
Rochester, New York 14642

Ruth McCorkle, R.N., Ph.D.
Associate Professor of Nursing
University of Washington
School of Nursing
Mail Stop SM-24
Seattle, Washington 98195

Michael M. Merzenich, Ph.D.
Director of the Coleman Laboratory
Professor of Otolaryngology
  and Physiology
University of California School
  of Medicine
Department of Otolaryngology
  863 HSE
San Francisco, California 94143

Bonnie J. Petrauskas
Professional Relations
Johnson & Johnson Baby Products
  Company
Grandview Road
Skillman, New Jersey 08558

Patricia Boudolf Rausch,
  R.N., M.S.N.
799 Torchwood Drive
Deland, Florida 32720

Martin L. Reite, M.D.
Professor of Psychiatry
University of Colorado
  Health Sciences Center
4200 East Ninth Avenue C268
Denver, Colorado 80262

Robert B. Rock, Jr., M.A., M.P.A.
Director of Professional Relations
Johnson & Johnson Baby Products
  Company
Grandview Road
Skillman, New Jersey 08558

Susan A. Rose, Ph.D.
Professor of Psychiatry
Department of Psychiatry
Albert Einstein College of Medicine
  of Yeshiva University
1300 Morris Park Avenue
Bronx, New York 10461

Paul Satz, Ph.D.
Chief of Neuropsychology
Neuropsychiatric Institute
University of California, Los Angeles
Department of Psychiatry and
  Behavioral Sciences
760 Westwood Plaza, C8-747/NPI
Los Angeles, California 90024

Steven Sawchuck, M.D.
Chairman, Institute for Pediatric
  Service
Director of Medical Services
Johnson & Johnson Baby Products
  Company
Grandview Road
Skillman, New Jersey 08558

Judith A. Smith, R.N., Ph.D.
Head, Family-Community Section
University of Pennsylvania
School of Nursing,
  Nursing Education Building
420 Service Drive S2
Philadelphia, Pennsylvania 19104

Stephen J. Suomi, Ph.D.
Chief, Laboratory of Comparative
  Ethology
National Institute of Child Health
  and Human Development
Building 31, Room B2B15
National Institutes of Health
9000 Rockville Pike
Bethesda, Maryland 20205

James R. Utaski
President
Johnson & Johnson Baby Products
  Company
Grandview Road
Skillman, New Jersey 08558

Renée Weber, Ph.D.
Professor of Philosophy
Department of Philosophy -
  Douglass Campus
Rutgers University
New Brunswick, New Jersey 08903

Sandra J. Weiss, R.N., D.N.Sc.
Associate Professor of Nursing
  and Associate Dean
University of California
School of Nursing
San Francisco, California 94120

Iris S. Wolfson, R.N., B.S., C.N.M.
Private Practice
Homebirth and Nurse Midwifery
  Service
5519 Greene Street
Philadelphia, Pennsylvania 19144

PREFACE

The interest of the Johnson & Johnson Baby Products Company in the subject of touch may, perhaps, be obvious; it is certainly long standing. The reason for this is inherent in the product-use relationship established between mother/caregiver and baby, which for years has been coupled with the concept of "a touch of love." However, the company's interest has been both broader and deeper in its desire to consider the many faceted connections between parental emotional attitudes expressed through touch and a scientific basis for growth and development.

Over the past decade the availability of new research data on the importance of touch, or its deprivation, to the bonding process between mother and newborn expanded the subject area to the point where there was keen interest in a broader scientific review. This took the form of the Johnson & Johnson Pediatric Round Table #10, the faculty for which was brought together to consider *TOUCH — The Foundation of Experience: Its Importance Through Life, With Initial Emphasis for Infants and Young Children.* The Round Table's stated objectives were "to focus on scientific data, through the medium of a multidisciplinary faculty, which will bring together meaningful information on the importance of touch to growth and development through the human life spectrum, with emphasis on its special significance for infants and young children."

The multidisciplinary faculty, composed of twenty-three of the world's leading authorities on broadly related subjects in this field, were appropriately positioned in the professional perspectives of nursing and medicine by the Round Table's co-moderators, Kathryn F. Barnard, R.N., Ph.D. and T. Berry Brazelton, M.D. Set against an unusual and perceptive philosophical background, the participants' comments emphasized neuroanatomical, developmental and clinical perspectives. The results of their presentations and related discussions — which were certainly the most intensive of any Round Table in this series — have led to this summary publication, *The Many Facets of Touch.* We hope its readers will feel as rewarded by its contents as all those associated with its publication.

Robert B. Rock, Jr., M.A., M.P.A.
Director of Professional Relations

INTRODUCTION

The round table summarized in this book is probably one of the first symposia that has addressed the modality of touch as a single entity. Despite its identified importance as a communication system and as an integral factor in survival, its effects are hard to isolate. Touch has been addressed empirically in combination with other systems — vestibular, pain, pressure, visuomotor. The difficulty in isolating its effects has prevented attention to its importance as a modality.

Yet, the complexity of this modality makes it a fascinating focus for research. In order to identify critical areas as one probes for the limits of this modality, one must first describe the various functions served by touch. In the area of passive touch (of being touched), the following functions come to mind: (1) pain, (2) alerting an organism to protect itself, (3) stimulating the organism to awaken and move on to an alert state for responsiveness, (4) communicating of such information as tenderness, caring, direction, (5) organizing for learning disabled, (6) controlling excessive input and hyperresponsiveness. Self-touching can be used for (1) exploration, (2) self-stimulation, (3) self-control. In the area of active touching, touch can be used (1) to explore, (2) to alert another, (3) to communicate with another, (4) to cement a word or a communication, (5) to modulate or calm another. These do not make up an exhaustive list but are suggestive of the complexity of this modality.

Our goal in setting up this seminar was to attempt to define this modality and to examine the implications of tactile stimulation and deprivation for the developing organism. By mapping the areas in the brain which represent this modality, we can begin to see what a violation of the expected and even necessary tactile input might mean at an anatomical level. Animal studies of deprivation and of enrichment could contribute paradigms for studies of the developing human. In the area of high-risk premature and underweight neonates, there is increasing evidence for autonomic as well as anatomical effects. Opportunities for recovery from impairment in immature brains are increasingly recognized to be much greater than we had previously thought, thanks to the redundancy of unassigned neurological pathways in immature humans. Tactile experiences need to be graded for their appropriateness versus their inappropriateness in providing organizing information to promote recovery from damage and functional assignment of the undamaged pathways. Cross-modal transfer from tactile to other modalities seems to enhance this recovery and may become a way of assessing for future competence in immature organisms. The use of touch as therapy in older, disorganized infants and children is beginning to be explored in more detail. In hypersensitive or disorganized hyperkinetic or even learning disabled children, touch can be seen as therapeutic. For sick or disturbed older children and adults, especially the elderly, the modality of touch can be of major therapeutic value. The nursing profession has become inspired recently with uses of therapeutic touch — a concept of the tactile and kinesthetic modalities in which the therapy focuses on touch as a major mode of communication and reorganization. Touch is having a new heyday.

My own thinking about touch and the newborn baby comes from my experience with neonatal assessment and is based on the idea that there is a kind of programming in the infant, apparent at birth, which demonstrates that in any modality there are three sources of energy for development. These sources are shown in Figure 1. Maturation of the central nervous system is the main force, and also the main limiter. The other two fuelers of development are the internal feedback system and the external feedback system.

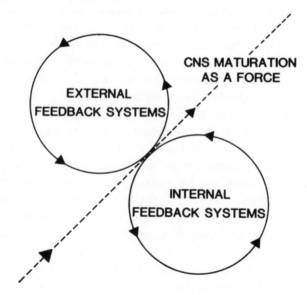

Figure 1. Three Sources of Energy for Development.

To illustrate how these systems interact, consider a newborn baby who puts together several reflex behaviors and pulls off a complex behavior. For instance, when an infant is coming from sleep to awake and about to lose control in crying, he will make massive efforts to try to keep himself under control. As you watch him, he'll throw off first a tonic neck reflex, then a Babkin reflex (bringing the hand up to the mouth), then a third reflex of rooting, and if he gets his thumb or finger into his mouth, a fourth reflex, sucking. He has used his own tactile areas of mouth and finger to complete an internal cycle of behavior. The touch completes his recognition of this. As he begins to suck and get himself under control so he can take information, which is my idea of what he was programmed for, he signs and brightens. You see the internal feedback system go off as he looks around the room as if to say, "Wow, this is what I was trying to do the whole time." If an adult is there to lean down, touch him, contain him, to say, "That was just great," the external feedback system is operating as well. This goes on throughout infancy.

Touch may be one of the main intersensory integrators, and one of the main consolidators or cementers of development. In the neonate, it can be either a stimulator or a reducer of stimulation, depending on the situation and the state of the infant. It can become a control system. In the nursery, you may see a baby who's losing control, and then somebody just puts a hand gently on her and she subsides. This shows how powerful touch is as a control. It can both instigate and maintain communication between the outside and inside feedback systems.

Obviously, it is difficult to separate touch from the things that go with it. In the infant, for instance, reaching, grasping, and manipulating all convey qualities of intentionality. There is satisfaction in anticipation and in achievement. These obviously affect the feedback from the outside. If the infant has intentionality, anticipation, and then finally achievement, the whole system of touch is reinforced in a very significant way. Linking his thumb with his mouth, a final achievement in producing a control system for himself, makes this program of primary importance.

Touch is a very powerful conveyor of messages. Just what message a touch conveys depends on the state of the organism, particularly in the infant. If the baby is in an alert state, touch means something very significantly different from what it means in other states — as information, control, or even pain. On the other hand, infants in a sleepy state may become alert if an adult touches them.

The quality of a touch — the location, rhythm, intensity, and so on — also determines its message. In a study we have been conducting of face-to-face interactions between parents and infants, we have found that babies, by six weeks of age, behave differently toward the mother, the father, and a stranger. They do this partly because mothers and fathers behave differently toward their infants. When mothers touch a baby, they do it to control, to facilitate alertness, and to smooth the baby down, and then they begin to react in a rhythmic way. Fathers never do that, even primary caretaking fathers. Their attempt in touching is to jazz the baby up. They are more likely to poke and to touch abruptly, going from lower extremities up to the baby's face. She, in turn, responds by laughter and excitement. The infant comes to expect these predictable behaviors from each parent. The mother and the father set up a different expectancy for touch as well as other kinds of communicative modalities starting at birth, and we find that their behavior is likely to be sex-linked.

The papers which follow represent the best of the scientists who are studying and attempting to identify this modality. They are from several disciplines. Their approaches vary in accordance with Kathryn Barnard's and my plan as co-moderators to start with anatomy and neurophysiology and then proceed through animal behavior to humans — both immature and mature. The last part of the book touches on the revival in nursing of utilizing this modality as specific therapy — therapeutic touch. It is not a new concept, as the reader will recognize, but its renewed use by nurses represents a vigorous attempt on their part to promote health and healing in at-risk patients of all ages, and to treat whole persons rather than particular pathologies. We hope this volume will enrich and further the investigation of touch as a vital modality for the human organism.

T. Berry Brazelton, M.D.

PART I
PHILOSOPHICAL
PERSPECTIVES

In "Philosophers on Touch," Renée Weber constructs a three-part philosophical framework for the varied scientific perspectives on touch presented in the papers and discussion that follow. Some of the Round Table participants, she would say, have adopted a physical-sensory model of human experience, as formulated by Hume and Descartes. Some prefer a second model, a humanistic-phenomenological approach that emphasizes subjective meaning as the ultimate reality. And some (the nurses whose papers on the healing technique called therapeutic touch appear in Parts VI and VII) have chosen a third model, the field model. Derived from Eastern metaphysics and buttressed by recent work in theoretical physics, this holistic world view maintains that physical boundaries separating "objects" from each other and from "space" are illusions, an idea that gives touch tremendous potential power.

PART 1
PHILOSOPHICAL PERSPECTIVES

PHILOSOPHERS ON TOUCH

Renée Weber, Ph.D.

What is a humanist to say to an audience of scientists and social scientists about touch from the philosophical perspective? To me, the unique task of the humanities is an integrative one. Humanism tries to synthesize what the sciences and social sciences must necessarily take apart in the course of their analyses and research. The focus of this paper is therefore holistic. It explores touch from a theoretical and speculative viewpoint and is not data-based.

Philosophical writing on touch is rare. Given the paucity of explicit material, I will look at some representative philosophical views and — though they may not deal with touch explicitly — extrapolate from their general position what their view on touch would most likely be.

Models of the Person and Nature

I intend to map the concept of touch onto three divergent models of the person and nature: the physical-sensory model, the psychological-humanistic model, and the field model. The last is a bold and intriguing view. Its offshoot, the theory of therapeutic touch, is the most novel philosophical framework applicable to touch and the only one which devotes itself explicitly to the subject.

What is touch? The dictionary distinguishes three relevant meanings. *Touch* can mean "to be in contact with"; "to reach and to communicate"; or "to lay the hand or hands on." These three definitions correspond roughly to the three models I have outlined. The physical-sensory model restricts its interest mainly to the contact definition. The psychological-humanistic model explores touch as a way of reaching and communicating with a self or inner person. The field model draws on this definition but also, in therapeutic touch (for example), sees touch as a laying on of hands.

These three models of touch can be correlated with distinct cultural and philosophical contexts. The physical-sensory model fits the aims and assumptions of Anglo-American philosophy. The psychological-humanistic model expresses the concerns of contemporary continental philosophy, especially phenomenology and existentialism. The field model and therapeutic touch best harmonize with Eastern philosophy and its

3

holistic world view.

Touch as an interactional modality has been neglected by Western philosophy. Especially in the last three hundred years, since the time of Descartes, only mental and verbal exchanges have been considered important. Since the eighteenth century and the work of the British empiricists, interest has shifted to sensory input. Contemporary Anglo-American philosophy, the heir of Descartes and Hume, tends to be reductionist, as is much of psychology. It tends to reduce touch to its constituent aspects.

To treat a holistic sense such as touch within a reductionist framework seems paradoxical. Existentialism and phenomenology provide a somewhat more hospitable climate for the humanistic implications of touch. But the richest and most holistic framework for a theory of touch comes from the philosophies of the East, from Hindu, Buddhist, and Taoist thought. Eastern philosophy depicts human beings and nature as inherently linked and even one, at some deeper level of their being. It postulates the existence of energies beyond those currently described by science, which — though not quantifiable or at present well understood — seem to play a distinct role in human well-being. One such vital energy is *prana*, postulated by virtually all Eastern philosophies to be a key factor in human health and well-being.

According to the theory of therapeutic touch, a healthy organism with abundant energy can deliberately and with conscious intent direct that vital energy to someone depleted of it or low in it. A Western precursor of this idea appears in Michelangelo's Renaissance masterpiece, The Creation of Man, in the Sistine Chapel. Michelangelo has God stretch out a dynamic hand toward the limp and lifeless hand of Adam in order to transmit the spark of life to it. This vision of touch as the bearer of vital energy may be an early and intuitive rendition of the principle of field touch. Its most arresting feature is the positioning of the hands, which are the focal point of the composition. These hands do not touch; they *nearly* touch.

The Ancient Greeks

Michelangelo's esteem of touch is shared by antiquity. The ancient Greeks held rival theories of touch. Plato espoused a nonlocalization theory; Aristotle, a direct contact theory. The Platonic concept of nonlocalization is a forerunner of the field theory of touch. It emphasizes that touch is something generalized, a synthesis of the function of the body, and perhaps of the body and mind, soul, or spirit.

For both Plato and Aristotle, human beings are rational animals, possessing a mind and a soul that make use of and direct the senses. This is most clearly brought out by Plato, who rejects the idea that knowledge is only sense perception. For example, in the *Theaetetus,* Plato observes that we perceive *through* the senses as well as *with* them, for the senses "all meet in some one nature, the mind, or whatever we please to call it, of which they are the instruments" (Jowett, 1937). The interesting question is, who or what is this "we" to which Plato refers?

Descartes and Hume

To Descartes, as to seventeenth-century rationalism in general, the perceiver is the inner person, self, or thinker whom he describes in his *cogito* doctrine: "I think, therefore I am." This entity is distinct from sensation and, indeed, from the body. The mind-body dualism that Descartes establishes in his *Meditations* has persisted largely until our day. Descartes confesses that he cannot really account for the interaction of body and mind. Moreover, he bequeaths to philosophy a doctrine of interpersonal difficulty that borders on alienation: his Cartesian solipsism. Since I can have direct access to and thus certainty only of my own mind (hence, self), I can never be certain that other minds or selves — that is, whole human beings — exist. Cartesian solipsism casts serious doubt on touch as a tool of genuine communication among people. Despite the primacy of consciousness and the irreducibility of the self in the *cogito,* Descartes' position belongs to the physical-sensory model.

The outstanding figure associated with this model is David Hume, the great British empiricist, whose universe is built upon the idea of sense impressions. Nothing but these are ultimately real, and all our ideas are just modifications of sense impressions. They are the building blocks of knowledge. Whatever ideas cannot be traced back to them are based on self-deception.

Hume's influence on contemporary philosophy is vast. By his criterion, touch would have to be explained as sense impressions impinging upon sense impressions, mediated perhaps by some neurologically complex mechanism for registering and encoding them. Touch does not involve the whole person but is explained in physical terms, as one set of stimuli approaching another set. The idea of reaching an inward self, as in the other two models, is ruled out. In fact, since we never have a sense impression of the self, Hume terms the notion a fiction.

The therapeutic role that intent associated with touch might play is incompatible with Hume's and other versions of reductionism. Behavior rather than intent or mind-set shapes human interactions, and it satisfies the definition of touch as "reaching" another. The reaching, in Hume, cannot apply to an invisible "inner" person, for that is reduced to a bundle of habits by Hume (as by Skinner, his heir).

Existentialism and Phenomenology

The psychological-humanistic model is more holistic than the physical-sensory model, less so than the field model. It concerns itself with the purposive interaction of self-conscious agents and focuses on such uniquely human feelings as sympathy, empathy, and love. Individuality, personhood, and the subjectivity and inwardness of consciousness are its building blocks. The power of human interaction derives from imaginative ways of relating to others, who are conceived as irreducible and autonomous agents like oneself. Their existence cannot be proved, but it is disclosed to us with the same certainty as is our own.

Meaning, for the psychological model, is as fundamental a datum as sense impressions are for the empirical model; it constitutes the core of the human experience. Our ecological niche is the interpersonal world, linked by symbols, social categories, and shared cultural contexts.

In the psychological model social exchange is considered the basic fact of existence. Communication and communion, or their breakdown in alienation and isolation, are the earmarks of the uniquely human world. They are irreducibles, and reducing them to a more primary set of explanations explains them away and loses their meaning.

Not all the figures that may be grouped within this model focus on the positive aspects of human interchange. For example, in Sartre's world, conflict and competition predominate. For Sartre, touch is a threat to autonomy, used to manipulate others. That is because Sartre transposes the power of the look — his central epistemological category and the tool for appropriating others — to the domain of touch. Phenomenologist Merleau-Ponty rejects this view. Touch, unlike the other senses, is inherently reciprocal. "In the very act of touching, one is touched in return.... In touch, the distinction between touching subject and touched object blurs" (Mazis, 1971).

I-It Versus I-Thou Relationships

If Sartre is the pessimistic end of the humanistic spectrum, its other extreme is Martin Buber. He distinguishes between an I-It and an I-Thou mode of relating to others. Manipulation and handling would be an I-It mode of physical interaction; touch would be an I-Thou mode. The I-It mode is object-oriented, reductionist, utilitarian, and judgmental. It reduces the other to qualities or components, like the parts of a watch, and treats the other as external to the self. The I-Thou relationship is holistic. It perceives the other as a total *Gestalt* within a framework of acceptance and mutuality. It is a living relationship, with its own dimensions of space and time that differ from ordinary space and from clock-time.

Buber notes that children, above all, live in the I-Thou dimension more than they live in the I-It. For Buber, it is part of our existential tragedy that we cannot remain exclusively in the I-Thou dimension but are forced through daily necessity to convert the Thou back into a utilitarian It, with which no genuine relationship — that is, mutuality — can exist.

Although Buber's theory furnishes a framework for touch, he does not address the topic directly. We come closer to this in a philosophical novelist like Tolstoy, in whose classic, *The Death of Ivan Ilych,* touch becomes the denouement of the whole work. Ivan Ilych, tormented on a lonely deathbed and wracked by pain, feels totally isolated from those around him. He asks himself, "Why, and for what reason, is there all this horror?" and finds no answer. As he struggles to die, he suddenly becomes aware of the touch of a hand upon his own, followed by a trickle of tears. This gesture by his school-boy son reverses the I-It status of their relationship and changes it to an I-Thou mode. The transformation enables Ivan Ilych to die reconciled with his family and at peace with himself. For the first time he feels love, not only for his son but even for his cold and calculating wife. Beyond this, Tolstoy hints that Ivan Ilych links up with a nonfinite level of being that transcends time and space, whose touch dissolves his fear of death.

Tolstoy's work is one of the few examples in philosophy and literature in which touch functions therapeutically, in the original Greek sense of the word. *Therapeuein* means "to take care of," and its humanistic roots are preserved in the word itself, for *therapon* meant "attendant," a living person. Thus, *therapeutic,* which today signifies "curative, having healing qualities," derives from the care shown to one person by another, the *therapon* or healing presence.

Therapeutic Touch

The theory of therapeutic touch rejects the dualistic view of Descartes and the simplified materialism of Hume. In their stead, it proposes "an energetic perspective, in which individuals are interconnected and local concentrations within a larger field.... Underlying this model is the assumption that the energies interchanged in ordinary human interactions are modulated in (via) a universal field which permeates all matter" (Kunz & Peper, 1982). In other words, human interactions are interpreted as field phenomena, not as atomistic exchanges by atomistically conceived units.

Preliminary studies show that therapeutic touch as a clinical technique has some promise in the alleviation of pain, anxiety, and other problems. Because of its soothing and noninvasive nature, therapeutic touch can be used from the moment the neonate emerges into the world and throughout the life spectrum. It may be especially appropriate with the terminally ill and dying, whom it can envelop in an affirming atmosphere even in the absence of language.

Ideally, therapeutic touch aims (as do all health strategies) at restoring order. It can be viewed as helping the body to speed up its innate healing powers and tendency toward homeostasis. Although the technique may seem to focus on the physical body, its emphasis is on the whole person. This harmonizes with current reform in medical education, where a less fragmented and more humanistic approach to patients is now being actively sought.

Emotional and other well-being may be as direct a consequence of therapeutic touch as physical improvement. At times, as was the case with the fictitious Ivan Ilych, it may not be possible to reverse the physical disorder. Yet Ivan Ilych, though he died, was helped — healed, Tolstoy implies — at other levels.

The objection could be raised that enhanced well-being in the absence of clinical concomitants can be attributed to the placebo effect. Certainly the physical-sensory model would legitimately voice this concern. However, if field theory is correct, the so-called placebo effect may be an instance of, and hence evidence for, field interactions that account for changes in the person. According to this reasoning, to attribute the changes to the placebo effect is to beg the question.

The point, of course, cannot be settled at this early juncture. One can note, however, that therapeutic touch is an area in which the positivist-physicalist model of proof may not be appropriate. New paradigms of explanation and proof may have to be devised, combining rigor of mind with intuitive sensitivity to subtler energies, and allowing for the human element which is carefully factored out in traditional research.

Quantum Mechanics

Asked about the applications of quantum mechanics to human interaction, physicist David Bohm offers a view similar to that of Kunz and Peper's field model. He says:

> There are two views of space. One view is to say the skin is
> the boundary of ourselves, saying there is the space without

and the space within. The space within is the separate self, obviously, and the space without is the space which separates the separate selves.... Therefore to overcome the separation you must have a process of moving through that space, which takes time.... Now if we took the view of (Bohm's implicate order physics), with this vast reserve of energy and empty space, saying that matter itself is that small wave on empty space, then we could better say that the space as a whole...is the ground of existence, and we are in it. So the space doesn't separate us, it unites us. Therefore it's like saying that there are two separate points and a certain dotted line connects them...or to say there is a real line and that the points are abstractions from that.... The line is the reality and the points are abstractions (Weber, 1982).

What common-sense naive realism takes to be empty space, Bohm says, is in fact teeming waves of energy. In that ocean of energy, as he terms it, everything is connected. All human beings, together with every particle in the universe, are the outcome of the history of the universe and store that history at some level of themselves. When pressed, Bohm insists that this is not a poetic metaphor but good physics.

Eros and Agape

A central premise of therapeutic touch is that compassion is the essential factor in healing. Touch with compassionate intent somehow synchronizes our innate energies with those found in nature. Like Plato, therapeutic touch assumes that we touch *through* our hands as well as *with* our hands. Alongside the emphasis on compassion, there is equal emphasis on nonattachment. The caring must be intense but not personal. This sounds paradoxical and admittedly is difficult in practice.

The idea of touch may appear inseparable from the idea of involvement in the sense of ego-investment, but this need not be so. A rich tradition in our heritage revolves around this very issue. In classical Greece, *eros* was identified with secular love, with the senses, desire, and self-interest. Giving was construed as inseparable from the hope of return. *Agape,* on the other hand, was sacred love, apart from the senses, not born of desire, and purged of self-interest. It came close to what we term compassion.

Like touch, *eros* has been narrowly interpreted in Western culture, equated with romantic and sexual love and restricted to it. In the twentieth century, it has increasingly been portrayed as narcissistic and self-seeking, and treated in an I-It context. For this reason it may have appeared an unlikely candidate for therapeutic functions. At the other end of the scale, *agape,* once sacralized all human relationships as expressions of God and frowned on sensory means of communication. Its effort was to purge itself of matter, which in some medieval philosophy as in Puritan theories held a quasi-sinful status.

The dissociation of *eros* from *agape* may account for the long delay in our awareness of the therapeutic power of touch. Far from seeing *eros* and *agape* as mutually exclusive, therapeutic touch reconciles and integrates them. Given compassionate intent, touch can become the most *agapaic* form of *eros.*

This view of the unity of love brings us back to Plato. For Plato, *eros* is the physical counterpart of a universal creative principle, much as it is in field theory, in Bohm, and in Buber. His seven-step ladder of love in the *Symposium* symbolizes a force that underlies all human desire and striving. The love that originates in the touch of one person ends in the embrace of the universe.

What begins with the particular leads to the universal. This outlook relates Plato to the field model. Field touch is the expression of the *therapon* that reaches across the boundaries by which we believe our world to be confined and links us to as yet mostly uncharted regions of nature and ourselves. Touch so construed is a resource which begins in human interaction and flows outward in widening circles to dimensions where nonordinary models of space, time, energy, and consciousness seem to apply.

DISCUSSION

Seymour Levine: Don't the philosophical models you've described apply primarily to Western medicine, which is only a small percentage of the world's medicine? They may have developed because of Western empiricism, and out of our whole set of cultural conditions. Eastern cultures have a complex of medical practices that are very aware of holistic approaches and organic medicine. These practices need to be considered in discussing the Eastern philosophical position, which may well have led to them.

Renée Weber: The third model I discussed, the field model, is the underlying assumption of Eastern thought. At some deep level in virtually all the Eastern metaphysics, we are all interdependent and interconnected. We're actually not separate entities. In contrast, Western philosophy since the time of Descartes has encouraged an atomistic and fragmentary approach in Western medicine. According to seventeenth- and eighteenth-century assumptions, people are like discrete little billiard balls. Twentieth-century physics denies this, but our ordinary language is still Cartesian and dualistic and does not reflect the new paradigm.

Seymour Levine: A new field is now trying to emerge called psycho-immunology. The term is bad — it illustrates your point about Cartesian language because again it implies a dualism — but the idea is good. A massive amount of information is available implicating psychologic issues in basic regulatory functions. However, there's tremendous resistance in the Western medical community to the viewpoint that there is an organism which is essentially in tune with its environment and whose environment very much affects its functions. Physicians have almost a vested interest in seeing those functions as autoregulatory rather than holistically regulatory.

T. Berry Brazelton: Is empiricism holding us back? Is it a symptom of where we were and what we are trying to break out of? Renée, I'm trying to relate Buber's I-It and I-Thou modes to what we see mothers do when they touch their babies. A mother in an I-Thou mode senses what's going on in the baby, what state the baby is in, and she adapts her touch to that. A complex unconscious regulatory system seems to be operating. The complexity of that system, it seems to me as a clinician, is what we ought to be after.

Seymour Levine: The behavior pattern you're describing is not exclusively human. If you spend enough time watching a variety of animals interact with their infants, as many of us here have, you tend to think of mother-infant behavior in terms of signals and communication. The system is tuned to the survival of the infant, and what goes into the survival of the infant is essentially a set of mutual dyadic interactive processes.

William Greenough: What do you think it was that led Eastern cultures, which long ago were ahead of us empirically and "scientifically," to choose such a different direction from the one we chose in the West.

Renée Weber: Why did Eastern thinkers come to the almost axiomatic notion of unity and interconnectedness, and why did they stress that rather than individuality and separation? If pressed, I would say it must have been experiential. It was empiricism, but inner empiricism, and the most appropriate word to describe that is meditation. I think they turned within (now I'm using Cartesian language, which is wrong again), and through inner empiricism they discovered meditation and yoga. They experienced something within, and that became the supporting premise of their metaphysics and their stated ethics.

William Greenough: Western science has an inner empirical method, too — namely, introspection — but that approach developed completely differently.

Renée Weber: But introspection is not meditation. Introspection is dualistic. It sets up an object and a subject. Meditation is a state of consciousness that cuts across the dualism of subject and object. Obviously, this is very difficult to understand and to handle verbally, but that's the important distinction. But, if we go a step farther back and ask, why did they stumble upon meditation and why did we not, I cannot answer.

T. Berry Brazelton: One of the reasons for this whole conference is that we'd like to get beyond the empirical approaches that we have at our fingertips now, so that we can learn more about interconnections, complex systems, and ways of communicating via them. I feel a tremendous need for more research on the field model, partly in order to understand it better and partly to support the work of clinicians who are trying to use a more holistic approach to healing. A gifted clinician who gets some scientifically credible research back-up suddenly feels on another level in terms of what he or she can provide for people in a dyadic interaction such as nursing or medicine. As we design studies to provide that back-up, I think it's very clear we need to get beyond the stimulus-response kind of empiricism that most of us have been trained in.

Neuroanatomical Perspectives

PART II
TOUCH AND BRAIN PLASTICITY

What happens in the neocortex of the brain in response to touch and other sensory experiences? In the first of three papers on this topic, Michael Merzenich describes studies from his laboratory showing that representations, or maps, in the somatosensory cortex continue to change in response to inputs from the skin even after an animal has reached maturity. Next, Marian Diamond reviews her classic work demonstrating that environmental enrichment, including contact with "toys" and conspecifics, can increase the weight of the neocortex in rats, whereas environmental impoverishment has the opposite effect. Finally, William Greenough reviews what is known about synaptic change in response to sensory experiences during development and adulthood and attempts to resolve an apparent contradiction.

FUNCTIONAL "MAPS" OF SKIN SENSATIONS

Michael M. Merzenich, Ph.D.

A large proportion of the neocortex of adult primates is occupied by topographic maps of the skin surface, the retina, and the cochlea (Merzenich & Kaas, 1980). The formation of these maps has been examined in a number of developmental studies. The findings have strongly reinforced the general conclusion that the anatomical projections distributing information to different cortical zones are established early in life, prior to the end of a postnatal "critical period," and are subsequently fixed (Hubel, Wiesel, & LeVay, 1977; Sherman & Spear, 1982; Killackey & Belford, 1979). Experience prior to the critical period is required for normal neuroanatomical development, but the experience need not be very specific. A monkey or rat with eyes open or whiskers intact will develop normal neuroanatomical connections in visual or somatosensory cortex after a few weeks (for vision) or a few days (for whiskers).

It has been thought that nervous system development is largely over at that stage, at least in the cortical zones that have been studied. All elements of the neural machine, this theory continues, have appropriate and inflexibly assigned functions. Cortical representations (maps) are completed in detail. Our mental development arises from appropriate algorithmic treatment of information delivered to this hard-wired machine. In other words, the establishment of *neuroanatomical* boundaries in the cerebral cortex has been thought to create *functional* boundaries.

Dynamic Nature of Functional Maps

Studies of somatosensory cortex in primates have revealed a hitherto unappreciated second stage of cerebral map development in that system (Merzenich et al., 1983; in press). Specifically, they have shown that functional cortical maps are *not* static but on the contrary are continuously altered by experience throughout life. The initial stage of development, during which neuroanatomical connections are established prior to the end of a critical period in early life, establishes limits on later use-dependent shaping of functional map detail. We hypothesize that:

1. There are a nearly infinite number of possible forms of cortical maps, when their structure is considered in detail.
2. Input correlations, and consequent changes in synaptic effectiveness and input "selection," underlie the lifelong dynamic shaping of cortical maps.
3. Map alteration by use constitutes the general physiological basis for the acquisition of skills.
4. It may also play a role in the process(es) underlying recognition and memory.
5. Map dynamism accounts in part for the recovery of function following brain injury.

In such a self-organizing system, common or repetitive idiosyncratic experiences would result in common or idiosyncratic directions of map alterations, and repeated experience would gradually stabilize cortical maps. In addition, changes in maps at one level would necessitate changes in projections to other cortical and subcortical zones. Under special circumstances, map instabilities and possibly hyperstabilization might occur, signaling themselves through mental instabilities (errors of association) and limitations in acquisition of new information, respectively.

Some of the evidence supporting these new concepts of brain organization and development is outlined below.

Map Alterations After Peripheral Nerve Injury

One simple way to determine the alterability of cortical maps in response to changes in inputs from the skin is to examine the consequences of peripheral nerve transection or amputation. These are common injuries in human beings, and their neurological consequences are well known (Dellon, 1981; Haber, 1958).

Some of our detailed cortical mapping studies have focused on the cortical zones representing the skin field of a digit or of the large nerves in the palm of a monkey's hand. After amputation or nerve transection, these zones are very rapidly occupied by inputs from surrounding skin surfaces (Merzenich et al., 1983; in press). That is, the central cortical map reorganizes. Figure 2 diagrams this process. In time, the nondeprived surrounding skin comes to be represented over a larger cortical territory, while the transected nerve(s) lose their central representational territory.

In such studies, the sites of representation of specific skin surfaces commonly shift hundreds of microns across the cortical surface. Cortical sites of representation move from their normal (predeprivation) zones to a territory that earlier clearly represented the now denervated or amputated skin field. In human beings, no errors in localization result from stimulation of skin fields surrounding such small hand lesions. This constitutes clear evidence that the cerebral cortex is "perceptually transparent" in regard to peripheral reference. That is, there is no static isomorphic relationship between the skin surface and its cortical representations.

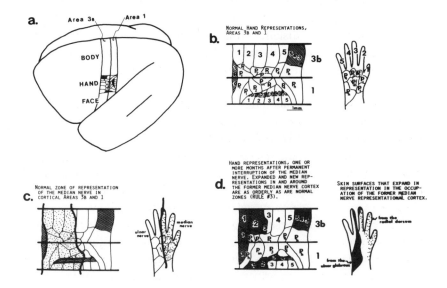

Figure 2. Cortical consequences of severe peripheral deprivation resulting from surgical transection of the median nerve. (a) Site of the hand representations in cytoarchitectonic Areas 3b and 1 of the brain of an adult owl monkey (lateral view). (b) The detailed pattern of representation of the hand in a normal monkey. The labeled zones correspond to receptive field centers on the skin surface, shown in the hand drawing at the right. Shaded areas are cortical zones in which the dorsal hand surfaces are represented. (c) The normal zone of representation of the median nerve (dotted). The skin field of the median nerve is shown in the hand drawing at the right. (d) The basic form of cortical maps derived one or more months after permanent transection of the median nerve. Neurons throughout the field of the nerve are driven by "new" inputs from adjacent skin surfaces. The cutaneous sources of these occupying inputs are indicated in the hand drawing at the right.

Remapping Rules

The remapping process appears to follow a series of functional rules.

Rule 1. As skin surface representations expand, receptive field sizes are correspondingly (inversely) reduced in area.

Rule 2. The extent (percentage) of receptive field overlap is actively maintained throughout reorganization over at least most (not all) reorganizing zones.

Rule 3. Overall topographic order is maintained throughout reorganization, and expanded and new representations in and around the reorganized area are as orderly as normal representations.

Rule 4. As outlined above, sites of representation commonly shift hundreds of microns in location during cortical reorganization. There must be a nearly infinite number of possible detailed forms of experience-derived cortical maps.

Rule 5. There is a distance limit for reorganization. These rules presumably directly reflect the neural processes underlying map establishment and alteration by experience.

Map changes are due to alterations in synaptic effectiveness, not to growth or movement of axonal arbors or dendrites. Our hypothesis is that, at any one time, neurons respond to only a small fraction of anatomically delivered inputs. The point-by-point selection of effective inputs is always influenced by surrounding sectors; that is, the selection is functionally determined. There is both neuroanatomical and physiological evidence that inputs from skin surfaces are delivered to areas far larger than the usually evident (overt) receptive fields. While these "surround" inputs do not effectively drive neurons, they do generate discernible postsynaptic potentials (PSPs) on cortical neurons (Zarzecki & Wiggin, 1982). That is important, as in this highly dynamic system temporarily ineffective inputs must define later forms of the somatosensory map.

Taken together, the relevant studies indicate that the *details* of cortical maps are established by experience from comparatively crude neuroanatomical maps. The first stage of map development, then, is the establishment of anatomical inputs and cortical architecture in the very young animal. The second stage is the establishment, adjustment, and maintenance of the details of cortical maps by experience. This second stage appears to be operational in monkeys throughout life.

How can this evidence for highly plastic somatosensory cortical maps be reconciled with developmental evidence for an early stabilization of cortical maps in the visual cortex of cats and monkeys and the vibrissal cortex of rodents? The models chosen represent instances of coincident functional and neuroanatomical boundaries. Movement across such boundaries, by our model, cannot occur: Alterations are possible only within the bounds of fixed neuroanatomical repertoires. The spread of anatomical inputs represents, in our view, the *potential* for map alteration through experience, and hence the potential for individual diversity. In the visual and vibrissal cortex models, neuroanatomical projection boundaries greatly limit that potential. In most cortical zones, the potential for experience-dependent map alteration is very great.

Individuality of Map Details

If experience can create substantial differences in cortical maps, then maps should be idiosyncratic in detail in different normal adult monkeys. A recently completed study of normal monkeys confirms this conclusion. The variation in representation of the dorsum of the hand is especially striking. Glabrous surfaces commonly vary up to about threefold in area in different monkeys in Area 3b and up to eightfold in Area 1 (these areas are shown in Figure 2). The size differences are consistent, again, with the ideas that there are many possible forms of functional maps and that the actual maps at any point in time have been shaped principally by the animal's tactual experience up to that time.

Developmental Implications

These observations have implications for the development of tactual abilities. Unfortunately, studies are incomplete. They do not define exactly what it is about inputs from the skin that alters the form of cortical maps. Given the maintenance of topographic order and shifted overlaps during map reorganization, it appears likely that input correlations underlie the maps, and that there is an optimal temporal sequencing of inputs across the skin. In this kind of system, task repetition would be a factor in generating a significant map change. However, the system is competitive. The refinement of one task limits the potential for the development of skills that compete for organizational space in the same cortical territory.

It is interesting to ask whether functional map changes might be *the* adaptive neural changes underlying cognitive processes. The basic features of the system are highly consistent with properties of self-organizing nerve nets, which have been hypothesized to account for recognitions, associations, learning, and memory. Indeed, the properties of the somatosensory system that we have defined are consistent in almost every detail with the hypothetical requirements of the recognition machinery described by Edelman (1982) and Edelman and Finkel (1984), as they are with most theoretical hypotheses as to the origins of higher brain functions.

It is highly probable that the dynamic properties recorded in the somatosensory system are general to other sensory and motor systems. The study of this functional dynamism should provide new insights concerning the development and later acquisition of skills; the mechanistic properties of neural systems underlying rules of cognition; the recovery from central brain injury; the functional origins of certain mental illnesses; and other aspects of behavior and perception hitherto largely unexplained by neuroscience.

DISCUSSION

Stephen Suomi: You mentioned finding differences between the cortical maps of different monkeys. Would you get variation of a similar order of magnitude if you examined the maps of the same monkey at, say, monthly or yearly intervals?

Michael Merzenich: The proportional differences might not be as great, but I would be surprised not to see the same range of differences over a period of years. Unfortunately, caged monkeys like the ones we study live in a relatively stereotyped tactile environment. If you watch them, you find that they spend much of the day hooking their hands over the bars of the cage, so that the outer part of the hand keeps striking the bars. As a result, the cortical representation of that part of the hand probably differs from what one would find in monkeys living in the more varied tactile environment of the wild. In general, we believe the variety you would see over time in an individual would depend on the amount of variety in the animal's tactile experiences.

Stephen Suomi: Suppose you could make your measurements on a macaque female before or during pregnancy, and then again after the birth, when she was holding the infant.

Michael Merzenich: We definitely believe the map would change. A simple human parallel would be that when you learn to smoke a cigarette, your map or representation of the parts of your fingers and thumb used to hold the cigarette probably changes dramatically. I believe that the map changes we see are probably general. They probably occur in motor as well as sensory cortical areas, and they probably account for the acquisition of skills.

Stephen Suomi: What about behavior that stops and then reappears? Take the macaque female that's holding the infant, which changes the architecture or the representation. Then the infant goes away, and the female is doing other things. A year later, she has another infant to hold.

Michael Merzenich: Certainly relearning would take place, though not instantly. It's the equivalent (which some of you may have experienced a number of times, as I have) of relearning to smoke a cigarette. At first the cigarette is extremely foreign and you handle it clumsily. But with each relearning (in my case, several of them), you are a little sooner back to a smooth performance of the task. Now, does that relearning constitute a remapping? We think so, and it's something that can be studied directly.

Seymour Levine: Are you convinced that the major differences in mapping that you've found reflect individual differences in behavior? Are these animals really using their hands in such different ways?

Michael Merzenich: Well, that's obviously the main question. We see enormous individuality, but we have no very strong links between the details of the form of the map and the behavior of the animal. That requires directed experiments in which you determine exactly what the animal is gaining or losing behaviorally as its maps change. We've been trying for about a year and a half to conduct such experiments, and we have some data. Some very simple links of this kind, such as the one between changes in field size and sensory acuity, very clearly do exist.

Seymour Levine: Why is it that you haven't used the word *plasticity?*

Michael Merzenich: I'm not opposed to using the word, but I think it carries the connotation that something is physically moving. We are not showing that any input arbors are growing or moving. Our findings are consistent with the idea of overlapping projections, but they are not consistent with the idea that something sprouts or moves from one place to another.

T. Berry Brazelton: Michael, your work has exciting implications for those of us who work with premature infants. The map changes you've found that result from individuated experience suggest great potential for recovery after sensory deprivation or trauma to the central nervous system. I think we're on the brink of understanding recovery from trauma in neonates very differently from the way we have in the past. The opportunities for early intervention, for bringing babies toward recovery after an insult, are way beyond anything we anticipated with our old fixed-deficit model of the central nervous system.

I have a question, though. Did your animals show a period of hypersensitivity following the surgery? In a baby with a CNS insult, there will be an in-rush of capillaries and blood vessels to the damaged area, trying to make up for the insult. Raw nerve endings are going to come into an area like that. What you see behaviorally is hypersensitivity. It may be generalized, but it is greater right around the lesion.

Michael Merzenich: Surgical trauma may have some influence on the map changes we see initially, but sometimes receptive fields do not change substantially many months after chronic recording electrodes are implanted. Such cases of delayed appearance of movement of representation, we think, could not have any relationship to the surgical insult.

T. Berry Brazelton: What I'm concerned about is that babies who've been through an insult may be hypersensitive to the very experiences they need to organize their nervous systems around. Unless we respect that hypersensitivity, the information we give these infants is going to overload them and our therapeutic efforts will go astray. In other words, the input preterm infants receive may have to be adjusted to their hypersensitivity in order to bring about appropriate function. Infants try to show us their threshold for receiving information behaviorally; the challenge for clinicians, which we'll be discussing later, is to learn to interpret and respond to these behavioral signals appropriately.

CORTICAL CHANGE IN RESPONSE TO ENVIRONMENTAL ENRICHMENT AND IMPOVERISHMENT

Marian C. Diamond, Ph.D.

Over the past twenty years much evidence has accumulated supporting the ability of nerve cells in the mammalian forebrain to change in response to varied environmental conditions. In the rat, environmental enrichment can increase the thickness of the cortex not only during infancy, but throughout life. Whether the increase is due to touch, pressure, temperature, or other factors is not known. All these modalities are probably involved when animals huddle together or investigate new surroundings and objects.

The first part of this report will consider the effects of environmental enrichment and impoverishment on the brains of very young (unweaned) male rats. The next section will deal with older (weaned) male rats. The third part will discuss changes in the brains of female rats and later generations.

Young (Unweaned) Male Rats

In the first series of studies (Malkasian & Diamond, 1971), a mother rat and three pups six days old were placed in one of three conditions:

1. The unifamily condition: The mother and pups remained in the standard small colony cage.
2. The multifamily condition: Three mothers with three pups each were placed together in a single large cage.

3. The multifamily/enriched condition: Three mothers with three pups each were placed together in a single large cage (as in 2) with "toys" or objects with which they could interact.

The animals were sacrificed for autopsy when the pups were between 14 and 28 days old. At 14 days, the multifamily/enriched condition rats had developed a somatosensory cortex that averaged 10 percent thicker than that of the unifamily animals. There were no significant differences between the cortexes of the unifamily rats and those of the multifamily rats with no toys. Therefore, it appeared that the stimulating interaction with the toys was the important factor in increasing the cortical dimensions.

The medial occipital cortex did not respond at this age, undoubtedly because the eyes had not yet opened. However, the most lateral region of the occipital cortex section showed a 16 percent increase. Evidently, a fair amount of sensory integration is taking place in this area at this stage of development.

At 19 days of age, again the somatosensory cortex displayed an increase in thickness in the multifamily/enriched condition rats compared to the unifamily rats. At this time the occipital cortex also showed significant increases. By 28 days of age, all areas measured showed a thicker cortex in the multifamily/enriched condition rats (see Figure 3). The occipital cortex appeared to be more responsive in the 28-day-old group than in any of the younger groups.

At 19 and 28 days, the area of the neurons and their nuclei in the somatosensory cortex showed large increases in the multifamily/enriched condition rats. In the occipital cortex, the increase in nuclear area reached as much as 25 percent.

In a previous study mapping the growth of the cortex from birth to 26 days of age (Diamond, Johnson, & Ingham, 1975), we learned that the cortex is growing most rapidly during this period. The present results indicate that the rate of growth can be accelerated with an enriched environment. The enriched environment brought about significant increases in the thickness of the cortex and in the area of its neuronal constituents. The true cause of these brain changes is not clear. Handling alone is not sufficient to change cortical thickness (Hoover & Diamond, 1969). One step in teasing out the components of the environment responsible for the changes might be to remove the whiskers of the rat, which are an important source of tactile stimulation.

Older (Weaned) Male Rats

During our early studies of rats past the age of weaning, only enriched and impoverished conditions were used. But after several studies it became apparent that we were dealing with two experimental conditions; there were no controls. Since then, a third group has been included for comparison, the standard colony condition.

In the standard colony condition, three rats lived together in a small cage. In the impoverished condition, a single rat occupied a small cage. This animal could see, hear, and smell other rats but could not interact directly with them or with "toys."

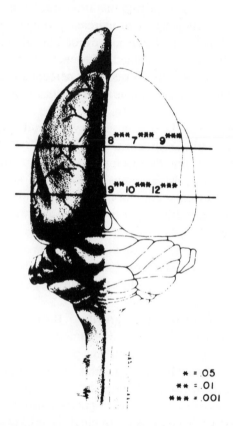

Figure 3. Percentage differences in thickness of the cortexes of rats living in enriched and nonenriched environments from six to 28 days of age. After 22 days of exposure, rats in the enriched environment showed very significant increases in thickness in all the cortical areas measured.

In the enriched condition, twelve rats (usually) lived together in a large cage. Several times a week "toys" were placed in the cage: small ladders, wheels, mazes, swings, jungle gyms — objects that provided novel stimulation as the rats explored them, very similar to those used with the younger animals. It was important to change the toys frequently, or the brain alterations were not as marked. As new toys were introduced, the animals would come to the front of the cage to investigate them. They sniffed, approached carefully, and climbed over the toys, thoroughly exploring them. The whiskers were the first part of the body to touch the toys, conveying information to the receptive barrels in the somatosensory cortex.

The animals were exposed to these conditions for various periods of time: 80 days, 30 days, 15 days, and 7 days. During each of these periods, brain changes were noted. The shortest exposure that brought about significant change was four days. One day was not sufficient to produce a change.

In adult rats, the occipital cortex was most responsive to the enriched environment. Impoverishment effects in adults took longer to develop than with the young. The effects of impoverishment on rats just past weaning age were marked. After just four days in the impoverished condition (days 26-30), all showed significant decreases in cortical thickness compared with standard colony animals. The decreases were more striking in the occipital cortex than in the somatosensory cortex.

It is apparent from these data that depriving an animal of the stimulation of companions and objects is more detrimental to the young animal than to the adult. Also, the occipital cortex is more susceptible to such deprivation than is the somatosensory cortex.

Female Rats and Later Generations

Soon after we learned the effects of the environment on brains of male rats, we were asked about the brains of their offspring. To study this question, we mated enriched males with enriched females and impoverished males with impoverished females. Cortical thickness was measured in both parents and pups immediately after the birth of a litter (Diamond, Johnson, & Ingham, 1971).

No significant cortical thickness differences were noted between the pups from the enriched and the impoverished parents. However, the body weights of the pups from the enriched parents were significantly greater than those of pups from impoverished parents. Upon measuring the cortical thickness of the parents, we found that the brains from the enriched males were 7 percent larger than those of the deprived males, as usual. No comparable difference was found between the brains of the females.

Closer examination of the data showed that the cortex of the impoverished, pregnant female had reached the same thickness as that of the enriched, pregnant female, and this was why no significant differences were seen between their brains. These data alerted us to the importance of looking at the brains of nonpregnant females exposed to the different environmental conditions. A new set of experiments was arranged, using 60- to

116-day-old nonpregnant females in order to duplicate the duration of the pregnancy experiments.

The results indicated that the pattern of change in cortical thickness in the nonpregnant female was different from that of the pregnant female or male. In the 116-day-old, sexually mature female, the somatosensory cortex showed a greater, more significant change than in the male. In addition, though the occipital cortex responded to the environmental conditions, it did not show as great a change as in the male, and this difference was statistically significant when compared with the male.

These experiments opened new doors. They showed that the female somatosensory cortex was more responsive to our environmental conditions than was the male somatosensory cortex, but the response was less than the male's in the occipital cortex. They also suggested that altering the environment during pregnancy could affect the body weights of offspring. This was an encouraging finding. If we could plan another experiment and allow the animals to reach maturity instead of taking the brains at birth, would we see differences? In other words, would greater body weight at birth give an animal an advantage in interacting with the environment? Would it bring more stimulation to the brain, creating greater cortical mass?

In our most recent set of experiments, we did not sacrifice the pups at birth but allowed them to reach 60 days of age. At that time, we sacrificed twelve rats to obtain baseline data and assigned others to enriched or impoverished conditions. After 30 days, enriched males were mated with enriched females and impoverished males with impoverished females. Twenty-one days later, we had a new generation of pups. Some were sacrificed at various times; others have been allowed to produce a third generation, which is now being raised. These pups will cycle through the contrasting environments before their brains are measured.

Preliminary findings show that the occipital cortex of males at 60 days is thicker than that of males in the two earlier generations. Overall, our results clearly indicate the plasticity of the cerebral cortex in response to stimulating and deprived environments. One might ask what changes are occurring in the cortex to account for thickness differences. The cortex consists of nerve cells, glial cells, and blood vessels. Any or all of these structures can respond to increased or decreased stimulation. Over the past twenty years members of our laboratory have identified many structures that increase their dimensions in response to stimulating environments (e.g., Diamond et al., 1966; 1975; Globus et al., 1973). Other investigators have demonstrated that rats that have experienced enriched environments can run a maze better than rats from less stimulating environments (Nyman, 1967). The increases in neuronal structure support the enhanced maze performance.

We are pleased to learn that the brains of our old animals respond to the enriched environment in a manner very similar to that of younger animals. In fact, our most recent data with animals exposed to the different environments from 776 to 904 days of age (very old for a rat) showed increases almost identical to those of young animals.

The significance of these results is manifold. The somatosensory cortex does increase its dimensions with our experimental design, and it does so at every age we have studied. Undoubtedly, touch plays a role in this somatosensory response, although this role has not yet been thoroughly investigated. There is no indication that the amount of touch our animals receive is excessive or disturbing to them. The adrenals do not show any significant difference between the groups (Rosenzweig et al., 1969), whereas experiments designed to stress rats do show such differences in the adrenal weights. With the present evidence one can conclude that touch and exploration induced by "toys" is beneficial to the individual as measured by brain and behavioral changes.

DISCUSSION

Allen Gottfried: Have you applied vestibular stimulation in any of your studies, Marian?

Marian Diamond: No, we have not specifically studied vestibular input, though undoubtedly it plays a role as the animals climb and balance in the cage and on the toys.

Allen Gottfried: So at present you define an enriched environment basically as more space and more objects?

Marian Diamond: Yes, definitely more objects. We have to change the objects at least twice a week because the animals get bored with the same ones. If the same toys are left in the cage, the cortical dimensions will decrease with time. The minute new toys are offered, the animals become alert and climb on and explore them. We have not yet placed toys in the standard colony cage to determine if space is definitely a factor or not.

Allen Gottfried: It's interesting that toys are so important. Several longitudinal studies in North America show that one of the most potent factors relating to human mental development is play materials. But perhaps it's not just toys. Perhaps crowding plays a role, or general activity?

Marian Diamond: General activity per se, no. This was studied some 20 years ago, when Rosenzweig and his colleagues put animals in running wheels for several hours a day to see if their cortexes would change. No cortical differences were found.

Stephen Suomi: Does the brain of an animal in the enriched condition actually change shape?

Marian Diamond: Yes. The soma increases, as does the nucleus. A nerve cell is shaped like a hand with dendrites comparable to fingers, and the dimensions of the dendrites change. Some increase in number and some in length. The postsynaptic thickening length changes, and so does spine number. In other words, all parts of the cell measured to date change size in relation to environmental input.

T. Berry Brazelton: When infants come into the "enriched environment" of the hospital, their head size increases rather rapidly. We've wondered why — is it nutrition, stimulation, or what? Have you looked at fluid intake and diet in your animals to see whether they're correlated with changes in brain size?

William Greenough: We have measured food consumption in animals that grow up from weaning in these sorts of environments. The isolates consume more food than the animals in the complex environment, and they also weigh more. But their brains are smaller, so I don't think a simple nutritional answer is appropriate.

Marian Diamond: We've found that the weight gain depends on the amount of time the animals spend in the enriched and impoverished environments. After 80 days, the animals in the impoverished environment definitely weigh more, but their brains are smaller. After only 30 days, the body weights of the animals in the two environments are the same, but the brains of the animals from the enriched environment are still larger.

Paul Satz: These are group effects you're getting, Marian, and they're very predictable and lawful, but I'd love to see the distributions. There must be some animals that are not showing the effect. Have you studied them?

Marian Diamond: That's a beautiful question. Our results are statistically significant, so the majority of brains do show the differences. Why some do not, I do not know. Some of the rats may not interact with the objects in the cages. Some rats may not be good at playing, just as some are not good at mothering. We would need to mark the animals clearly; videotape their behavior; and then correlate behavior with cortical dimensions.

Peter Gorski: You really allow the rats to determine the best use of the enriched environment, don't you? So the effect you get is different from the one you might obtain by actively employing touch or handling in order to enrich.

Marian Diamond: Yes, though we did have an experiment on touch per se. The animals were held for around five or ten minutes a day (admittedly this was a small amount); after 30 days, there was no change in cortical thickness compared to untouched littermates.

T. Berry Brazelton: A finding that fascinated me, with my bias, was that the size of the female cortex goes up during pregnancy. Might it continue to increase during nurturing?

Marian Diamond: This we have yet to examine, but we now have the brains of mothers who nursed their pups for 23 to 25 days after birth. It will be many months before we have the results from this experiment, but they will indeed prove interesting.

Kathryn Barnard: Some very interesting new data from the University of Oklahoma (Ramsey is the principal investigator) show that a major contributor to prematurity or low birth weight is a condition called family enmeshment. It isn't hard to see a parallel between the impoverished environment in your studies and the enmeshment of families that are socially isolated and closed off rather than being open systems.

T. Berry Brazelton: The environment of newborn premature infants may also resemble your deprived environment. Our problem as clinicians is to differentiate between stimulation that is appropriate and enriching and stimulation that is inappropriate and perhaps overwhelming.

BRAIN STORAGE OF SENSORY INFORMATION IN DEVELOPMENT AND ADULTHOOD

William T. Greenough, Ph.D.

Three decades of work have made it clear that mammalian brain function can be profoundly affected by experience, particularly during development. Although the majority of the evidence comes from studies of sense modalities other than the somatosensory, especially vision, the "rules" of neural development identified in visual system studies seem to apply in general (e.g., Feng & Rogowski, 1980). For example, some aspects of sensory system development appear to take place during relatively brief periods of sensitivity to experience and to be followed by stabilization. Other aspects, as the papers by Merzenich and Diamond make clear, remain sensitive at least to some types of experience. In addition, in all sensory systems so far assessed in detail, there is evidence that numbers or patterns of synaptic connections between nerve cells are affected by differential experience. That is, the effects of experience are stored in the "wiring diagram" of the brain.

My purpose here is to focus on these two aspects of sensory system development, transient versus lasting sensitivity to experience and associated synaptic change. Although my speculations on how these may be related are derived largely from information on vision, they seem likely to apply to the somatosensory system as well. I will concentrate on studies addressing the number of synapses, though it should be acknowledged that evidence also exists for changes in the characteristics of previously existing synapses.

Studies of Nonsomatosensory Systems

Research on the early development of the visual systems of various mammals has revealed the importance of experience at the time the modality first begins to function. One measure that seems particularly sensitive to very early manipulations is the frequency with which spines (postsynaptic structures on the dendrites of most types of brain neuron) occur along the dendritic membrane. Deprivation of light or patterned vision has generally been found to reduce the frequency of spines on visual cortex in rodents (e.g., Rothblat & Schwartz, 1979) and to reduce dendritic field size in visual cortex neurons in cats (Coleman & Riesen, 1968). When only one eye of a monkey or cat is deprived, the number of synaptic contacts associated with that eye is reduced while the contacts of the other eye increase (LeVay, Wiesel, & Hubel, 1980).

Our laboratory has followed up on the pioneering work described by Diamond in the preceding paper concerning the effects of environmental complexity and deprivation. Our initial studies showed differences in the size of the dendritic fields of animals that had experienced various conditions. Rats reared with other rats in a complex environment had more extensive dendritic fields than did rats reared in isolation without toys. Rats reared in pairs without toys had intermediate values, but generally closer to those of the isolated rats. The effects were most pronounced in the outer part of the dendritic field, suggesting that this region may be more sensitive to experience. The difference between the environmental-complexity animals and the isolated animals was considerably greater than the difference typically reported between light- and dark-reared animals.

These and other results suggest that the number of synapses per neuron in a variety of brain regions (maybe most) is determined to a significant extent by the circumstances under which the organism develops. We speculate that these changes are involved in storing information arising from experience.

Altering the number (or pattern) of synapses is one of the two most frequently proposed ways in which the functional circuitry of the nervous system could be changed by experience. The other is by selectively altering the strength of individual connections. There is evidence for experience-dependence in both the number and the structural characteristics of synapses in nonsomatosensory brain regions, beginning as early as the time the regions begin to function and extending, as Merzenich and Diamond have explained, well beyond maturity. These data suggest that the brain may use more than one mechanism to alter its functional organization in response to experience.

Studies of Somatosensory Development

As noted earlier, studies of the role of experience in the development of the somatosensory system have been rare. The dominant developmental model in the somatosensory system has been the large snout whiskers (myastacial vibrissae) and associated cell groupings called barrels in the cortex of the mouse. The aggregation of neuronal cell bodies into barrels, one barrel for each whisker, occurs postnatally, as cell bodies move into cell-dense walls and cell-sparse hollows. If whisker follicles are destroyed within a few days of birth, cell aggregation into corresponding barrels is disrupted (Woolsey & Wann, 1976). However, merely removing the whiskers does not prevent cell aggregation (Van der Loos & Woolsey, 1973). The implication of these results is that mere deprivation does not affect organization of this somatosensory system — physical damage is necessary.

There is some behavioral evidence that later vibrissal function may be affected by functional demands during development. Rogowski (unpublished) reared mice blind from shortly after birth with sighted counterparts in a complex environment. Informal observation indicated that while both the blind and sighted animals used their vibrissae extensively, whisking them back and forth to sense objects as they moved about, the blind animals used their whiskers more, particularly in situations of apparent uncertainty about the safety (or wisdom) of the next forward step. To assess whether whisker function had been altered by this apparently increased reliance upon whiskers for orientation in the physical environment, Rogowski examined the placing response (forelimb extension toward a surface) triggered by whisker contact. The performance of the mice suggested that whisker contact with the platform was more effective in triggering placing in the blind mice. This study, as well as a long history of studies suggesting enhanced somatosensory function in blind humans, indicates that the somatosensory system can respond to functional demand by providing information normally available through other modalities.

One study of relative deprivation of body sensation in which detailed brain measures were made involved the cerebellum (Floeter & Greenough, 1979). Macaque monkeys were reared alone or with other monkeys in environments that differed in complexity. In one condition, the monkeys were raised in individual enclosures that prevented contact with other monkeys. These animals showed a behavioral pattern termed the isolation syndrome: Extensive bouts of repeated stereotyped motor behaviors, inappropriate social behavior, and so on, as described in the next paper by Suomi. We examined the cerebellum, a sensory-motor integration region, both because of the effects of these rearing conditions on motor behaviors and because involvement of the cerebellum in the isolation syndrome and behaviorally related human disorders had been postulated (Prescott, 1970). The results suggest that the development of the cerebellum, which appears to be involved in translating sensory information about body position for the coordination of movement, is sensitive to experience. However, they do *not* indicate involvement of the cerebellar regions studied in the isolation syndrome: There was no cerebellar difference between individually reared monkeys, which did exhibit isolation syndrome behaviors, and monkeys reared in pairs, which did not. In addition, our data do *not* implicate tactile input per se in the cerebellar effects.

In general, the literature provides only sporadic evidence that postnatal tactile stimulation affects early development of CNS regions that process tactile information. This does not mean that the somatosensory system is somehow impervious to structural experiential influences in early development, of course, for several reasons.

1. We simply have not found the proper combination of situation and species to demonstrate widespread structural experience effects.
2. The effects of early deprivation in, for example, the visual system are often surprisingly small, smaller than those of complex environments versus individual housing on estimates of synaptic number, for example. What we don't know is the degree to which the *pattern* of synapses differs between light- and dark-reared animals. It may be that there is a strong tendency for synapses to form and that the primary effect of early experience is to determine *which* synapses form (or survive).
3. Subtotal deprivation (which seems to be all that can be achieved for tactile sensation) may have little effect on basic somatosensory

developmental processes.

4. The visual, auditory, and olfactory stimulation provided by complex environments may actually *detract* from somatosensory effects. If information storage requires the involvement of some overriding or permissive central process, as suggested by some recent reports (e.g., Kasamatsu & Pettigrew, 1976; Mirmiran & Uylings, 1983), it may be that the complex environment diffuses this "attentional" process.

5. Except perhaps in whisker studies, the timing of experience manipulations may not have been right for assessing cutaneous sensitivity to early experience. In mammals and birds, the cutaneous sense matures early, followed by vestibular, auditory, and visual sensation (Gottlieb, 1971). Thus, the period of greatest sensitivity to tactile manipulations might occur earlier in development than the period of greatest sensitivity to manipulations affecting other modalities.

Two possible reasons have been suggested for this sequencing of sensory system development (Turkewitz & Kenny, 1982). First, some common resource, such as attention to the modality by other brain systems or metabolic resources, might be limited in availability, as suggested in number 4 above. Second, sequencing of maturation of the sensory modalities could allow better integration among them. Information acquired by one modality could be used in the development of others and in establishing relationships among them with regard to aspects of the environment (visual-tactile relationships, for instance). The cutaneous sense, early to develop, might thus be of great importance to the later-developing modalities.

Later Somatosensory Plasticity

There is considerable evidence such as that presented by Merzenich that neural substrates of cutaneous sensation remain capable of reorganization in adulthood. Plastic responses to experience have been demonstrated in several adult mammalian brain systems in recent years (e.g., Juraska et al., 1980; Uylings, Kuypers, & Veltman, 1978); the somatosensory system appears to be no exception. Thus, we face a possible contradiction between evidence for the early maturation of cutaneous sensation (and possible subsequent reductions in sensitivity to experience) and evidence for the continuing sensitivity of this system to experience in adulthood.

One explanation for this apparent contradiction, which has arisen from behavioral research, posits that developmental effects of experience and adult-like learning and memory are distinguished by their ability to be retrieved as memorial events (Campbell & Spear, 1972). In human beings, developmental events that have profound effects upon later behavior or ability are often not remembered; adults rarely remember much from the first few years of life, though later childhood memories may be abundant. Similar phenomena have been demonstrated in animals (Campbell & Campbell, 1962; Nagy & Murphy, 1974). Campbell and others have argued that adult-like learning and memory capacity emerge at a relatively specific point in development. The implication is that the neural substrates of developmental organization processes and adult memory are different.

In apparent opposition to this view, evidence is accumulating that similar neural substrates exist for developmental experience effects and adult memory phenomena. Experience manipulations in adult, even aging, animals can bring about changes in the structure of neuronal dendritic fields that are remarkably similar to those produced by the same or other experience manipulations during development (Green, Greenough, & Schlumpf, 1983; see also preceding paper by Diamond). Moreover, the dendritic field changes in adult animals trained on traditional psychological learning tasks such as mazes are qualitatively similar to those seen after developmental experience manipulation (Chang & Greenough, 1982; Larson & Greenough, 1981). This evidence suggests that the neural mechanisms of developmental information storage retain at least some capacity for functional reorganization during adulthood.

Early Versus Late Plasticity: A Hypothesis

A view that allows for both the development-versus-memory distinction and a common final mechanism proposes that developmental experience may be of two types, that is, that the developing nervous system may receive two different sorts of information from the environment. (Similar categories were proposed by Piaget, 1980). *Experience-expectant* developmental interactions involve experiences common to all normally reared members of a species. In contrast, *experience-dependent* interactions involve experiences that are unique to the individual — information about sources of food and safety, the social system, and so forth. This latter type of interaction could blend into the sort of information storage process traditionally referred to by the terms learning and memory.

It seems at least possible that the nervous system could distinguish between these two types of information on the basis of its ability to prepare for them in advance. If information is expected, then the developing nervous system could be arranged in such a way as to take advantage of it efficiently. If information is unexpected — or at least unpredictable at the individual level — it may be more difficult for the nervous system to store it quickly.

There is evidence that can be interpreted to indicate that the nervous system recognizes this distinction, or a similar one. Early in development, in some pathways of developing somatosensory cortex and in other systems, there are more synaptic connections than exist in the adult system (e.g., Ivy & Killackey, 1981). The connections that survive in these systems apparently do so because they have successfully competed with other connections for sites on, and control of, the postsynaptic cell. In the primate visual cortex, for example, adjacent patches of synapses associated with each of the two eyes are formed from an initially overlapping distribution. If one eye is deprived of experience, synapses from the other take over part of its space, rendering the deprived eye's patches smaller (LeVay et al., 1980). From such results it has been proposed that experience acts in part as a sculptor during early development, preserving adult forms while pushing irrelevant scraps of connections away.

In contrast, there is little evidence for synapse overproduction in later development and in adulthood. A low level of synaptic turnover has been detected in some regions of the undamaged adult brain (Sotelo & Palay, 1971). However, it is not clear whether this turnover is constitutionally generated, with some sort of selective preservation process operating as in development, or activity-dependent, with synapses being generated as a result of neural information processing or the need for information storage. In the latter case, a mechanism for postdevelopmental plasticity of a different sort from that of early development would exist — potentially one with the capacity to encode unpredicted information in nervous system organization. It may be this form of neural plasticity that is tapped by experiments indicating morphological change in sensory systems in later development and adulthood. It may be, too, that experience-expectant and experience-dependent information storage processes adapt the individual to the environment through different mechanisms — synapse selection versus synapse formation — but with the same ultimate end, alteration in the functional wiring diagrams of the nervous system.

DISCUSSION

T. Berry Brazelton: Bill, reminding us of Piaget's concepts with your terms *experience-expectant* and *experience-dependent* is an important contribution. Experience-expectant, as I understand it, refers to the preparation the nervous system has for experience — the basis for environmental sculpturing of the brain's organization. Experience-dependent refers to the building of new structures upon this species-characteristic baseline, that is, to the incorporation of individual experience. Since experience-dependent development is individual, it may be more at risk.

William Greenough: Yes and no. Individual development can be maladaptive — witness the truly crazy individuals who disrupt society — but extreme laboratory situations indicate that disruption of experience-dependent processes can be disastrous. Touch is the modality that develops first, at least in mammals. However, we know very little about it, because we can deprive an animal of most sound and all vision, but how do you deprive an animal of touch?

T. Berry Brazelton: Other kinds of experiments might give us more information. I really look forward to seeing other kinds of experiments with animals besides deprivation experiments, and I'm happy that you seem to have that in mind, too.

Peter Gorski: Bill, what happens at the opposite extreme from deprivation—if you put the animals into an overly complex environment, a chaotic, "crazy" one?

William Greenough: Presumably there is a point beyond which the rule "If a little is good, more is better" ceases to hold for our rats, but we haven't found it yet.

Peter Gorski: Are you sure you're getting meaningful cortical growth in the complex-environment animals rather than disorganized change?

William Greenough: Our approach is anatomical rather than physiological, and a problem when you're doing anatomy is that although you can count things, the pattern and meaning of neural connections is very hard to discern with a microscope. The question you're asking should be answered by using physiological recording techniques. At a higher level, though, behavioral studies certainly imply positive changes in brain organization with complex environments.

Michael Merzenich: An important issue that you've raised is the relation between the kind of work you and Marian Diamond have done and the kind of work we've done. From our point of view, the real question is: Exactly what is the cortical circuitry underlying the map changes that we see? We believe that the map changes we've observed result primarily from changes of input. However, there is probably also a system in the brain that is modulating the process, and thereby controlling the rate at which things can change.

Some exciting new evidence from Dr. Evart's laboratory, in experiments done by Randall Nelson, demonstrates a powerful relationship between the motor act of the animal and the potential for organization of the somatosensory field. What they've seen specifically is that in Area 3b, during voluntary movement, the stimulation of the skin counts just as it would in a passive situation. However, Area 1 is dramatically suppressed when the animal is actually moving; only in the passive situation is Area 1 activated. We believe that these differences between the maps of Area 3b and Area 1 are due to the fact that stimulation from movement per se is not allowed to *change* Area 1. When you find changes in spine density or dendritic branching, then, the question is: Which process or combination of processes do they relate to?

William Greenough: New connections might be involved in longer-term changes, or in stabilizing the changes.

Arnold Scheibel: Sorting out exactly how changes in cortex morphology relate to function is an exciting issue. What strikes me about our discussion is that Bill Greenough and Mike Merzenich think of input systems to the cortex as primarily relating to information. As you know, however, some extremely important parallel systems deal with the import or impact of the information on the animal, quite independent of its content. The reticular activating system may have a tremendous influence on what the cortical cells will and will not listen to at a given moment.

William Greenough: As well as perhaps on whether they change or don't change on a longer term basis. Let me elaborate briefly on some relevant work mentioned in my paper. First, Kasamatsu and Pettigrew have done some very nice work on a plastic change of a permanent nature in the visual system. The change is dependent for its occurrence on experience, and also, apparently, on the presence of catecholamines, norepinephrine in particular. Second, Mirmiran and Uylings have recently shown that morphological effects of complex environments are significantly reduced by injection of anti-adrenergic compounds. So there does appear to be a neuromodulatory system there. Frankly, the number of neurotransmitters and other potential modulatory compounds that have been discovered over the last ten years is frightening. It's going to be a real maze figuring out what they all do.

T. Berry Brazelton: Human newborns use state as a way of modulating and screening information. For a preterm or small-for-gestational-age (SGA) baby who has not developed the capacity to modulate appropriately, a stimulus that a full-term neonate can accept may be too much. If you say "How are you doing?" to a full-term, she'll probably search for your face and find it. But a premie might avert, go into an arched state, and perhaps spit up, have a BM, and become cyanotic. You might get more cells with that second avoidance response, but the question I guess would be one of appropriateness.

William Greenough: There is something about modulation and the environment of premature babies that I would like to bring up. It's my understanding, though maybe this is changing, that the intensive care nurseries in many hospitals are kept lighted 24 hours a day. If you did that to a rat and it happened to be an albino, you would destroy its entire retina in four days. Even more important, an infant rat needs an opportunity to track its mother's rhythms during early development. I'm concerned about the fact that all sources of natural rhythms are removed from the environment of these premature newborns. These rhythms govern very important things, such as patterns of growth hormone release.

T. Berry Brazelton: We'll be discussing the nursery environment in detail later, Bill, when we focus on the preterm infant. Many nurseries are now trying to simulate natural light rhythms, and I think this is a very constructive trend.

Developmental Perspectives

PART III
TOUCH AND ATTACHMENT

In the quarter of a century since Harry Harlow's compelling demonstration of the importance of contact comfort to infant rhesus monkeys, much has been learned about the role of touch in early development. For example:

- If an infant rhesus monkey is taken from its mother at birth and raised in a cage alone, with no chance to touch other monkeys, its social behavior during adulthood is very abnormal. For instance, a female isolate will probably become an abusive or neglectful mother, refusing to accept her infant's efforts to cling and nurse.
- If mother and infant squirrel monkeys are separated for half an hour, both experience a sharp rise in a stress-related hormone called cortisol. Reunion, which is always accompanied by the renewal of physical contact, moderates this hormonal response.
- If pigtail monkey infants are taken from their mothers at an early age, they go through a series of behavioral and physiological reactions that resemble human responses to bereavement or separation from a loved one. The mechanisms involved may help explain why touch with compassionate intent (in particular, therapeutic touch) might have positive effects on human health.
- Human one-year-olds, like maturing infants in many species, seek physical contact with their mothers when frightened. A mother who rejects her baby's efforts to climb into her arms or onto her lap increases the baby's anxiety while withholding his best means for alleviating it, with negative effects on psychological development.

These and other findings relating touch to attachment are presented in Part III.

THE ROLE OF TOUCH IN RHESUS MONKEY SOCIAL DEVELOPMENT

Stephen J. Suomi, Ph.D.

In 1958, Harry F. Harlow presented for the first time the results of a series of experiments designed to identify the features of rhesus monkey mothers that were most important for their infants' development of social attachment bonds. Conventional wisdom at the time was that human infants (and probably most neonatal mammals) formed social attachments with their mothers via association with the feeding process through nursing. Harlow stunned his audience by reporting that he had reared rhesus monkey infants on pairs of artificial (surrogate) "mothers," one providing milk and the other providing instead what Harlow termed *contact comfort* — a terry-cloth ventral surface. The infant monkeys consistently formed lasting and functionally important attachments to the cloth-covered surrogates that provided no nourishment (Figure 4), and they consistently failed to develop attachment-like behavior toward surrogates that provided milk from a baby bottle attached to a wire-mesh-covered body (Harlow, 1958).

Later investigators of primate behavior have been acutely aware of the importance of contact or touch in the social life of their subjects. This paper describes the types of social contact that rhesus monkeys and other macaques routinely display in the course of normal development and discusses their importance, as revealed by the now well-documented consequences of early touch deprivation. It concludes with a brief review of some comparative data on other primates.

Role of Contact in Normal Development

Of the approximately 200 primate species still in existence today, rhesus monkeys are almost certainly the second most successful. Except for Homo sapiens, they have a higher world-wide population and inhabit a larger geographical area with greater climatic variability than any other species of primate. In the wild, they usually live in troops numbering 15 to 100 individuals. Each troop is a complex society that encompasses several distinct matriarchally organized kinship lineages.

Figure 4. An infant rhesus monkey in one of Harlow's early studies clings to its terry-cloth "mother."

Figure 5. Mutual clinging and ventral contact in an infant rhesus monkey and its mother.

Even brief and casual observation of these wild-living troops reveals extensive physical contact of a variety of types involving all the troop members at one time or another. For rhesus monkeys (as for all species of nonhuman primates), extensive tactile contact with conspecifics begins essentially at birth. Rhesus monkey infants invariably spend the vast majority of their first days and weeks of life in intimate physical contact with their mother. Most of the time this contact is mutually ventral (ventro-ventro) in nature, as shown by the mother-infant pair in Figure 5.

Under normal circumstances rhesus monkey infants rarely if ever engage in prolonged mutual ventral contact with anyone but their biological mother. Moreover, once past infancy relatively few rhesus monkeys are ever seen in ventral contact with any other conspecifics, with one prominent exception. The exception occurs when rhesus monkey females give birth to infants of their own. In other words, mutual ventral contact is a universal characteristic of rhesus monkey mother-infant relationships, but it is almost universally absent from other normal social relationships.

Nevertheless, there is considerably more to normal rhesus monkey mother-infant relationships than mutual ventral contact. After an infant's first month of life, when the duration of time spent in such contact with the mother begins to decline sharply (Hansen, 1966; Hinde & Spencer-Booth, 1967; Hinde & White, 1974), other forms of tactile contact between mother and infant emerge with increasing frequency. One of the most important of these is social grooming.

At the same time that infants are developing grooming behavior, they are also learning to use tactile contact with the mother for a new purpose — to establish and maintain a secure base for exploration of the environment. From their second month on, infants venture away from the mother's immediate reach on exploratory forays that become increasingly frequent, longer, and farther from the mother. Each foray typically ends with the infant scurrying back to its mother for a brief period of tactile (and not necessarily mutual ventral) contact with her. When an infant is experimentally denied tactile access to its mother, all exploratory activity immediately ceases — even if the mother remains in visual, auditory, and olfactory contact with the infant (e.g., Seay, Hansen, & Harlow, 1962).

For young rhesus monkeys (as for juveniles of most primate species), interactions with peers differ considerably from interactions with mothers. One very obvious difference is that the type of tactile contact most prevalent in normal mother-infant interactions — prolonged mutual ventral contact — is virtually absent in normal peer relationships. Social grooming does occur between peers, and its incidence tends to increase as the peers grow older. The initial form of contact between peers — brief exploratory touching via hands or mouth — is fundamentally different from the extended, whole-body contact that characterizes the mother-infant relationship. Perhaps most importantly, the activity that accounts for the bulk of peer interactions among juveniles — contact-oriented social play — rarely occurs between mothers and offspring older than four months of age (Suomi, 1979a; 1979b).

By four months of age a rhesus monkey's play repertoire includes both rough-and-tumble play and approach-withdrawal play, in which the primary role of one of the participants is to avoid all physical contact with the other (Harlow & Harlow, 1965; Hansen, 1966; Harlow, 1969). By one year of age, virtually all forms of social contact that characterize social interactions between adults can be identified in an individual's normal play with its peers (Suomi & Harlow, 1975), including obvious precursors of both sex and aggression (Harlow, 1975; Suomi, 1979b). Contact-oriented social play remains the predominant form of peer interaction among young monkeys until they reach adolescence, usually at about four years of age, when the incidence of play and other interactions with peers drops precipitously.

At this point the life histories of male and female rhesus monkeys diverge, at least in natural environments. Females tend to spend more time in the general proximity of their mothers and increase their interactions with mother-related kin, especially older sisters and cousins. Males, on the other hand, almost always leave the troop in which they grew up. Eventually, each male that survives will join another troop of rhesus monkeys.

These sex differences in social roles and troop affiliation among young adult rhesus monkeys are reflected in their use of tactile contact. Most contact between adult males takes the form of grooming, physical aggres-

:n to the point of wounding), and very occasional play. Adult female-
ontact is usually restricted to grooming, passive nonventral body
e.g., two females might lean side-to-back), and aggression (usually
toward nonkin females and adolescents). Of course, when these
young females have infants of their own, mutual ventral contact will again
become an important part of their overall contact repertoire.

Thus, for rhesus monkeys, social contact with conspecifics is ubiquitous
from the moment of birth throughout maturity. How important are early
contact experiences for normal later development? A large body of data,
to be reviewed next, suggest that they are crucial.

Consequences of Contact Deprivation

Prior to Harlow's 1958 surrogate studies showing the importance of contact comfort, most laboratory researchers studying nonhuman primates
routinely housed their subjects in individual cages. These researchers, and
their veterinary staffs, assumed that single-cage housing would reduce the
risk of disease and aggression-induced injury for the monkeys without in-
troducing any other major hazards. Adolescent and adult monkeys imported
from the wild appeared to show few ill effects from long-term single-cage
housing. They seemed to behave normally when permitted to interact with
other wild-born monkeys (e.g., for breeding purposes), and they displayed
no obvious cognitive deficits in standardized learning test performances
(Harlow et al., 1971).

On the other hand, when infants born in the laboratory to females
imported from the wild were placed in single cages, it soon became apparent
that something was very wrong with their behavioral development. During
the first few months of life they developed patterns of self-clasping and
self-orality seldom seen in wild-born monkeys. In succeeding months,
almost all single-cage-reared infants began to display idiosyncratic patterns
of repetitive, stereotyped activity. Moreover, they seemed unusually timid
and reluctant to explore new toys or other objects placed in their cages.
When these monkeys were finally introduced to a group of age-mates, they
did not exhibit spontaneous exploratory or play behavior. Instead, they
typically withdrew from all social contact and engaged in self-directed
stereotypic behavior (Figure 6).

We now know that this clearly abnormal pattern of behavioral development was a direct consequence of single-cage housing initiated shortly after
birth. Such housing, of course, allowed the laboratory-born infants to see,
hear, and smell other monkeys, including socially normal adults, on a con-
tinual basis, but it precluded tactile contact and kinesthetic stimulation
from conspecifics almost completely.

Figure 6. Self-clasping and avoidance of social contact in single-cage-reared rhesus monkeys placed in a cage together for the first time.

Formal study of rhesus monkeys reared from birth in single cages or under conditions of visual as well as tactile deprivation revealed long-term deficits that seemed to persist even after the monkeys had been introduced to group living. It was consistently found that rhesus monkeys reared in tactile isolation from conspecifics for at least the first six months of life actively avoided most social contact as adolescents and adults, and in their infrequent social interactions they tended to be hyperaggressive. In addition, though single-cage-reared rhesus monkeys as adults were reproductively normal in the physiological sense, they developed gross abnormalities in their sexual behavior (Harlow, 1962b; Goy, Wallen, & Goldfoot, 1974). Finally, even though many single-cage-reared females eventually became pregnant (often by artificial insemination), some three-fourths of them failed to provide adequate care for their firstborn offspring. Most of these "motherless mothers," as Harlow called them, failed to nurse their offspring, while over a third were physically abusive, making it necessary for the nursery staff to remove the infants for the sake of their survival (Seay, Alexander, & Harlow, 1964; Ruppenthal et al., 1976). In summary, single-cage rearing had severe negative consequences for the development of normal social behavior, and the adverse effects continued well into adulthood.

Mother-Only Versus Peer-Only-Rearing

The devastating effects of tactile isolation during early infancy have become well known to primatologists over the past two decades, and few laboratory-born rhesus monkeys are currently reared under conditions of complete isolation from conspecifics, at least in this country. Nevertheless, many infants continue to be reared in social environments that maintain some degree of tactile isolation from certain classes of conspecifics, while permitting unlimited contact with others. Two such environments are represented by mother-only and peer-only-rearing conditions.

Neither the short- nor the long-term consequences of these conditions are nearly as severe as those associated with single-cage rearing. However, certain social abnormalities are evident. Generally speaking, the longer the period of early deprivation, the greater the likelihood that such abnormalities will appear and the greater their severity. Moreover, the deficits appear to be closely related to the nature of the early contact deprivation. Peer-only-reared rhesus monkeys tend to have problems in activities that normally have their genesis in mother-infant interactions, such as exploratory behavior, while mother-only-reared monkeys typically display deficits in activities normally originating with peers, such as play. When females bear their first offspring, those reared by their mothers only are competent mothers. In contrast, peer-only-reared females are almost as likely to abuse their firstborns as are females isolated from all conspecifics during their first six months of life.

Each of the rearing environments discussed above — single-cage rearing, mother-only-rearing, and peer-only-rearing — involves some degree of tactile contact deprivation initiated at or shortly after birth and maintained for at least six months. Extensive study of the consequences of much shorter periods of touch deprivation has also been carried out with rhesus monkeys and other nonhuman primates over the past 20 years (for a comprehensive review, see, e.g., Mineka & Suomi, 1978).

A large number of studies have convincingly demonstrated that short-term physical separation from a current attachment object typically results in immediate and often dramatic behavioral disruption and intense physiological arousal. These reactions do not appear to be moderated when subjects are able to maintain visual, auditory, and olfactory contact with their attachment object(s) during the period of physical separation. Indeed, in many cases, the availability of such nontactile contact seems to exaggerate the intensity of the separation reaction (e.g., Seay & Harlow, 1965). On the other hand, access to limited tactile contact — for example, through wide-gauge mesh — appears to attenuate the separation reaction (e.g., Suomi et al., 1976).

Cross-Species Comparisons

Taken as a whole, the results of numerous studies of contact deprivation in young rhesus monkeys provide a compelling complement to the general findings from investigation of the role of contact in normal social development in this species. In a nutshell, tactile contact is obviously a very basic and necessary component of normal rhesus monkey social life: The stimulation provided through tactile contact with conspecifics seems crucial for normal development.

In most cases, the results obtained in deprivation studies with other primate species have paralleled the findings for rhesus monkeys. However, there have also been some notable, indeed puzzling, exceptions (Sackett et al., 1976; Berkson, 1968; Sackett et al., 1981). In addition, there appear to be substantial species differences among primates in the nature and intensity of reactions to brief social separations and substantial individual differences between members of the same species in both long-term consequences of single-cage rearing and short-term reactions to separation (e.g., Suomi, 1983).

We hope that eventually studies of tactile contact between nonhuman primates, even though they're not furry little human beings with tails, will give us some insight into the role tactile contact may play at the human level. However, the discovery of major species and individual differences in response to single-cage rearing and brief social separation belies easy explanation or interpretation and makes it difficult to generalize across species with confidence.

DISCUSSION

Seymour Levine: How do you explain the comparative data showing relatively transient effects of long-term social isolation in some species?

Stephen Suomi: Some species, such as pigtails, appear to show essentially spontaneous recovery after isolation when they are introduced to a social group. This is a very puzzling finding. My hunch is that it may be explained in part by the reception isolates get from their conspecifics when they're first put into the group. By macaque standards, rhesus monkeys are unusually aggressive; pigtails are less so. So it may be that pigtail isolates get more appropriate social stimulation when they enter a group than rhesus monkeys do.

William Greenough: Are there sex differences in the profundity of isolation effects?

Stephen Suomi: For rhesus monkeys, the data suggest that social deficits are more pronounced for males reared in isolation than for females, perhaps because the normal adult role requires the male to leave his troop of birth, operate independently for a while, and then join a new troop, which usually isn't eager to have him.

T. Berry Brazelton: Have you found ways to reverse the effects of long-term tactile isolation — to rehabilitate monkey infants that were reared alone?

Stephen Suomi: About ten years ago, Harry Harlow and I did a study in which we attempted to rehabilitate animals reared for the first six months in tactile and visual isolation. We let our isolates, when they came out of isolation, interact with socially competent individuals only three months old, that is, much younger than the isolates themselves. The three-month-olds were socially normal, but still small and too young to be aggressive, so they didn't pose a physical threat to the isolates. Even more important, they were still at an age when ventral contact with another monkey was a major part of their behavioral repertoire.

When the isolates were first introduced to the three-month-old "therapists," they would retreat to the corner of the play room or test cage and roll up into a ball. And the first thing the younger therapists would do was run over and start clinging to the isolates, interacting in essentially the same way they would have with other, normal three-month-olds. We noticed very quickly that with this sort of activity the incidence of abnormal, self-directed behaviors on the part of the isolates began to decline. They began reciprocating and sometimes even initiated contact.

As the therapists grew older, ventral-oriented behaviors began to disappear and were replaced by simple play patterns. During the time they spent with the isolates each day, the therapists would use these play patterns in social interactions. After four or five months of this, there were essentially no statistical differences between the isolates and their younger therapists on any behavior. We had seen what seemed to be pretty complete recovery.

T. Berry Brazelton: What about the "motherless mothers" that abuse or neglect their first infants? Can you rehabilitate them — teach them to be better mothers?

Stephen Suomi: In looking back over the data, one finds that the best predictor of whether a female that abused or neglected one infant was going to be a good mother to another was the amount of time the female spent with the first infant. Specifically, females that spent at least two days — 48 hours — with their infants, no matter what the quality of care, virtually always became good mothers to the next infant.

My speculation is that what is missing from the early experience of the inadequate mothers may be ventral contact with another individual. An inadequate mother that spent 48 hours with her infant, even if she rejected the infant and pushed it away, did experience some ventro-ventro contact. This little bit of experience, even later in life, may be sufficient to make such contact acceptable to the female after subsequent births. It may be like a priming mechanism.

We've instituted some therapeutic approaches based on this idea. In one approach, we give motherless females access to females with infants when they themselves are adolescents or young adults. Another approach uses foster grandparents: male-female pairs that are past reproductive age. These individuals, even though they're too old to reproduce, turn out to be excellent parents. When the motherless infants get frightened, they can run to the older female, who gives ventral contact; the older male often breaks up fights among peers, especially as the isolates grow older. When infant females reared in this way become mothers, the incidence of inadequate mothering is no greater than with females reared by their biological mothers.

Elizabeth McAnarney: Despite the importance of ventro-ventro contact, monkey mothers and infants don't seem to look at each other's faces much. Do you have any comments about that?

Stephen Suomi: To the best of my knowledge, both eye contact and vocal communication are exceedingly common in normal human mother-infant interactions but very rare in rhesus monkeys and other Old World monkeys. Chimpanzees, being great apes, spend a lot more time in eye contact with their infants.

Susan Rose: I'm curious about the differences between the monkey mothers whose infants were taken away right after birth and the mothers who spent at least 48 hours with their infants. Were the monkeys in the latter group less abusive? In other words, is their improved performance with the next infant really a matter of time and ventral contact, or is something else involved?

Stephen Suomi: That's a good question; the data aren't broken down that way. I can tell you, though, that some females have been separated from their infants immediately after the birth because the infants were to be reared in peer-only groups — that is, for experimental reasons having nothing to do with the adequacy of the female's maternal behavior — and these females do not show improvement with subsequent offspring. If a female's first two infants are both taken away at birth, not because of any improper care on her part, there is still a fairly high probability that she'll be a poor mother to the third infant.

T. Berry Brazelton: Steve, do you ever see the biological grandmother prohibit certain maternal behavior toward the infant, or give her daughter directions about it?

Stephen Suomi: I wouldn't call it giving directions, exactly, but you do see grandmothers taking an interest in the maternal behavior of their daughters, and older sisters as well. To what extent these older females are shaping or encouraging certain types of behavior hasn't been tested, but some of that does appear to be going on.

T. Berry Brazelton: Do you have any idea why young monkeys past infancy develop sex-typed behavior patterns? Can you see social prohibitions operating, or something like that?

Stephen Suomi: It's a complicated issue. There's plenty of evidence for a biological basis for some sex-typed behavior differences, but there's also evidence that the differences can be exaggerated by the behavior of those around, especially adults. For example, rhesus adult males ordinarily take little part in caretaking activity and interact very little with infants or youngsters, except that they seem to encourage, if you will, sex-appropriate behavior. These animals will encourage young males, especially those not their own, to engage in rough-and-tumble play, and they'll play back. If a young female tries to initiate rough-and-tumble play, many times the male will swat it or otherwise discourage it. Similarly, you see males intervening when some of the juveniles are engaging in precursors of reproductive behavior, especially if the mix is not right. So I think there's clear evidence of social influence, even though you may be starting off with a biological difference.

Patricia Rausch: Do the females involve themselves in rough-and-tumble play as infants?

Stephen Suomi: Some do at first, but after a few months females tend to avoid that sort of interaction, and if a male tries to initiate it they won't reciprocate. On the other hand, in experimental situations in which a single female is growing up with a group of male peers, this female's play will be rough-and-tumble, for the most part. So it depends on the social situation.

Michael Merzenich: In the unusual case in which a female engages in rough-and-tumble play for several years of life, is she as solid maternally as other females?

Stephen Suomi: Every one that I've seen has turned out to be a perfectly fine mother.

THE HORMONAL CONSEQUENCES OF MOTHER-INFANT CONTACT IN PRIMATES AND RODENTS

Seymour Levine, Ph.D.
and Mark E. Stanton, Ph.D.

When one observes the behavior of mammalian females and their off-spring, with very few exceptions one finds that there is an initial period of time when mother and infant are in constant contact. Aside from reproductive behavior, few other behavior patterns occur as universally. The period varies in length, depending on the species. Rat mothers and their infants remain together almost constantly until the pups are from 8 to 14 days old. For the squirrel monkey, the period lasts approximately one month; for the chimpanzee, approximately six months.

The data we will present suggest that close mother-infant contact has important functional consequences during development. It may be a crucial mechanism whereby infants can modulate their level of arousal.

Primate Studies

The squirrel monkey is an arboreal South American primate that breeds seasonally under natural conditions. As a result, the year is divided approximately into a mating-gestation phase and a birth-rearing phase. At birth, the infant monkey climbs onto the mother's back with minimal assistance, and it remains in continuous contact with her until the onset of independent activities. Nursing is accomplished by the infant shifting to the mother's ventrum and rooting for the nipple. This technique is usually mastered by the second day of life.

As in most primate species, the biological mother is normally the primary caretaker, and a specific attachment relationship appears to develop soon after birth. After the first day, the mother recognizes her own offspring and usually will not accept another infant. Infant selectivity of attachment does not develop as rapidly but is evident by several weeks of age (Kaplan & Russell, 1974). The rapid formation of an attachment relationship appears to occur through the performance of caregiving behavior by the mother and complementary expression of behavioral reflexes (such as clinging, rooting, and suckling) on the part of the infant.

As the infant becomes attracted to other aspects of the environment after the first month of life, there is a fairly rapid decline in affiliative behavior between mother and infant. However, one very characteristic behavior following even mild environmental perturbations is the infant's immediate seeking of proximity and reestablishment of contact with the mother. Thus, even as late as six and seven months of age, when a disturbance occurs in the environment the infant can be observed on the mother's back.

Hormonal Sequelae of Separation

A number of years ago, our laboratory began a systematic series of investigations on mother-infant relationships in the squirrel monkey. We were concerned with the hormonal as well as the behavioral sequelae of brief periods of separation. Pituitary-adrenal activity is an extremely sensitive indicator of the organism's detection of environmental changes, including minor changes in novelty (Hennessy & Levine, 1977; Hennessy et al., 1979a). In addition, this hormonal response often provides evidence of the state of the organism that is difficult to obtain by strictly behavioral measurements (Hennessy & Levine, 1979). For example, the literature on primates indicates that it is difficult to determine any long-term gross behavioral change on the part of the mother following the loss of her infant. We introduced measurement of the hormonal response to alterations in the mother-infant relationship in the hope that we could detect a physiological change.

The data we have obtained lead to a different interpretation of the separation process from the traditional one, which emphasizes infant protest, agitation, and despair (Mineka & Suomi, 1978). Instead, we see the infant's behavior during separation as a set of coping responses that seek to establish reunion with the mother (Levine, 1983). The infant utilizes the mother as its primary mechanism for arousal reduction, and contact with the mother can eliminate or attenuate both behavioral and endocrine responses to arousal-inducing stimuli. In the context of reunion after separation, contact (and therefore touch) may be crucial to the infant's capacity to modulate its own level of arousal.

Of the many stimuli that can induce arousal in the infant, separation from the mother is perhaps the most potent one. In what is now a large number of investigations, we have found that under most circumstances the infant shows a dramatic elevation of plasma cortisol when separated from its mother. Many variables affect the magnitude of this response, including length of separation. Even so, the cortisol response tends to be a much more reliable and invariant response to separation than are behavioral responses.

We investigated the arousal modulating properties of maternal contact and touch in a series of studies that employed a separation-reunion condition (Mendoza et al., 1978). In this procedure, mother and infant are removed from the home cage, separated, and immediately reunited and returned to the home cage for thirty minutes.

Somewhat surprisingly, we found no change in plasma cortisol after thirty minutes of reunion in either the mother or the infant. Two hypotheses were offered to account for this. The first was that mother and infant have the capacity to "buffer" each other from stress; that is, under some conditions contact between mother and infant prevents an increase in arousal as measured by pituitary-adrenal system activity. The alternative explanation was that cortisol levels of both mother and infant were significantly elevated initially but by thirty minutes after reunion had returned to basal levels. We conducted another study, which indicated that the first explanation — that mother-infant contact buffers each member from the stress response — more accurately describes the process (Levine et al., 1978).

In this experiment, mother and infant were separated for thirty minutes and then reunited for thirty minutes. Blood samples were taken at the end of the separation and reunion periods. They showed (Figure 7) that the mother's cortisol level was lower after reunion than after separation. The infant's cortisol level, though it did not decline after reunion, was modulated

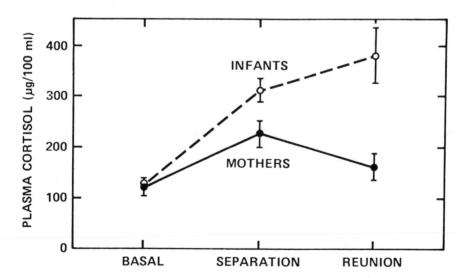

Figure 7. When squirrel monkey infant-mother pairs are separated and reunited, contact modulates the arousing effects of separation stress for both members of the pair.

that it did not show the continued steep rise that characterizes prolonged separations. In general, then, under conditions of separation stress it appears that proximity, and particularly contact with the mother, results in a reduction of both the infant's and the mother's arousal levels.

One of the most important aspects of adaptive behavior in response to stress is control (Levine, 1983). The concept of control plays a central role in coping theory. An organism's capacity to exert control over stressful stimuli results in either an attenuation or an absence of the usual behavioral and hormonal responses. We have proposed that very early in development the infant learns to control its environment by making use of contingent relationships between its responses and outcomes — outcomes which, at this early stage, usually involve the modification of maternal behavior. Thus, the infant's responses to stress, whether vocalization to facilitate contact or high activity levels leading to even more rapid contact, represent mechanisms whereby the infant learns that it can exert some control over its environment and thus maintain some homeostatic balance within the endocrine system.

Contact Comfort and Attachment

Mason (1970) has developed an elaborate theory based on contact comfort as the predominant factor in the establishment of attachment relationships. To quote Mason, "We know from Harlow's celebrated experiments that contact is a significant factor in the development of filial attachment. We have reason to conclude that the affected mechanism is reduction in emotional arousal." Mason's theory of development of filial attachment in monkeys is based primarily on the phenomenon of clinging, and therefore touch. The data indicate that the presence of a surrogate in an unfamiliar environment can ameliorate the behavioral and physiological responses of the surrogate-reared infant placed in a novel condition.

Cortisol studies show an important difference between surrogate-reared and mother-reared primate infants, however (Hennessy et al., 1979b). In a mother-reared infant, only the mother appears to be capable of reducing the infant's cortisol response, whereas in a surrogate-reared infant, almost any object the animal can cling to reduces the response. These data emphasize the importance of clinging in surrogate-reared infants but also raise issues about the attachment process. For the mother-reared infant, only contact with the primary attachment figure appears to reduce arousal levels.

Rodent Studies

Whereas primates are precocial species, rodents are altricial species;

that is, they are born in a highly underdeveloped and helpless state. The response characteristics and sensory capacities of the neonatal rat pup are, at best, restricted. Many physiological functions are regulated by the mother, upon whom the newborn pup is extremely dependent.

During the first 10 days of the neonatal rat pup's life, when it is most helpless, the mother determines when and for how long bouts of mother-infant contact occur. Beginning at 15 or 16 days, the pups begin to eat and drink independently, and the mother spends increasingly less time with them. However, suckling and maternal contact remain important to pups as old as 20 days of age. Thus, although many aspects of development in the infant rat are clearly different from those of the squirrel monkey, a pattern of intensive continued mother-infant contact and subsequent maintenance of that contact (even after a period of independence) appears to be common to both species.

There is now a large body of literature dealing with arousal and pituitary-adrenal system activity in the rat. Most developmental research has been concerned with the processes whereby young rodents increase their pituitary-adrenal output. However, in recent years it has been demonstrated that there is also a central inhibitory process. In adults, certain consummatory behaviors (such as drinking and eating) appear to have a rapid and pronounced suppressive effect on pituitary-adrenal activity (Levine, Weinberg, & Brett, 1979). In examining mother-infant behavior, we therefore decided to assess the possible suppressive effects of suckling on infant arousal.

At 12, 16, and 20 days, rat pups were exposed to thirty minutes of novelty (they were placed individually in a small, heated test chamber they had never encountered before). Pups were then assigned to one of four experimental conditions. The infants in two conditions spent the test period suckling an anesthetized dam, one group receiving periodic milk infusions through an oral cannula, the other not. The infants in the other two conditions spent the test period alone in a test chamber (no dam was present); again, one group received milk infusions while the other did not. After half an hour in these conditions, blood was collected for assay of plasma corticosterone.

The results showed that at all ages the opportunity to contact and suckle an anesthetized dam markedly lowered levels of plasma corticosterone compared to levels shown by pups placed alone in the novel chamber. In contrast, consumption of milk delivered through an oral cannula had no significant effect, regardless of whether it occurred at the same time as suckling or not.

These results show that pituitary-adrenal activity in infant rats can be inhibited by maternal reunion and suckling. They do not, however, show whether suckling is necessary for this inhibitory effect or whether maternal contact is sufficient. We therefore performed a second experiment examining the role of these factors under the experimental conditions used in the previous experiment. The findings showed that maternal contact per se is sufficient to produce the effect, at least at the younger ages studied.

The Importance of Contact

Although our data implicate contact and touch in the infant's ability to regulate its own responses to stress, these studies were clearly not designed specifically to examine touch. They are confounded by a number of other potentially important variables, particularly the simple proximity of a familiar conspecific — the mother. What is impressive, however, is that contact seems to be an invariant response to novel or disturbing environmental conditions. This has been demonstrated most clearly in the monkey, but there is also evidence of similar behavior in the rat.

A major difference between the squirrel monkey and the rat is that, for the squirrel monkey, once an attachment relationship has been established only contact with the mother appears to buffer the response to stress. In the rat, there is no evidence of attachment in the traditional sense. Thus, rats resemble surrogate-reared primates in that almost any lactating dam that the infant rat can contact and suckle has the capacity to reduce the infant's pituitary-adrenal output. Nevertheless, contact with a maternal object, or with an object to which an infant can cling, does play an important role in the infant's capacity to modulate its response to stress.

In the case of primate mother-reared infants, we believe that this role has long-term consequences for the development of coping mechanisms. The data we have obtained on rodents are less fully developed. However, since the processes appear to be generally similar, it is reasonable to hypothesize that the long-term consequences in terms of adaptive mechanisms would also be functional in this, as in other, species.

DISCUSSION

T. Berry Brazelton: Your work really brings out the importance of tactile contact as a control system. Touch helps one learn how to deal with inner stress responses as well as outer ones. It's fascinating to me that contact regulates the mother's responses as well as the infant's. Of course, in parent-child work like mine, we can't just look at the baby and ignore the mother's intentions and actions and feedback systems.

Seymour Levine: The very concept of mother-infant interaction, of a mutual relationship, requires that one look at both members of the pair. The mother-infant relationship is the primordial social system. This is where the infant begins the whole process of being able to utilize the elements of its environment to become a socialized organism, and touch is vital to that process.

William Greenough: As Renée pointed out, touch is always reciprocal. You don't have to look at someone who's looking at you, but it's impossible not to touch someone who is touching you.

T. Berry Brazelton: We often see a grief-like reaction in mothers who give up their babies to daycare in early infancy. Do you think they experience a rise in cortisol that they habituate to over time?

Seymour Levine: My interpretation emphasizes coping rather than habituation. Coping involves an active set of mechanisms — psychological defenses that appear to be effective in reducing the cortisol response. Essentially, the mother develops a set of skills to deal with the new situation.

Susan Rose: Do you think uncertainty plays a role in elevating cortisol?

Seymour Levine: Cortisol levels are very sensitive to specific psychological events that seem to have an element of uncertainty, such as loss of control, novelty, exams, impending surgery.

Susan Rose: Has anyone looked at cortisol levels in human infants?

Seymour Levine: No. Technically it could be done, but practically there are a lot of problems. It is known, though, that adult women show a dramatic cortisol elevation as a function of the birth process itself. It would be very nice to determine how rapidly cortisol returns to a basal level, with and without contact with the infant. How effective the infant is in modulating the mother's response is a very important question.

Michael Merzenich: I'd like to make a couple of physiological points that relate to your paper and to Steve Suomi's. One is that there are differences in the distribution of receptors on the body surface, and a mammal — a primate, like a rhesus monkey or an owl monkey — has a very high proportional representation of what are called slowly adapting afferents on the belly skin. These receptors are excited continuously when the belly skin is depressed, as during ventral contact between mother and infant. An increase in these slowly adapting afferents on the breast is one of the secondary sex characteristic changes of female primates.

Second, I think it's obvious that there are differences of affect when different forms of stimulation are applied to the skin. Touch can be calming or irritating; tickling the feet has different results from stroking the belly.

We think of the qualitative aspects of sensation as being among the highest aspects of our behavior, but from a neurological point of view I don't think they're hard to understand. There is a unique mix of tactile inputs, with unique qualitative sensations evoked, from different skin regions on the body. Neurologically, it's fairly easy to see how I might imagine that some kind of contact with my stomach is a good thing!

Seymour Levine: That's not quite enough, because it suggests that contact is all, which it clearly is not. As the work with surrogate monkey mothers shows, contact serves a lot of functional purposes, but contact alone will not give you an infant that develops adaptively. Something else is involved, something related to the infant's capacity to utilize what is going on in the environment.

Michael Merzenich: There are certainly differences in the feedback situations of an infant with a surrogate and an infant with its mother. With the surrogate, there are obviously some things missing from this mutual feedback.

Seymour Levine: That's one useful way of looking at things, but I don't think it gives you the whole picture.

TOUCH, ATTACHMENT, AND HEALTH—IS THERE A RELATIONSHIP?

Martin L. Reite, M.D.

Touch is a magic word, loaded with meanings and connotations. The Oxford English Dictionary devotes over 1,800 lines to definitions of touch. One very important connotation of the word *touch* is an association with healing, as in the laying on of the hands to effect a cure. The Bible is replete with references to the healing powers of touch. For example:

> When he was come down from the mountain, great multitudes
> followed him. And behold, there came a leper and worshipped
> him, saying, Lord, if thou wilt, thou canst make me clean. And
> Jesus put forth his hand and touched him, saying, I will; be

thou clean. And immediately his leprosy was cleansed (Matthew 8:1-3).

This meaning of the word extends from early history up to and through the present day. It forms a significant part of this conference.

It is the purpose of this paper to examine a possible mechanism whereby a basis in science might be found to underlie such folklore. My thesis might be stated as follows: Touch is a fundamental, possibly necessary, component of the development of the earliest social attachment bonds. Attachment bonds are central to the normal development and integrative functioning of high primates, especially human beings. Their presence is associated with pleasurable states and good physical health. Their absence, or disruption, is associated with discomfort and increased risk of impaired health. Their inappropriate disruption may constitute a major psychobiological insult to the organism. The strong belief that touch has healing powers may be related to the fact that, having once been a major component in the development of attachment bonds, it retains the ability to act as a releaser of certain physiological accompaniments of attachment — specifically, those associated with good feeling states and good health. The exhaustive treatment of this subject would require a volume of its own, but I will attempt to sketch it in outline form here.

Touch and the Development of Attachment

In high primates, both human and nonhuman, one of the fundamental and earliest attachment relationships is the bond between mother and infant. Physical contact — touch — appears central to the development of this relationship. Harlow (1962a) stated,

> Our research on the first affectional system indicated that there are multiple variables operating to tie the infant monkey to the mother, and they are similar to those described and stressed by Bowlby for the human being. The most important single variable disclosed by our research is sheer bodily contact between infant and mother (p. 210).

Others in this symposium have presented empirical data that bear on this issue (see preceding papers by Suomi, and Levine and Stanton). In short, converging data from many sources implicate touch as central to the development of attachment in primates.

Much less is known about human beings. Klaus and Kennell (1982), after examining observational data from a number of investigators on the patterns and sequence of the way in which mothers touch their newborns, stated,

> Thus we have fragmentary evidence for what we believe is a significant principle — that human mothers engage in a species-specific sequence of (touching) behaviors when first meeting their infants, even though the speed of this sequence is modified by environmental and cultural conditions (p. 73).

Perhaps also relevant is the observation that infants classified as "anxiously attached" (as opposed to "securely attached") frequently have mothers who demonstrate an aversion to close body contact (Ainsworth et al., 1978). Such individuals tend to show up disproportionately in samples of abused or neglected children (Gaensbauer & Harmon, 1982). The current situation with respect to human beings has perhaps best been summarized by Montagu (1971):

> We do not have much evidence of a direct kind that tactile stimulation or its absence affects the growth and development, physical or psychological, of the human infant. Such direct evidence is largely lacking for the simple reason that it has never been sought in man. We do, however, have as we have seen, plenty of direct evidence of this sort for nonhuman animals. Also, we have a great deal of direct evidence in human infants which thoroughly supports the extrapolation that tactile stimulation is at least as important in the physical and psychological growth of the human infant as it is in the nonhuman infant (p. 191).

Physiological Correlates of Mother-Infant Separation

In this section I will briefly examine the physiological correlates of mother-infant separation in several species of macaque monkey. One aspect of separation, although certainly not the only one, is deprivation of touch. Our data relate to clinical issues and may begin to provide a viewpoint for conceptualizing the role of touch in healing.

Early work in monkey mother-infant separation was a direct outgrowth of the description by Spitz (1946) of anaclitic depression and the descriptions of protest-despair behavior in human infants and children separated from their mothers (Robertson, 1953; Bowlby, 1953; 1960). A series of monkey studies followed, performed in several laboratories during the 1960s (see

Reite & Short, 1983, for review). These studies demonstrated that monkey infants, separated from their mothers, exhibited a protest-despair or agitation-depression behavioral reaction that looked quite similar to the reaction of human infants and children. While most of the altered behavior resolved following reunion with the mother, long-term effects apparently due to early maternal separation experiences could be demonstrated as long as 24 months after brief separations in rhesus monkeys (Spencer-Booth & Hinde, 1971).

During the past decade, our laboratory has been examining the physiological correlates of the agitation-depression behavioral reaction following maternal separation in young pigtail monkeys (Reite et al., 1974). In a typical experiment, infants are born and reared in their natural social groups. Extensive behavioral data are collected from birth on. At about four to six months of age, a multichannel biotelemetry system is surgically implanted in the infant under general anesthesia and begins transmitting multivariable physiological data around the clock. The data are processed by an on-line dedicated computer system (Reite & Short, 1983).

After a baseline period of four to seven days, the mothers are removed from the social group. The infants immediately become quite agitated and upset. They search vigorously for the mothers and exhibit frequent cooing, the distress call of the young macaque. The period of behavioral agitation is accompanied by marked increases in both heart rate and body temperature, characteristic of generalized physiological arousal. Studies in other laboratories have shown that the initial period of protest or agitation is accompanied as well by prominent increases in serum cortisol (Gunnar et al., 1981).

Agitation is followed in a day or two by a profoundly different reaction, distinguished by a slouched posture, little or no play behavior, a slowing of motion with evidence of impaired coordination, and a sad facial expression. This period of behavioral "depression" is accompanied by decreases in heart rate and body temperature (Reite et al., 1978), increases in cardiac arrhythmias (Seiler et al., 1979), and disturbances in nocturnal sleep patterns, including more time awake, more frequent arousals, less rapid-eye-movement (REM) sleep, longer REM latencies, and a fragmentation and shifting of slow wave sleep to later in the night (Reite & Short, 1983).

Figure 8 shows an implanted infant during the baseline period prior to separation. The infant is being enclosed by the mother, and its concomitant physiology is presented at the left of the photograph. Figure 9 shows the same infant after separation, exhibiting the slouched posture and sad facial expression characteristic of depression. Once again, the simultaneous physiology is illustrated at the left.

Several recent studies from our laboratory have suggested that separation experiences, both peer and mother-infant, may affect immunological

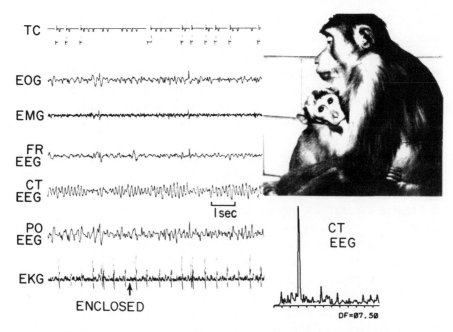

Figure 8. A 22-week-old pigtail infant enclosed by its mother, with the simultaneously transmitted physiological data illustrated on the left. TC = time code; EOG = eye movement; EMG = posterior nuchal muscle activity; FR EEG = frontal EEG; CT EEG = central-temporal EEG; PO EEG = parieto-occipital EEG; EKG = electrocardiogram. The photo was taken at the time indicated by the arrow beneath the EKG tracing. A power spectral plot based upon a fast Fourier transform (FFT) of the illustrated epoch of CT EEG is illustrated at the lower right. Dominant frequency was 7.5 Hz.

function as well as autonomic physiology (Reite, Harbeck, & Hoffman, 1981; Laudenslager, Reite, & Harbeck, 1982). This constellation of physiological changes is compatible with an alteration or impairment in central autonomic homeostasis; we have suggested it may represent a disturbance in hypothalamic regulation of autonomic activity and immune function.

Primate Separation and Human Loss

It is interesting to examine these findings in relation to symptoms of grief in human beings, since the separated monkey infants appeared to show a grief response. Typical somatic symptoms of grief in human beings include loss of appetite and weight, insomnia, cardiac irregularities, shortness of breath and sighing, and either apathy and withdrawal or restlessness (Lindemann, 1944; Averill, 1968; Parkes, 1972). While we have no independent measures of appetite or respiration, young monkeys undergoing

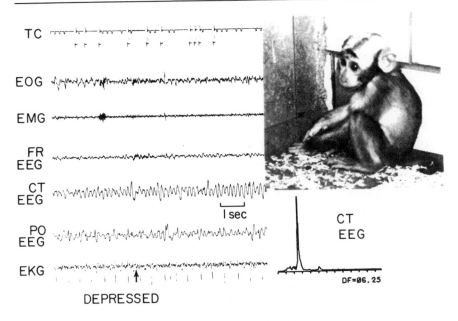

TC

EOG

EMG

FR
EEG

CT
EEG

| 1 sec

PO
EEG

EKG

CT
EEG

DF=06.25

DEPRESSED

Figure 9. The same infant during the period of behavioral depression following maternal separation. The CT EEG activity is still present but has decreased in frequency to 6.25 Hz.

separation from the mother show clear changes in heart rate, sleep patterns, and motor activity, in directions similar to those just described for human beings.

There have now been several reports of alterations in cellular immune function following bereavement in human adults (Bartrop et al., 1977; Schleifer et al., 1983). These alterations are similar to those we have found in pigtail infants separated from their peers and in bonnet mothers and infants separated from each other.

The presence of impaired physiological homeostasis, with disturbance in immunological function, following separations and losses may provide the beginning of an explanation for the by now well-established increase in morbidity and mortality following bereavement (Epstein et al., 1975; Jacobs & Ostfeld, 1977). It may also help explain the mounting evidence implicating separations and losses in the etiology of various nonpsychiatric medical disorders (Reite & Short, 1983). In a nine-year major epidemiological follow-up study of 6,928 randomly selected adults in Alameda County, California, Berkman and Syme (1979) found that people who lacked social and community ties were more likely to die in the follow-up period than were those with more extensive contacts. In a similar vein, the presence of social attachments has been linked to improved health (Cassel, 1974; 1976).

A major function of social attachment may be the promotion and facilitation of psychobiological synchrony between individuals. Implicit in this notion is that such synchrony would be associated with optimal functioning of physiological systems, which could well result in improved health. This idea, expressed initially by Bowlby (1973), has recently been reviewed with supporting evidence by Field (in press) and Reite and Capitanio (in press). Further, attachment behaviors may well be mediated by specific CNS anatomical and neurochemical systems, involving especially limbic and hypothalamic regions (Reite & Capitanio, in press; Steklis & Kling, in press; Panksepp, Siviy, & Normansell, in press).

How might all this be related to touch? It seems that touch is instrumental in the development and maintenance of attachment, at least in the early life of high primates. Subsequently, the experience of touch in appropriate situations may exert a regulating or signal influence on physiological systems similar to that afforded by the process of "being attached." To the extent that this experience promotes improved physiological functioning and ultimately improved health, touch could be viewed as a signal stimulus capable of evoking or reactivating a more complex organismic reaction, one component of which is improved physiological functioning.

The mechanisms that might underlie such a relationship remain obscure. The evidence for behaviorally conditioned immunosuppression described by Ader and Cohen (1975) does suggest, however, that the immune system may be responsive to conditioned learning. Similarly, considerable evidence now exists suggesting that many physiological symptoms, including autonomic, are capable of being influenced by learning (Miller, 1978; 1981). Thus, a set of data exists that would provide an explanatory basis for relating touch to altered physiological function. We hope continued work in this area will clarify our knowledge of the relationship between touch, attachment, and health.

DISCUSSION

Judith Smith: In discussing loss and human illness, what do you mean by loss?

Martin Reite: I mean loss in a comprehensive sense. I think the best illustration of loss in terms of its increasing one's susceptibility to illness was Robert Burton's *Anatomy of Melancholy,* published in 1621, in which he first related loss to the development of depression or affective disorders. He included under loss not only the loss of a person, as through bereavement, but the loss of health, a major symbolic loss, a loss of self-esteem. Loss is very stressful.

There is ample evidence that separations and losses, or the disruption of attachment bonds, can lead to impaired health. There is also evidence that the presence of attachments promotes health, and that tactile stimulation is important to the development of attachment bonds. What I'm suggesting is that perhaps on some symbolic level touch invokes mechanisms associated with attachment that ultimately can lead to optimal physiological functioning.

Kathryn Barnard: In your series of studies, did the monkey infants that were separated from their mothers recover?

Martin Reite: Some animals recover completely and others don't. They show long-term changes for some four to six weeks after reunion with the mother.

T. Berry Brazelton: Does that have anything to do with the mother's behavior?

Martin Reite: It may. We haven't studied it directly, but we have noticed that the mothers of animals that have not recovered seem less interested in the infants after reunion than they were during the baseline period.

T. Berry Brazelton: In our work, we often see a reaction that looks like grief in mothers who must put a child in the hospital or in daycare. This is something that we've ignored for too long. I know from experience that when a young baby goes into daycare, we can expect the child to have sleep problems, feeding problems, and immunological problems for the next few months, until the adjustment is made. And I know the same thing will happen to the mother: she too will have sleep problems, eating problems, and immunological problems for a while. Maybe we can play a preventive role and somehow aid the homeostatic system that we're dealing with.

Martin Reite: We have here a response system that we've sort of taken for granted for a number of years. We've been implicitly aware of its importance, and what we're trying to do now is to work out the biology of the system. I think we're going to find out that there's a lot of biology involved, and one of our goals should be to try and look at it from both a comparative and a phylogenetic standpoint. If we can understand the biology, then the psychology will make more sense.

MATERNAL AVERSION TO MOTHER-INFANT CONTACT

M. Louise Biggar, Ph.D.

I begin with a simple observation. There are individual differences in parents' feelings regarding physical contact with their infants, differences that become manifest when an infant is frightened or apprehensive and attempts to approach the parent. Under these conditions, a majority of parents adopt an open posture and gladly accept the infant in mutual ventral contact. But others adjust their bodies so that the infant is barred from access, or actively turn the approaching infant's body so that the infant's ventral surface does not touch theirs, or simply push the infant away.

A given parent's response to close bodily contact with an infant is stable over fairly long periods. This has been demonstrated in a study based on the narrative records of mother-infant interaction made by Ainsworth and colleagues as they visited the homes of 26 Baltimore families throughout the first year of infant life. One set of judges made ratings of a mother's apparent aversion to physical contact with her infant during the infant's first three months. An entirely independent judge observed the mother's response to the infant's active efforts to initiate contact nine months later, at about one year of age. This judge simply tallied the number of times the mother actively rejected the child's bids for contact. The correlation with mother's earlier aversion to physical contact with the infant was very high (.72).

This impressive stability seems likely to be echoed in our own longitudinal study. In this study we began by rating parents for observed aversion to contact with their infants at 12 or 18 months of age. Because we were videotaping, we were able to observe parental facial expressions as well as postural responses. While, again, most parents welcomed infant approaches (both posturally and otherwise), some showed facial expressions of distaste and some winced or suddenly pulled away. In addition, we found a relationship between aversion to contact with an infant and anger toward the infant, that is, a positive correlation between aversion to contact observed in one setting and rough handling of the infant's body observed in another.

We are now bringing families into our laboratories while the children are six years of age. Although the data are not all in, we think we see a remarkable stability over the five-year period. The parents who showed the greatest aversion to physical contact when their children were infants now seem to avoid even mutual ventral body orientation. Returning to a room in which the six-year-old has been examined, these parents approach the child from behind, speak to the child from behind, and touch the child only gingerly. Infants whose parents showed strong aversion to close bodily contact might still try repeatedly to make contact. At six, the children seem to join the parents in avoiding a mutual ventral orientation, even across a distance.

Having reported considerable stability in individual differences in parental aversion to physical contact, I am ready to present both some theory and some empirical results. First, I examine some implications of attachment theory, which suggest that an attached but physically rejected infant is placed in a conflict situation similar to the double bind described by Bateson and his colleagues (1956). Next, I review some empirical work from my laboratories showing anger and conflict in physically rejected infants. Finally, I report briefly on our search for an understanding of individual differences in parental response to close bodily contact.

Attachment in Primates

Startled, threatened, and frightened primate infants instinctually seek their attachment figures. For this reason, acts of physical rejection by the primate mother often lead to a peculiar response on the part of the infant (e.g., Kaufman & Rosenblum, 1969). Rather than simply withdrawing, the primate infant often tries again to approach the mother or clings to the mother all the harder. It seems, in fact, that the immediate effect of a mother's rejection of her primate infant is to draw the infant toward her. The mother both repels and at some level simultaneously attracts the infant.

This situation should be expected to create an ultimately self-perpetuating conflict for the infant. It should also lead to aggression, avoidance, and conflict behaviors on the part of the infant. On what grounds can we predict these specific consequences for a mother's rejection of physical contact with her infant? The ethologically oriented theory of infant-mother attachment developed by Bowlby (1969; 1973; 1980) seems to explain two of them, angry or aggressive behavior and conflict behavior.

This theory suggests that human and many nonhuman primates (providing they are not subjected to grossly abnormal rearing conditions) develop one or a few specific and focused attachments to caregiving adults by the time of the onset of locomotion. Once these attachments have developed, we may speak of the working of an attachment behavioral system (Bowlby, 1969). This is an internally constructed system that functions to track the accessibility of attachment figures as a basis for exploration and a haven of safety in times of trouble. The system is considered to be as vital to survival, and hence to reproduction, as is the sexual behavioral system.

Now let me derive what I see as some unexamined consequences of ethological or evolutionary attachment theory. As we normally conceive the working of the attachment behavioral system, the child who is alarmed — whether by thunder, predators, or threats from conspecifics — inevitably seeks the primary attachment figure as a haven of safety. But if alarm stemming from *any* source activates a system designed to bring the infant and attachment figure into close proximity, then the system can be activated even by the attachment figure herself.

Therefore, a child whose mother roughly pushes him or her away will experience a desire to approach the mother even though she is the "predator." At the same time, the child will experience some fear of the mother and some desire to withdraw from her. What is peculiar to the situation in which the attack comes from the "haven of safety" is the arousal of conflicting tendencies. From this single threat or signal at least two conflicting messages are received: to go away from, and to come toward, the haven of safety.

The conflict created is self-perpetuating. Rejection by the attachment figure activates attachment behavioral systems which are necessarily frustrated, and therefore still more strongly activated. This is positive feedback. At the same time, withdrawal tendencies conflict with approach tendencies, and the impossibility of approach arouses anger. Eventually, the physically rejected child may feel fearful and angry in every situation that normally arouses love or longing.

A Double Bind

The conflict situation just described resembles the double-bind situation described by Bateson and colleagues (1956) and implicated by them as an environmental contributor to the development of schizophrenia. Their original example concerned a schizophrenic son observed while his mother was visiting him in the hospital. The mother stiffened and withdrew as her son attempted to embrace her in greeting; at the same moment, she asked, "Don't you love me?" Thus, she gave simultaneous conflicting signals to her son, one nonverbal and the other verbal.

The physically rejecting mothers in our study gave the same nonverbal signal as the mother in Bateson's example. But the opposing message, namely the instinctual injunction to *approach* the attachment figure when threatened, comes from the infant's own inner state, that is, from the infant's attachment to the mother. In addition, this signal as well as the mother's is nonverbal. Despite these differences, the situation described by Bateson and the situation I describe are basically analogous.

Infant Anger and Conflict

If this formulation is correct, we should expect to observe certain behavioral consequences on the part of the physically rejected, attached infant — specifically, anger and conflict. To test this prediction, we undertook a study of three independent samples of infants and mothers. In sample 1, we videotaped 38 mothers actively interacting with their 21-month-old infants in Baltimore during a 10-minute play session. Sample 2 was the Baltimore sample studied by Mary Ainsworth and described earlier. Here we had available narrative records of 24 hours of home observation for 26 mother-infant pairs. Sample 3 was 30 mother-infant pairs who were observed during a 10-minute interaction with a stranger.

The mother's aversion to contact with the infant was rated, with special attention to the parent's attitude toward ventral contact. In the infant, conflict behavior was identified as any behavior that seemed odd, disturbing, or worrisome to observers. Although the coder was instructed to score only "odd" behaviors, a review of these showed that they could also be described largely as conflict behaviors (see Hinde, 1966). Examples include hand-flapping, echoing of the speech of others, sudden fear of a toy, and laughter in a false manner into empty space.

We found a significant relationship between mother's observed aversion to physical contact with the infant and infant conflict behavior in all three samples. Indeed, in Ainsworth's Baltimore sample, mother's observed aversion to contact with her infant in the first three months of life predicted infant conflict behavior nine months later.

It was also possible in the Baltimore sample to compare mother's aversion to contact with the infant in the first months of life to infant anger and aggression between nine and twelve months of age. We found that the greater the mother's observed aversion to physical contact with the infant during the first three months, the more anger seemed to direct the infant's mood and activities nine months later. In addition, the more the mother had shown an early aversion to physical contact with the infant, the more frequently the infant struck or angrily threatened to strike the mother in relatively stress-free situations.

Touch as a Facet of Development

A natural consequence of an interest in touch as a facet of early experience might be a search for individual differences in development as a consequence of differing absolute *amounts* of touch as a sensory experience. In this paper I have tried to demonstrate another approach.

Evolutionary attachment theory suggests we set aside the notion that touch as a purely sensory experience, apart from questions of who and when and how, can have much meaning for human infants who have reached the stage of forming attachments to caregivers. From that time forward, the physical and hence tactual accessibility of certain persons (including, of course, daycare caregivers) is continually monitored by the infant and becomes an organizing principle in infant behavior. Rejection of physical contact *by attachment figures* has specific consequences, as I have shown. It leads initially to increased approach efforts and eventually to anger and conflict. Rejection of physical contact by mere acquaintances or strangers does not usually have these consequences. Touch, by late infancy, has meaning chiefly in terms of physical contact with attachment figures. We will not be able to understand the influence of touch on early human development unless we understand these issues.

DISCUSSION

T. Berry Brazelton: Louise, tactile accessibility is an elegant idea, and the sensitivity of your observations is very impressive. Intention and the ability to perceive intention in others are critical to the nurturing process, whether mother-infant or nurse-patient. I think what you're demonstrating about attachment is that it can be studied scientifically. It doesn't need to be mystical anymore.

Susan Rose: When you assessed the children in your study at six years of age, did you use an attachment paradigm?

Louise Biggar: Yes. We assessed the apparent security of the relationship during a three-minute reunion with the parent after an hour of separation. At six, the children who had been called very secure at one year initiated conversation with the parent, spoke to the parent in a personal way, or were highly responsive conversationally. They initiated some physical contact as well, but verbal communications seemed to substitute for body contact some of the time.

The six-year-olds who had been deemed very insecure as infants showed three main patterns of behavior. One group was linguistically avoidant. These children responded minimally to questions, tried not to engage the parent in conversation, and talked only about things, not personal state. As I mentioned in my paper, these children might even avoid ventral orientation with the parent, by crossing the room or moving away. Another group was quite rejecting of the parent, saying "Don't bother me" or "Why don't you go sit over there." The third pattern, which was rare, we called inappropriate caregiving. Children in this group seemed to become parental toward their parents, reflecting another kind of organization of attachment in infancy.

Sandra Weiss: Are you assuming that mutual ventral contact is the healthiest behavior?

Louise Biggar: Not necessarily. I'm just showing that there are individual differences in mothers' preparation for it and response to it.

T. Berry Brazelton: Certainly it's a form of accessibility. I'm intrigued that you studied attachment using mutual ventral contact as your variable. I could do the same using rhythmic or matching behaviors on the part of the mother, her sensitivity to the baby, I think. Perhaps you could look at almost any system and find similar nonverbal signals operating.

Louise Biggar: I certainly don't believe that touch is the ultimate answer, the only modality.

Attachment may be biological at first, but I think it moves to be representational. A part of our study demonstrated this. When the children were six, we transcribed their conversations with their parents after reunion — only the words, with no attention to stress or intonation. Then I asked a sociolinguist to try to match the transcripts with our records of nonverbal interactions between the same mother-child pairs during infancy. She was able to do so correctly for 52 of our 66 pairs. This shows the absolute translation of nonverbal behavior into a new, representational system.

Elizabeth McAnarney: Were the infants in your study firstborns or laterborns? Having raised other children might make a difference.

Louise Biggar: The sample was mixed.

Seymour Levine: The parity issue is interesting. We lose many more of our firstborn primate infants than we do laterborns. Roughly half the first infants of young mothers die, whereas almost all laterborns survive. Monkeys in the wild show a similar pattern — a fairly large loss of firstborns. Monkeys don't wait through the whole socialization process before they begin to mate and reproduce, and the youth of first-time mothers may have something to do with their lack of skill. What is your experience, Marty?

Martin Reite: Our firstborn mortality is not that high, but it is higher than with laterborns. Even more interesting to me than parity is the effect on maternal behavior of being raised in isolation during infancy. Very few monkeys that have been raised in total or severe social isolation become good mothers with their first infants, but a few of them — maybe one in four — do fine. The implications of the system's being activated in the absence of any relevant experience at all are very significant. It's very much as if you're looking at a strong biological system.

Another interesting thing is that so little experience with a firstborn is required for the mother to do better with the second infant. As Steve Suomi pointed out in his paper, as little as 48 hours of contact with the first infant is enough to turn the monkey into a good mother later.

Seymour Levine: Yes. The infants that don't survive are lost very early, a day or two after birth. There isn't time for the mothers to gain much experience.

Paul Satz: Is there any evidence that human mothers who do badly with their firstborns do better with later children? Is there a human parallel to the primate behavior we've been discussing?

Kathryn Barnard: We've found that mothers get much more efficient with experience — that may be relevant. In addition, Thoman's research shows that mothers take a lot more time around feedings with a first infant than with laterborns. One reason may be that the experienced mother has less to learn.

T. Berry Brazelton: Even in the supposedly mystical area of mother-infant attachment, there are variables that can be rather clear indicators of outcome. This should give hope to those of you who work with therapeutic touch, another supposedly mystical area in which outcome research is badly needed.

Martin Reite: I think Louise's work demonstrates beautifully that if you're very careful, use sensitive instruments, and are a good scientist, you can measure things that are hard to measure.

Developmental Perspectives

PART IV
PRETERM INFANTS—
TOO FRAGILE TO TOUCH?

Part IV concerns the touch needs of a special group: tiny preterm or small-for-date infants with immature nervous and respiratory systems. The first two papers, by Jerold Lucey and Peter Gorski and colleagues, suggest that the care routinely provided in neonatal special care units may be too "intensive" for very immature infants. In contrast, intervention studies described by Susan Rose, Patricia Rausch, and Anneliese Korner suggest that gentle tactile and kinesthetic stimulation benefits the development of most preterms. Allen Gottfried relates these data to known sequences of prenatal sensory development, and to his own findings on the tactile environment of the neonatal nursery.

THE SLEEPING, DREAMING FETUS MEETS THE INTENSIVE CARE NURSERY

Jerold F. Lucey, M.D.

Thirty years ago, when I first entered the premature nursery at Bellevue Hospital as a frightened intern, I was confronted by a head nurse who announced "the rules." One of them was, "Don't touch the babies unnecessarily!" Over the next 30 years I was often confronted by nurses asking, "What are you doing to that baby?"

We really didn't do very much, but everything we did was regarded rather critically. The dogma of that era was that small infants were best left alone, isolated from infection. The nurse was the protector, and the incubator was the infant's protective cocoon.

As new treatments emerged, our attitudes changed. The pendulum may have swung too far toward the other extreme. Small, sick infants are now subjected to dozens of diagnostic procedures and handled over 100 times a day. Survival rates have certainly increased. I do not want anybody to interpret my remarks to mean that I am not a believer in intensive care. I am, but I am having second thoughts about how "intensive" it should be. There must be an upper limit to the amount of handling an infant can take, and I suspect we are probing that upper limit now.

A New Technique

Ten years ago, we were preoccupied with the problem of how to measure blood gases in small infants. Microsampling techniques were becoming widely available, and we were trying to figure out how they should be used. It was considered good care to do three or four blood gas studies a day. Then in 1972, the German physicians Huch and Huch developed a special electrode that measured oxygen tension (PO_2) on the skin. You could leave it on for hours and record continuously. In 1978 this concept of using the skin as a window through which to monitor oxygen tension, and later carbon dioxide and bilirubin, came to America, where it is now widely used.

We've learned a great deal with transcutaneous oxygen monitoring. First we learned that the blood oxygen tension wasn't stable at all. It was changing rapidly. When we looked for reasons, we discovered that virtually every procedure that disturbed an infant or caused pain resulted in a fall in oxygen tension in the blood, including diapering, weighing, overfeeding, circumcision, drawing a blood sample, and various other diagnostic procedures (Figure 10). These events can have a cumulative effect on an infant and drive the oxygen tension down to levels that require assisted ventilation (Figure 11). We began to get the message: Sick infants are very sensitive to all procedures.

We wondered if oxygen tension was also unstable in healthy infants and found that it was, but only to a *very* minor degree. We then wondered whether soothing touches or breastfeeding would cause oxygen tension to fall. They don't.

We decided to see if we could quantify how much time an infant spent with a low blood oxygen tension or a high oxygen tension (Long, Philip, & Lucey, 1980). We studied 15 control and 15 experimental infants for 20 hours of continuous O_2 recording. The people caring for the control group were blind to the $TcPO_2$ measurements. The results showed that the control infants spent 40 minutes out of 20 hours in "undesirable time." The experimental group was identically monitored, but the nurses and residents used the monitors to decide on care. In other words, when they saw a falling oxygen level because of a procedure, they stopped and gave oxygen.

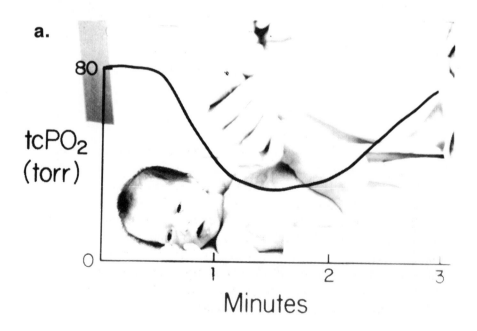

b.

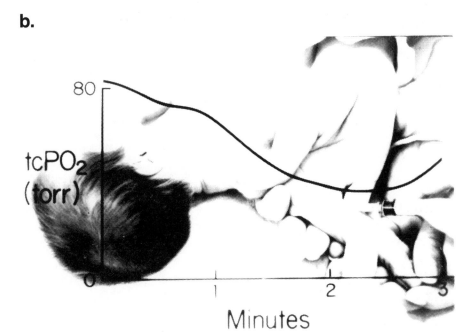

c.

Figure 10. The effect on TcPO₂ of (a) diapering an infant, (b) drawing a blood sample from a radial artery, and (c) crying.

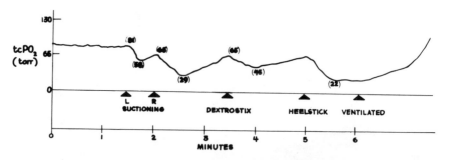

Figure 11. The cumulative effect of events that depressed TcPO$_2$ resulted in this infant's being placed on a respirator — unnecessarily?

Causes of "Undesirable Time"

Our conclusion was that the procedures, personnel, and equipment of the premature nursery itself had caused at least 50 percent of the undesirable time. How? One cause was noise (Long, Lucey, & Philip, 1980). For example, a sick infant in one of our studies showed a profound dip in his TcPO$_2$ whenever a telephone rang. At the same time, his heart rate went up, as did his intracranial pressure (Figure 12). We decided that loud noise was probably not good for sick infants.

Another cause was more subtle. We noticed that some infants were having apnea — a common problem. It is perfectly logical that blood oxygen should fall when a baby stops breathing for 20 seconds, and apneic spells accounted for a lot of the time in hypoxemia we were seeing. These apneic spells set off alarms.

We noticed another kind of spell that caused hypoxemia but did not set off the alarms, which we called disorganized breathing (Peabody et al., 1979). In this situation, the infant looks fine and appears to be breathing, but although the chest is moving, *no* air is passing through the nostrils. These are very common spells in sick infants. They can occur 20 to 80 times a day. They are completely missed if caregivers rely only on apnea alarms.

What's so bad about recurrent bouts of hypoxemia, you may be wondering. Maybe that's normal? First, disorganized breathing rarely occurs in normal infants. Second, apneic spells start in expiration. The infant goes into them with the residual capacity of the lungs low. If you force all the air you can out of your lungs and then don't inhale for 20 or 30 seconds, you will experience quite a stress. Yet your O$_2$ will have dropped only 10

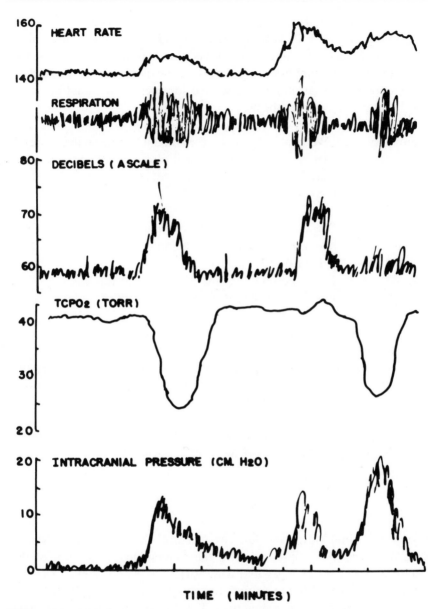

Figure 12. The effect of loud noise (telephone) on heart rate, TcPO$_2$, and intracranial pressure in a sick infant.

or 15 torr from about 90. In infants we see a drop of 30 or more from a starting point of 40 or 50. Airline pilots and mountain climbers pass out at 20 to 40 torr.

I think these spells are bad. They exhaust infants. We should do everything possible to avoid them.

During apneic spells, an infant's intracranial pressure goes up; the blood pressure rises; and CO_2 goes up. These are all events that cause abrupt changes in the neonate's intracranial blood flow. These stresses, combined with the fact that infant brain capillaries are easily ruptured, would seem to be a good explanation for why we see so much intracranial bleeding. It's the best current hypothesis.

When an infant is in quiet sleep, O_2 is steady — a straight line. This is probably good. We want to maximize the amount of time an infant spends in this state of quiet sleep. The current goal of our treatment is to avoid events that might have cumulative effects and cause hemorrhages. Several approaches are possible.

1. We can modify our behavior. As the nurse told me thirty years ago, if you don't have a good answer to the question, "Why are you touching that baby?", don't do it!
2. We could sedate the infant. Some places are trying this.
3. We can try to reduce the effects of our painful touching by using O_2 to prevent hypoxemia.
4. We can use treatments to avoid spells of apnea (CPAP, water beds, xanthines).
5. We can try to modify our procedures so that they do not produce pain. This would seem to be the most sensible (Long et al., 1980; Lucey, 1981; Peabody et al., 1979).

Judging whether such "less intensive care" is as effective or even superior to current care will take several more years, at least.

DISCUSSION

Seymour Levine: Measuring blood oxygen through the skin is a marvelous technique, and I'm impressed with the tremendous sensitivity of the response. It reflects changes in a wide variety of events, some of which appear to have very little to do with breathing. In a premie who has very little autoregulation of many functions, I'm curious about what else might be going on, either hormonally or autonomically.

Jerold Lucey: The respiratory system is extremely sensitive to any kind of ill effects on the infant. You can study respiratory movements in utero, and if the mother smokes one cigarette, the fetus stops breathing for five minutes. If her glucose goes up and down, respiratory movement stops. I think there's a message here about the sensitivity of the respiratory system.

Besides oxygen, you can measure CO_2, pH, and bilirubin

transcutaneously, as I said in my paper. Other chemistries can be developed. I think the first chemical that will be measured will be sugar.

Kathryn Barnard: How long does it take the oxygen level to go back to normal after a blood sample is drawn?

Jerold Lucey: A lot depends on how sick the baby is. For a well baby, it's a matter of a minute or so. For a seriously sick baby, it can take as long as half an hour.

T. Berry Brazelton: Does the transcutaneous oximeter give you an oxygenation reading immediately, or is there a delay?

Jerold Lucey: There's a delay in the electrode. When the PO_2 in the blood changes, it takes approximately 12 seconds for the change to show up in the skin.

T. Berry Brazelton: Our nurses at Boston Children's Hospital have really picked up on your ideas, Jerry. They have been watching the $TcPO_2$ levels of the babies, and before they do a procedure they use stroking techniques to soothe the infant and raise the PO_2. They think they can tell behaviorally whether the baby is responding positively or negatively, so they go by that and then watch the $TcPO_2$ too. They tell me they've cut two weeks off an 8-week-old premie's hospital stay by watching these things, and that the well-being of average infants has also been enhanced. But that 12-second delay worries me. I'd be more comfortable with a truly current reading.

Jerold Lucey: We used to wait an hour or two for blood oxygen tensions and then adjust the respirator on the basis of that reading! A 12-second delay doesn't bother me at all.

Allen Gottfried: As I'll point out in my paper, there are some mediating mechanisms operating here, such as crying and pain, which are resulting in these PO_2 drops. Are you saying that there are also forms of handling or soothing techniques that will bring the PO_2 back up?

Jerold Lucey: We have not engaged in any of these except randomly. Certain nurses are known to be better with the infants than others. When a nurse who tends to be rough with the babies sees what happens to blood oxygen as a result of her handling, she can often learn to do better.

T. Berry Brazelton: We've been able to keep the dips to a minimum by both stroking and talking to the babies. They seem to show positive behavioral responses to these techniques as well.

Kathryn Barnard: In our nursery, we have been experimenting with stroking the infant's head before (but not during) gavage feeding, and that seems to keep the oxygen level up. Also, Gene Anderson in Gainesville has some good evidence that non-nutritive sucking during gavage feeding minimizes PO_2 dips. He's found that infants are consistently discharged three or four days sooner when they have been given this sucking than when they have not. So I think there are all sorts of ways to work on it.

Susan Rose: Jerry, some people interpret your work to mean that any kind of tactile stimulation is bad for preterm infants. However, as we've just heard, and as the literature demonstrates, many interventions with a tactile-kinesthetic component seem to have good effects. Could you clarify your position?

Jerold Lucey: Pain and suffering are bad. This is what I'm really talking about. I'm not saying don't touch these infants at all; I'm saying we need ways of not causing pain. I think neonatal technology from now on will be aimed at doing things without going through the skin, and that these methods will be increasingly successful.

Kathryn Barnard: In a longitudinal study of preterms, we obtained a curious finding that your work helped us think about. We found a striking positive correlation between blood gas drawing during the newborn period and mental development at two years of age. Bagging (used when a baby becomes apneic and needs to be resuscitated) was also positively correlated with mental development at two years of age. It occurred to us that the infants who received blood gas drawing and bagging may have been the most organized infants, in that they were able to show symptoms of their problems. Your data suggest that some of the most disorganized or immature infants are not giving evidence of the hypoxia that's actually going on. In other words, the reason for the positive relationship between the medical procedures and IQ in our study may be that the procedures were an indirect measure of organization.

Jerold Lucey: I've never thought of it that way, but I have noticed that if you watch for seizures in the nursery, the smaller babies do not show them to you. If you put an EEG on, then you'll see patterns that would be called seizures, and they'll be associated with apnea. So there's a precedent for your idea.

T. Berry Brazelton: Jerry, I'd love to have you comment on something else we're doing in our premie nursery. We put a gown over the crib for an hour out of every three to cut down on the ambient light and provide a light-dark cycle. We're trying to reduce noise, too. Allen Gottfried will talk about this, but we think the ambient stress on the babies in a premie nursery is so great that the infants are at a sort of tip-over point.

Jerold Lucey: I agree with you. The baby who reacted so strongly to the ringing of the telephone is a classic example. There's a lot of noise in utero and a lot of noise in an incubator. It's sort of a bland background noise. What causes startling in some infants is sudden noise, like the clunk of a foot hamper closing or a telephone ringing.

T. Berry Brazelton: The overall message I get from your work, Jerry, is that the manipulations we're performing may prolong hypoxia and cause iatrogenic disease that none of us means to be causing. Despite our good intentions, we may not only be doing harm but causing infants to miss major opportunities for organization of the central and autonomic nervous systems.

Jerold Lucey: As a neonatologist, I feel I'm sort of trapped, because we're responsible for creating these very abnormal environments. We did it with a goal in mind and we've had some success. We really can't operate (1) without a lot of people, or (2) silently or in the dark. We're in a spot. If we do a lot, we can be criticized for doing too much, and if we don't do anything, then we're back to where we were before.

But I think the name of our game is rapidly changing. In the next decade, I think nobody will die of prematurity. Brain care will be the name of the game, as it really is now. All our efforts are to insure that the brain has an adequate supply of oxygen and doesn't have periods of no-flow. We hope that when we pass on these neonates with intact brains, those of you who work with older babies will be able to help reorganize them after this temporary trauma into functioning individuals. If a monkey can learn to be a good mother in a few hours by watching someone else, maybe people will be able to cope with this, too.

CARING FOR IMMATURE INFANTS — A TOUCHY SUBJECT

**Peter Gorski, M.D.
and colleagues***

How, when, how much, and even whether to touch fragile preterm infants are challenging questions for professional caregivers and parents in hospital nurseries. They reflect concern for the dialectic or delicate balance between the organizing and disorganizing effects of handling on stressed babies with immature nervous systems.

Does the intensive care nursery offer too little sensory stimulation to hospitalized infants, or too much? Clinicians and researchers differ on this question (e.g., Scarr-Salapatek & Williams, 1973; Cornell & Gottfried, 1976). Others wonder whether the contingency of stimuli might be more influential than the amount or type (Lawson, Daum, & Turkewitz, 1977; Gottfried et al., 1981). Such situations as infant sleep/wake state, position, and energy level might contribute to an individual infant's positive or negative response to any caregiver intervention.

The Premature Behavioral Research Project at Mount Zion Hospital and Medical Center in San Francisco takes aim at these questions. This paper, drawn from work in progress, describes our search for the relationship early in life between sensory experience and physical health.

Overview of the Study

We are conducting observational analyses of infant behavioral and physiological responses to interactions with caregivers. The nine premature infants whose responses are described here had a mean gestational age at birth of 31 weeks; at observation, their mean postmenstrual age was 33.4 weeks. The infants chosen had experienced minimal medical complications in the neonatal period and were considered convalescent. Each baby was observed for a total of 30 hours, divided into sessions of about five hours each.

*C. Leonard, D. Sweet, J. Martin, S. Sehring, K. O'Hara, P. High, M. Lang, R. Piecuch, and J. Green

All data were collected at the infant's bedside in the intensive care nursery with an unobtrusive, cart-mounted microcomputer system. This device records physiological data automatically; at the same time, an observer can enter behavioral and other codes on a typewriter-like keyboard.

Our results will be presented in two parts. First, we will report ecological data about caregiver behavior toward infants, with special attention to touch. Second, we will report associations between bradycardia (abnormally slow heart rate) and antecedent patterns of heart rate, $TcPO_2$, caregiver touch, and infant sleep/wake state.

Since part of our analysis focused on identifying events that might predict bradycardia, we grouped our data into periods as follows:

1. Pre-bradycardic periods (the five minutes prior to bradycardia)
2. Post-bradycardic periods (the five minutes after bradycardia)
3. Baseline periods (all other continuous five-minute periods)

For each group of periods, we analyzed data on heart rate and $TcPO_2$, on sensory stimulation (tactile and auditory), and on the touching infants received during caregiver interactions.

We counted 50 separate episodes of bradycardia, but they were not distributed equally among the babies in our sample. Baby 9 experienced half the episodes; the remaining eight infants had approximately an equal number of bradycardias each. Therefore, it was not desirable to combine the data from all nine babies into a single analysis and we did so in only a single instance, as noted below.

Caregiver Behavior Toward Infants

Thirteen percent of total observation time included some form of caregiver touching of infants. We classified the touching as medical or social (Table 1). The amounts of medical and social touching were roughly equal. The data on state showed that medical interventions occurred similarly often in sleep and awake states whereas social touch was significantly more frequent when infants were awake.

Infants spent most of their time on their stomachs, in a prone position. However, they were most often touched when they were supine, and this trend was even stronger for interactions in which the caregiver talked to the infant during handling. Although it may seem natural for social interactions to take place face to face, researchers have found that PaO_2 levels are higher in the prone position than in the supine (Martin et al., 1979). Further study is needed to show whether handling in positions that compromise oxygenation or perfusion compounds the risk of bradycardia.

Table 1. Categories of Medical and Social Touching

Medical Touching

Resuscitative stimulation	Ultrasound testing
Bag and mask breathing	Chest physical therapy
Physical examination	Injection
Blood drawing	Suctioning
Applying tape	Transfusing
Measuring blood pressure	Measuring abdomen
Stethoscopic examination	Thermometer
Weighing	Tube adjustments
Passing/removing gavage tube	Wrapping foot for laboratory test

Social Touching

Touching	Combing
Kissing	Washing
Rocking	Covering
Diapering	Stroking
Burping	Holding out
Placing in or out of infant seat	Changing
Patting	Bottle feeding
Holding close	En face positioning

Nurses were present for only 20 percent of the total observation time. For 71 percent of the time, no caregiver was present. These statistics may reflect staffing patterns that assign one nurse to several convalescent infants at a time.

After an intervention, the median length of time spent near the infant by nurses was only 64 seconds. This finding concerned us, since we have previously reported that infants can register signs of distress up to five minutes after an intervention (Gorski et al., 1983). We believe that caregivers may be missing important preventive opportunities. Electronic monitoring systems such as apnea alarms recognize and respond only to profound infant distress or instability. Learning to recognize early signs of distress, especially behavioral ones, means that time must be spent watching for them.

Antecedents of Bradycardia

When we tried to find out whether touch tended to precede a bradycardic episode, we discovered that more than half the pre-bradycardic periods included at least one instance of touch whereas only a third of the baseline periods included touch. However, in order to obtain this significant difference we had to include Baby 9 in the analysis (see Table 2). This baby, as mentioned earlier, showed an extraordinary susceptibility to bradycardia.

Table 2. Occurrence of Touch in Pre-bradycardic Periods

		Touch	No Touch
Babies 1-8		11/25	14/25
Baby 9		18/25	7/25
	Total	29/50*	21/50

* $p < .001$

Infants whose bradycardia was preceded by touch had borderline cardiorespiratory function and were therefore more vulnerable to stress from caregiving interventions. If we could reliably predict when an infant's autonomic controls were depleted and unable to respond to further challenge from the environment, these bradycardic episodes might be preventable.

Talking or singing to infants occurred significantly *less* often before bradycardia than during the rest of the day. This finding teases us with the notion that clinicians have yet to learn to use the stabilizing power of certain human sounds, perhaps because of the animate and inanimate cacophony so characteristic of intensive care nurseries.

For Babies 1-8, social forms of touch (and also simultaneous medical and social touch) occurred significantly less often before bradycardia as well. In all but two instances when social touch did precede bradycardia, we found that the infant's mother had been the source of stimulation. Perhaps this proves that parents are more exciting than doctors and nurses, even for infants too weak to handle excitement. A different thought is that because parents can spend so little time with their hospitalized infants, they may inadvertently pack loads of active stimulation into their short visits.

Heart Rate, TcPO$_2$, and State

Curiously, only two of our 16 heart rate and TcPO$_2$ variables exceeded chance in predicting bradycardia. However, the combination of touch in the pre-bradycardic period and low values on three $TcPO_2$ variables did predict bradycardia. When no touch occurred during a pre-bradycardic period, one heart rate variable and one $TcPO_2$ variable emerged as significant predictors.

We were fascinated to discover that heart rate variables were such poor predictors of very low heart rates. $TcPO_2$ fared only slightly better. We hope we are serving the interests of neonates by trying to develop fine measures of heart rate and $TcPO_2$ that might someday be easily monitored as early warning signs of autonomic disintegration or destabilization. If we could recognize subtle distress minutes before gross events, such as bradycardia or apnea, we might support infants in time to spare them the cumulative effects of repeated crises. ·

For Babies 1-8, more than half the bradycardic episodes occurred during active sleep. Another quarter occurred during awake non-fuss states, and the remainder occurred during quiet sleep. This distribution roughly parallels the amount of time spent in these states on days when no bradycardia occurred. Baby 9 became bradycardic significantly more often while in active sleep than the other infants.

Although the small number of instances of bradycardia in our sample makes it risky to generalize from our analysis, we believe we can already declare that human touch is not always therapeutic for premature infants. Some infants are exquisitely sensitive to, and perhaps easily overwhelmed by, tactile intervention.

As we accumulate larger data files, we plan to analyze more specific and complex interactions between type of touch and infant physiology and state. In this way, we hope to move toward our ultimate goal of learning to read preterm infants' response signals and act on them in support of optimal neurological and behavioral outcome.

DISCUSSION

Susan Rose: What first made you think that the nursery environment might be responsible for problems like apnea and bradycardia?

Peter Gorski: When I was studying with Dr. Brazelton and consulting in the nursery at the Boston Hospital for Women, I was asked to see a particular baby who was having a lot of apnea and had not responded to pharmacologic intervention or physical stimulation. I simply observed the baby in the caregiving environment for a day. Then, thanks to the nurses' records of when the baby was having apneic and bradycardic episodes, I noticed that the episodes clustered around the times when the health care team made rounds at the beginning and end of each day. I asked them to divert rounds from that particular baby's isolette, and the number of apneic spells plummeted to near zero.

Susan Rose: What was it about rounds that caused the apnea?

Peter Gorski: There was a huge increase in the noise and activity level. The group would go right up to the isolette, and a few people might lean on it to see if the baby was really responsive. A few minutes later, there would be an apneic episode.

This time lag is very important. Babies often respond minutes after an intervention with disorganized breathing or heart rate. Because the response is not necessarily immediate, its direct relationship to prior intervention is not always obvious.

The point is not that we need to worry every time we approach or handle a premature baby. I think we can develop some predictive capacity to know when an infant can make use of our efforts.

Seymour Levine: May I ask a naive question? Is there such a thing as a healthy premature infant, or are "healthy" and "premature" mutually exclusive categories?

Peter Gorski: Some preterms, even those born two or three months before term, are phenomenally healthy, meaning that they require minimal support.

Seymour Levine: But even a "healthy" premie who requires minimal support does not have the more fully developed regulatory mechanisms that a full-term infant would use to modulate environmental events.

Peter Gorski: Absolutely. Preterm infants do show disordered regulation. They are responsive to our support efforts, but unfortunately the response may come in the form of disorganized behavior or outright catastrophic physiological events.

Seymour Levine: Your data show that a lot is happening to the infant very quickly, very intensively. A lot of caregiving goes on in a short period of time. These bursts of activity represent a dramatic change from the background stimulation level, as the phone bell did for the apneic baby Jerry Lucey talked about. The preterm infant may not have the autoregulatory system to deal with sudden change, sudden increases in stimulation. Gradual-onset stimulation is a very different kind of thing.

T. Berry Brazelton: If premies are already at a stress level, which I think Peter's and Jerry's data show us that they are, then even a small increase in stimulation might push them into disorganization.

Stephen Suomi: Peter, I'm concerned about Baby 9, the one in your sample who had so much bradycardia. Let's assume you can find some predictors of bradycardia and apnea, at least for most of your population. What about the exceptions — the babies whose reactions are different? Shouldn't we be paying attention to them?

Peter Gorski: Exactly, Steve. I think that's the opportunity available through our way of analyzing. It allows you to individualize your clinical response to the infant.

T. Berry Brazelton: Are you coming up with any behavioral indicators of individual reactions? Our nurses find that after they get to know an infant — using the four developmental lines of the Brazelton Neonatal Assessment Scale (autonomic, social, attentional, and motor) to guide their observations — they can predict from the baby's external behavior whether a stimulus is positive or negative. Sometimes they know just from the look on the baby's face.

Peter Gorski: The BNAS categories you mention have been very useful to us. In very immature babies, autonomic changes seem to reflect the infant's energy level and organizational level. I think next we see changes in motor behavior. An infant who responds to any sensory or tactile stimulation with a long period of jerky, uncontrolled movement is wasting a huge number of calories. That baby's energy is being depleted. You can see the loss of facial tone, expressing fatigue, and autonomic exhaustion is not far behind.

Much closer to term, attentional capacities and the ability to sustain alert states for a relatively long time do seem to be markers of physiological stability. A preterm infant, however, is much more vulnerable autonomically at 40 weeks conceptional age than is a full-term newborn, who can coordinate the physiologic, motor, state, and interactive capacities that your scale defines for us. Sometimes, when you have a preterm baby who can finally alert and watch you, you can actually cause a bradycardic or apneic episode, and I have on occasion. The costly effect of social interaction can easily overburden the nervous system.

T. Berry Brazelton: You seem to be on the verge of a breakthrough in finding reliable behavioral-observational indicators that we can use to back up our clinical intuitions, which to me is very exciting.

Peter Gorski: I hope that at least we are beginning to offer a systematic approach to observing the caregiving environment and the infant's simultaneous behavioral and physiological responses. Eventually, of course, we want not only to be able to observe interactive events but to anticipate the infant's response and intervene supportively.

T. Berry Brazelton: I'm especially eager for behavioral indicators of problems in these fragile babies because we are sending them home so much earlier than we used to. Sometimes the parents work to get organized, attentional behavior from the baby and right afterward, the baby collapses. We're trying to train nurses, who can then train parents, to look for the hyperalertness and other signs that precede exhaustion.

Peter Gorski: In talking with parents about this problem, we try to put things in a positive way. We explain that an exciting stimulus — pleasant as well as unpleasant — may overwhelm a baby with low energy levels. The child may be so excited by interaction with the parents that it's more than the nervous system can handle. We don't want parents to feel that they're bad for the child or that the child is rejecting them, and we don't want them to be afraid to approach the baby at all. They simply need to understand how taxing social interaction can be for a weak infant.

PRETERM RESPONSES TO PASSIVE, ACTIVE, AND SOCIAL TOUCH

Susan A. Rose, Ph.D.

The word *touch* and its common synonyms, *feel* and *contact,* refer to a complex set of sensations that can be narrowly or broadly conceived. Although touch often refers to cutaneous sensations aroused by stimulation of receptors on the skin, sensations of the muscles and joints (proprioceptive sense) and sensations of movement (vestibular sense) are closely linked. Moreover, the experience of touch is complex, encompassing as it does separate sensations of warmth, pressure, pain, weight, location, and so on.

Similarly, the roles imputed to touch encompass a broad spectrum of phenomena. At the broadest level there is *social touch* (Kennedy, 1978), which treats the role of touch in promoting social bonds, attachment, and emotional integrity. Research on social touch generally concerns the effects of social deprivation and social stimulation. Since preterm infants spend their early days and weeks in the atypical environment of incubators and intensive care units, social touch may have special significance for them.

At a more basic level, we can consider what touch tells us about the external world. Here, touch plays two roles. *Passive touch* involves excitation of receptors in the skin and underlying tissue (Kenshalo, 1978). *Active touch* includes modes of exploration in which the skin, joints, and muscles function together in obtaining information (Gibson, 1962).

Theoretical accounts of tactual perception suggest that social touch, passive touch, and active touch can be considered separately, and that investigation of each will increase our knowledge of the various facets of touch. In this paper I will describe some of our work contrasting the responses of preterm and full-term infants to passive and active touch. Next, I will describe an intervention program that used social touch to foster preterm development. Finally, I will briefly raise the issue of whether touch plays a unique role in preterm development.

Passive Touch: Differences Between Preterm and Full-term Neonates

Children born before term are known to be at high risk for a host of developmental problems. Recent studies of the very young preterm have examined the possibility that environmental factors contribute to this risk. Some studies question the appropriateness of the stimulation provided in the newborn intensive care unit and indicate that preterms' problems may be caused or exacerbated by the characteristic high intensities of light and sound in the ICU, the lack of rhythmic day-night cycling, or perhaps the lack of contingent stimulation (Gottfried et al., 1981; Lawson, Daum, & Turkewitz, 1977). Others have sought to determine whether preterm infants benefit from changes in the quantity, quality, or patterning of environmental stimulation.

Somewhat less attention has been given to learning about the sensory organization and perceptual processing characteristic of the young preterm. Yet in order to understand how the environment can influence or shape the development of young organisms, it is important to understand what aspects of the environment they are capable of perceiving.

For this reason, we decided to investigate the preterm infant's sensitivity and responsivity to external stimuli. Our interest in using tactile stimuli stemmed from the significance imputed to this modality in development.

The first study was designed to investigate infants' responsivity to tactile stimulation and their ability to discriminate different intensities of such stimulation (Rose, Schmidt, & Bridger, 1976). Twenty healthy full-terms and 20 preterms were touched with plastic filaments of varying diameters during active sleep, while their cardiac and behavioral responses were monitored. These assessments were done when the preterm infants were close to term age, that is, close to 40 weeks from conception. Their mean gestational age at birth was around 33 weeks and their mean birth weight around 1,660 grams.

Analyses of the results revealed that preterms were considerably less responsive to tactile stimulation than were full-terms. The preterms showed no significant heart rate response to any of the stimuli, while the full-terms responded with significant heart-rate acceleration to the two stronger filaments. The striking failure of the preterm to respond was confirmed by supplementary beat-by-beat analyses of heart rate. Both groups gave a significant behavioral response to the strongest plastic filament (and only to that one), but the preterm gave a decidedly weaker response than did the full-term.

In addition to the overall dampened responsiveness of preterms, their pattern of cardiac and behavioral activation was different from that observed in full-terms. In full-terms, heart rate was a more sensitive index of stimulus perception than behavior. Whereas full-term infants responded behaviorally only to the strongest stimuli, they responded with heart rate acceleration to weaker stimuli as well. In preterms the relation was just the opposite. These infants showed no significant heart rate response to any of the stimuli but did show a behavioral response to the strongest of the three.

In a second study (Rose et al., 1980), the responsivity of 30 full-term and 30 preterm infants was examined over a longer period of time, so that infants were tested in both active and quiet sleep. Although several changes were introduced in the design of the study in an effort to enhance responding in preterms, the results for stimulation during active sleep were very similar to those found in the earlier study. In quiet sleep, full-term infants again responded with a significant cardiac acceleration. The response shown by preterms, though significant, was small — about one beat per minute. The behavioral responses were again significant for both groups in quiet sleep, but significantly greater for the full-terms than the preterms, as were the correlations between behavioral responsivity and cardiac change scores.

For the preterms, two aspects of risk, namely, birth weight and gestational age at birth, were correlated with cardiac responsiveness. Thus, infants who were heavier and more mature at birth were more responsive during testing.

Active Touch: Differences Between Preterm and Full-Term One-Year-Olds

Gibson (1962) argued that active touch is not simply a blend of two modes of sensation, kinesthesis and touch proper, but rather an exploratory movement used to gain information about the shape and other characteristics of the object being touched. Whereas passive touch involves only the excitation of receptors in the skin and underlying tissue, "active touch involves the concomitant excitation of receptors in the joints and tendons along with new and changing patterns in the skin" (p. 478).

We have carried out two studies investigating infants' use of active touch to gather information about the environment, particularly about the shape of objects. In the first study (Rose, Gottfried, & Bridger, 1978), we examined the ability of infants to recognize by sight objects they have experienced only by active touch. This ability to extract information about an object in one modality and transfer it to another is called cross-modal transfer.

In order to examine cross-modal transfer in infants, we adapted a paradigm commonly used to study visual recognition memory. In this paradigm, a stimulus is displayed for a period of visual inspection; then this stimulus is shown to the baby with a different (novel) one. Infants usually look longer at the novel stimulus, showing a preference for it and providing evidence of recognition memory. In adapting this paradigm, we presented our stimuli either tactually or orally during familiarization and visually during testing.

We tested three groups of one-year-olds: 28 predominantly lower socioeconomic status (SES) preterms, 39 high SES full-terms, and 27 lower SES full-terms. The preterms were tested at twelve months corrected age, that is, age estimated from expected date of birth.

Three cross-modal tasks were used, one oral-visual and two tactual-visual. The members of a stimulus pair differed primarily in shape. In the oral-visual task, the first stimulus was placed in the infant's mouth for familiarization, whereas in the tactual-visual tasks, it was placed in the infant's hand. In each case, the experimenter shielded the object from the infant's view. During the test period, the infant was shown the familiar stimulus and the second member of the pair, and the times spent looking at each were compared. At the end of the test period, the infant was permitted to reach for one of the two stimuli.

Analysis of the results revealed that preterms (and lower SES full-terms) failed to show any evidence of cross-modal transfer whereas middle-class full-terms looked significantly more at the novel stimulus, and reached for it more as well. These findings indicate that middle-class full-term infants can gain knowledge about the shape of an object by feeling it and mouthing it, and they can make this information available to the visual system. They were able to do this after only 30 seconds (or less) of handling or mouthing the object. Preterms, on the other hand, seem not to know that the object they explored with their hand or mouth and tongue is the same as the object they see. Despite the fact that this is a period in life when infants are busily engaged in learning about the world around them by manipulating and exploring with their hands and mouths, preterms are having difficulty acquiring information in this fashion.

In the second study (Rose, Gottfried, & Bridger, 1979), we examined the possibility that, although unable to achieve cross-modal transfer, preterms might be able to use active exploration to enhance visual recognition. Would infants obtain more information about the form of an object by both touching and seeing it than by seeing it alone?

Contrary to our expectations, manipulation turned out to impede rather than facilitate subsequent visual recognition. Even more noteworthy is the finding that the negative effects of interference were accentuated in preterms. At twelve months of age, full-terms achieved significant novelty scores in all conditions even though the percentages were somewhat attenuated in conditions where manipulation was permitted during familiarization. Preterms, on the other hand, showed evidence of memory only in the two visual conditions. In the two conditions involving manipulation, their scores dropped to chance.

Overall, preterms show evidence of difficulty in perceiving passive touch and in effectively using active touch to explore their world. As neonates they proved relatively unresponsive to pressure exerted on the skin. At one year of age, they had difficulty using information available through active touch to recognize objects visually, and this was true whether the tactual exploratory activity was accomplished in the presence or absence of visual cues.

Social Touch: Fostering Development in the Preterm

The rationale for many interventions designed to enhance development in the preterm is that birth before term deprives the infant of the regulatory influence of maternal biorhythms and of the sensory stimulation that characterizes the uterine environment (Dreyfus-Brisac, 1970). Thus, intervention studies have generally attempted to provide compensatory stimulation. While some early studies have only small sample sizes and various methodological inadequacies, they nevertheless provide important leads for further research. At least temporary benefits have been noted in physical, neurobehavioral, mental, and motor development, and in the reduction of apneic episodes. The most consistent improvements have been in perceptual and neurobehavioral functioning.

Our own regimen of stimulation (Rose et al., 1980), administered while infants were in the intensive care unit, emphasized tactile, proprioceptive, and vestibular stimulation. The core of the intervention was a systematic program of gentle massaging and rocking, initiated within two weeks after birth and ended a day or two before discharge. Three times a day for 20 minutes each time, the infant was massaged with the palm and fingertips of one hand in a cephalocaudal sequence: head, shoulders, back, arms, legs, and feet. When the infant was well enough to be removed from the incubator, one of the sessions was replaced by rocking in a rocking chair, to emphasize vestibular stimulation. Opportunities for direct visual contact and talking were optimized.

One major result of this intervention was an increase in the preterm infant's cardiac responsiveness to tactile stimuli during active sleep. In the intervened preterms, the magnitude of the cardiac response actually approached that obtained from full-term infants. A second major result was that visual recognition memory was found to be enhanced when the infants were retested at six months of age. Here, too, their performance was indistinguishable from that of full-terms. These results are congruent with those of several other investigators who have found that early handling affects visual exploration (e.g., McNichols, 1975; Siqueland, 1973; White & Castle, 1964).

Overall, however, the design of intervention programs is complicated by the fact that there is no compelling theoretical rationale for selecting any specific type, quantity, or patterning of stimulation. Relatively little is known about the preterm's thresholds or capacities for sensory processing. Furthermore, with the exception of our own study, I know of no study that included a full-term control group. Inclusion of such a control is of critical importance since it provides the norm against which the effects of intervention can best be assessed. And finally, we have practically no idea of the underlying mechanisms that might mediate the effects of the various interventions. Despite growing support for the efficacy of stimulation programs in changing behavior, the exact nature of these changes remains unspecified.

Touch: A Unique Role?

Although touch, whether passive, active, or social, clearly has important functions, it is not clear that it plays any sort of unique role in preterm development. Deficits are reported during infancy in other facets of development as well, including neurobehavioral functioning, visual processing, auditory processing, and infant-caregiver interaction. Similarly, while it has been reported that tactile intervention is effective, so are other modalities of intervention.

Lags or deficits in preterm infants' sensory functioning and information processing are found in various modalities, and intervention in various modalities can influence development. Perhaps the deficits are more commonplace, pervasive, or severe in the tactual modality, but we do not know this. It may very well be that preterm infants have higher thresholds for external stimuli, slower rates of information processing, poorer memory, and so on, and that these deficits are not modality-specific, that is, do not depend upon the channel by which information arrives. Only more research will tell us whether touch has a unique role in development.

DISCUSSION

T. Berry Brazelton: Susan, I especially like the idea of distinguishing between active and passive touch because to me it relates to the concept of state. In extreme states, such as crying or deep sleep, passive touch may add to an infant's ability to initiate and maintain control. Active touch, in contrast, acts as an alerter and as information. It helps the infant come to a receptive alert state and begin to process information.

The idea of differences in organization between preterms and full-terms is also critical, I think. It takes preterms longer to develop organizational systems. They may get there, but the cost to them of reaching out for something complex like cross-modal transfer is very great. The fact that these problems are not modality-specific is important, too. Your intervention seemed to point out that perhaps any modality can provide fuel for organization, so to speak.

Susan Rose: I agree with you, Berry, that perhaps intervention in any modality can provide the "fuel for organization." That is a tantalizing idea, and one that is compatible with the results of many intervention studies. I'd also like to emphasize a point made in my paper, that intervention studies should routinely begin to include full-term control groups for comparison.

Anneliese Korner: May I add to that? I think if we want to make comparisons with full-term infants, they should be older than the ones we usually study in the hospital. Recent evidence suggests that while two- to three-day-old full-term neonates differ greatly from preterm infants tested at term, the full-terms begin to look more like the preterms when they are five days old. Behaviorally, the just-born full-terms have a good deal more flexion and tone than they have at five days. In using just-born full-terms as controls for preterms at term, we tend to forget that the full-terms have just emerged from a very crowded environment and have gone through the birth process, with all its attending physiological adaptations. Thus, five-day-old full-terms may be more appropriate controls for preterm infants at term than the younger ones we usually study.

Susan Rose: That's a cautionary note. It suggests that the most valid comparisons may depend on our obtaining more knowledge about developmental processes in both preterms and full-terms.

William Greenough: Gottlieb's idea that modalities develop better if they develop in sequence might help explain the results of your intervention study, Susan — both the increased responsiveness to passive touch, which you expected, and the enhanced visual recognition skills at six months, which you didn't. Perhaps, at the time when cutaneous or somatosensory development would normally have been occurring in utero, your intervention helped the infant focus on that. Then later, with that development as a base, attention could be fully devoted to the visual modality.

Susan Rose: You mean the infants could more readily or efficiently devote their attention to exploring the visual world because our intervention had already facilitated development of the earlier-maturing somatosensory system?

William Greenough: The idea is based on the Turkewitz and Kenney notion of sequential development of modalities that I sketched out in my paper.

Susan Rose: Although to my knowledge there is no evidence that fetuses can see, or that there is much to enchant them visually in utero, a lot of visual development goes on before birth. Turkewitz's work comes from a school that said infants are sensitive to proximal stimulation before they are sensitive to distal stimulation, such as vision or audition. While there is no doubt that the proximal systems develop before the distal ones, or that the somasthetic system becomes functional before the visual system prenatally, it is also clear that preterm infants are exquisitely sensitive to their auditory and visual world.

Allen Gottfried: Should intervention follow the same sequence as sensory system development?

Susan Rose: That's a very important empirical question. So many different types of intervention seem to bring about some sort of improvement, it is hard to know. Since many of these interventions do have a strong vestibular or tactile component, we may in effect be providing intervention in such a sequential manner.

William Greenough: Yes, that is my point.

Susan Rose: Alternatively, infants may self-select the stimulation that fits their stage of development. I think that some, like Turkewitz, might argue that preterms lack the multimodal contingencies available to normal infants, and that these are especially critical. For example, the preterm infant in the incubator often hears speech when no one is in sight. In this case, a good intervention would be one that built in the proper contingencies between modalities, so that if you're talking to a baby in the ICU, you're looking at her or touching her as well.

T. Berry Brazelton: Susan, you may be putting your finger on the biggest problem preterm infants have. There is a kind of disorganization at the base of their systems that interferes with learning and with adaptation to the environment. We have found essentially the same thing in our study of the face-to-face rhythms that mothers and babies develop when the babies are between three- and five-months old. At the age of five months plus 40 weeks, preterms are very much like three-month-old full-terms in the ways they interact and communicate with their mothers.

Susan Rose: I think you're describing something very similar to what we're seeing. At six and twelve months, preterms are slow. But if you give them more time to process the stimuli, they often perform like full-terms. We've done some recent work on visual recognition memory that shows preterms can take in information, store it in memory, and retrieve it from memory, but they seem to need much more time to process and encode the original information.

T. Berry Brazelton: If you see the tactile modality as an organizer rather than just an information source, it would make a certain amount of sense to say that infants are learning by the tactile modality to organize themselves and then to pay attention. I think it's a very big job for preterm infants to get their systems working together — to establish basic rhythms of attention and withdrawal, sort of homeostatic systems. And it is very hard for people in the environment to learn those systems of the premie, because the keys we depend on in more organized infants just are not available.

Susan Rose: Studies that have used tactile, kinesthetic, or vestibular stimuli seem to have the most pronounced effect on development, but many other effective interventions have also been used — a heartbeat sound, for instance. I would like to suggest that these various interventions may be working through a common mechanism, perhaps having to do with improved state organization or greater regularity of state.

T. Berry Brazelton: Stability of state is one of the best markers of optimal development in prematures that we have.

Susan Rose: Many infants are discharged from the hospital while they are still unable to maintain stable states. I'm concerned about these babies. My hunch is that they are not in very good shape when they go home, and that follow-up studies will keep finding deficits.

T. Berry Brazelton: One reason we like to send them home is that our nurseries don't give them much opportunity to develop stable states. We certainly are not reinforcing them in any natural sort of way.

We ought to all have in our minds that prematurity, immaturity, CNS insult, or any of the things that make for difficulties in getting going do not stop costing a baby. Disorganization doesn't stop costing the baby after it's over. It costs for a long time afterward, and the fact that the baby can overcome it is what's remarkable. A great deal of energy goes into its overcoming.

However, children beyond infancy who are growing up with state problems, cross-modal transfer problems, learning disabilities, and the like are dogged less by their deficits than by their poor self-image and expectation to fail. We need to provide an environment that reinforces their self-image and sense of competence. In the long run, deficits in these areas may be a lot more important than any organic problems.

A TACTILE AND KINESTHETIC STIMULATION PROGRAM FOR PREMATURE INFANTS

Patricia Boudolf Rausch, R.N., M.S.N.

The problems of prematurely born infants include unstable temperature regulation due to decreased body fat and inadequate respiration due to immature lung tissue. Feeding difficulties are frequent because of the infants' immature gastrointestinal tract and poor sucking reflex.

In 1960, Kulka began extensive research to determine the effects of kinesthetic stimulation upon infant weight gain. Her theory states that a kinesthetic drive developmentally predates the oral drive, and is satisfied by means of stroking, fondling, cuddling, swaying motions, and rocking (Kulka, Fry, & Goldstein, 1960). My study, which was based on this theory, assessed the effects of a ten-day regimen of tactile and kinesthetic stimulation on the weight gain, caloric intake, and stooling of small premature infants.

The 40 infants selected for the study weighed 1,000 to 2,000 grams at birth and were of appropriate weight for their gestational ages. The sample was divided into treatment and control groups of 20 infants each. The groups were matched for weight, gestational age, sex, race, and ability to breathe spontaneously.

Both groups were cared for according to the usual nursery routine at the study hospital. This routine includes feedings every two to three hours via nasogastric tube or bottle. Babies fed in incubators are handled during bottle feedings, but virtually no handling occurs during nasogastric tube feedings. Vital signs (temperature, pulse, and respiration) are recorded every one to two hours, and bedding changes are made as needed. Parental visiting is encouraged, and parents may touch their infants as frequently as they wish.

In addition to the customary routine, the treatment group experienced a fifteen-minute tactile-kinesthetic stimulation regimen each day for ten days. The treatment began when the infants were between 24 and 48 hours old. It was given each morning, at a time when the infants were awake and receiving no therapy or feeding. The infants remained in their radiant warmer beds or incubators. Stimulation was given in three five-minute phases.

Phase 1 (five one-minute parts): gentle rubbing of the infant's neck, back or chest (depending on the baby's position), legs, arms, and head.
Phase 2 (five one-minute parts): gentle flexion and extension of the infant's right arm, left arm, right leg, left leg, and both legs simultaneously.
Phase 3: same as Phase 1.

Stimulation Effects

Our data on weight, caloric intake, and stooling for each infant over the ten days of the treatment period revealed, first, that the infants in the control group experienced a mean weight loss of 48 grams while the infants in the treatment group had a mean weight gain of 25 grams. This difference, though suggestive, was not statistically significant. However, the mean feeding intake of infants in the treatment group on Days 6 through 10 was significantly greater than that of the control group. Significant differences were also found in frequency of stooling.

These findings suggest that compensatory tactile and kinesthetic stimulation improves the clinical course of premature infants. Although the evidence on weight gain was not statistically significant, the curve in Figure 13 suggests we might have found a larger weight difference if the study had continued longer than ten days.

There was conclusive evidence that the feeding intake of the premature infants increased as a result of the stimulation program. Although this effect was statistically significant only for Days 6 through 10, it was present to some degree during the first half of the study period as well.

The increased stooling frequency in the treatment group can be attributed in part to the increased feeding intake. However, significant differences in stooling frequency began to occur a day *earlier* than significant differences in feeding intake. This finding supports the proposal that tactile-kinesthetic stimulation, which most infants experience as the result of normal maternal-

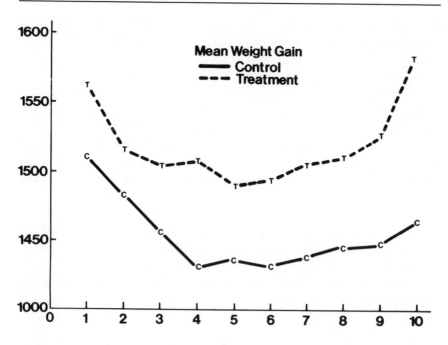

Figure 13. Mean weight gain in the control and treatment groups over the ten days of the study.

newborn interaction, improves gastrointestinal functioning. It promotes peristalsis and expulsion of waste products, thereby decreasing gastric retention and abdominal distention. Sucking, another component of infant-caregiver interaction, also appears to result in improved gastrointestinal function in premature infants.

Future Investigations

Although this research shows that stimulation has positive clinical consequences for premature infants, long-term effects of the treatment — and the effects of treatment that continues for longer than ten days — remain to be investigated. Since it is generally assumed that increased physical stimulation increases the activity of the heart and lungs, it would be advantageous to examine respiratory and cardiac function in infants who have been given stimulation.

It would also be interesting to know whether the stimulation treatment affects the relationship that eventually develops between parent and child. Ideally, stimulation treatments should be administered by parents. The contact would offer them a special opportunity to touch and fondle their premature infant and to become familiar with him or her as a unique individual.

The mortality and morbidity of premature infants has decreased with advanced technology. However, increased technology has also caused the environment of the premature infant to become more mechanized. Continued research in the area of infant stimulation supports the importance of early parental contact. The quality of that contact might be improved by giving parents the opportunity to provide stimulation that will positively affect the infant's clinical course.

DISCUSSION

Allen Gottfried: Did your touching and movement regimen seem to soothe the babies? Did it make them feel relaxed and comfortable?

Patricia Rausch: Yes, but not always at first. At the beginning of the treatment, some babies would startle and cry. It was a very individual matter—some were more sensitive than others.

Michael Merzenich: Where do premature infants seem to want to be touched, by behavioral sign? Do they seem relatively indifferent to touch in some places and more sensitive in others?

Patricia Rausch: I've found that babies tend to calm more when there is stimulation on the belly and the back. It seems to be more overwhelming, more "right now."

T. Berry Brazelton: In performing the stimulation, were you sensitive to the baby's reactions? Did you try to synchronize your own rhythm with that of the baby?

Patricia Rausch: We tried not to vary our behavior much in response to the baby because we wanted our procedures to be repeatable. In a clinical situation, I would be much more inclined to adjust my behavior to the baby's.

Anneliese Korner: It is difficult to know whether to attribute the effects of the program to the tactile or the kinesthetic stimulation, is it not?

Patricia Rausch: Yes, it is. Frankly, the reason I included the kinesthetic procedures was that I was afraid tactile stimulation alone would not produce an effect.

Peter Gorski: Pat, I think so well of your cause that I worry about the methodological oversights in this particular study. They undercut the strength of your findings. In addition to the problem Anneliese just mentioned, some of your outcome measures are open to criticism. You need to demonstrate not just weight gain but meaningful weight gain because, as you know, premature babies are very prone to fluid overload. I think protein metabolism consumption is a much more compelling measure of utilization of intake than stooling frequency or intake volume.

Patricia Rausch: On the very last day of my study, I learned something else that will affect the outcome measures I choose next time. I had finished the last treatment on the last baby, and as I began to walk away from the bed a respiratory therapist came by and remarked, "Oh, you're all done — what a pity. This baby's going to have bradycardia now, and apnea." I said, "What?" And she said, "Yes, I've been observing that a few minutes after you do these treatments, the babies have bradycardia and apnea." Obviously, I did not look at that in this study, though I wish I had.

Kathryn Barnard: In a study by Schaffer, she put her hand on the infant's abdomen four times a day for 12 minutes each time, and one of her findings was an overall increase in apneic episodes in the infants she touched. Because of that, when one of my graduate students wanted to try gentle touch with the preterms recently, I suggested she keep track of the babies not only while she was touching them but for half an hour afterwards. Sure enough, there was absolutely no apnea while the hand was on the belly, but in the next 30 minutes there was a lot. It is as if the cutaneous stimulation serves as an organizer for the system, and when it is removed the system goes through a period of extreme disorganization.

T. Berry Brazelton: Touch is not only a cutaneous system but a sort of motor control system, too. If you have an agitated baby and you put a hand on her, she's likely to quiet.

Patricia Rausch: Yes. Touch has an encasing quality, which goes back to the uterus.

Stephen Suomi: Do conditions that simulate the intrauterine environment offer optimal stimulation for preterms, in your opinion?

Patricia Rausch: Absolutely. I wish we knew more about exactly what the infant experiences in utero, and what we can do to simulate it. We need to remember that these babies who are born early are would-be fetuses; they are prepared to live in the uterus, not the intensive care nursery. Putting a gown over the bed for one hour out of every three, as Berry said they do in his nursery, I think is wonderful (though it could also be a problem, since we need to watch skin color and things like that). If we could leave an infant in an environment that was dark all the time, there's no telling what we might accomplish.

Allen Gottfried: I'm not at all sure that's the direction interventions should take. Although some programs have tried to simulate the uterine environment (often by using sound, such as the mother's voice or heartbeat), many others have been based on the axiom that the preterm infant is sensorially deprived. They often offer multimodal stimulation and "enrichment" — a mobile in the incubator, for instance. The rationale behind this approach is that the infant is a very different organism after birth than before, and a visual environment that is dark all the time is no longer appropriate.

William Greenough: As we were saying earlier, there is an order to the development of sensory systems. Vestibular, olfactory, auditory, visual — the exact sequence depends on the species. Some central resource — maybe attention, maybe a metabolic process — may be devoted sequentially to these systems. Multimodal interventions might actually overload the central resource so that each of them would develop more poorly.

Allen Gottfried: That was the thrust of much research in the 1940s, '50s, and '60s. It may explain why so much emphasis is now being placed on touch.

T. Berry Brazelton: Pat, I particularly like the fact that one aim of your stimulation program was to model behavior that could be passed on to parents. I am very much in favor of involving parents with their preterm infants, and we've known for a long time in our work that parents learn a great deal from watching someone with skills like yours interact with the baby.

I have one warning, though. A long time ago, Marshall Klaus and John Kennell introduced parent rooming-in in their nursery, but Marshall told me that most parents were so anxious that they couldn't stand to spend a full 24-hour period with their baby at the hospital. This made me aware that encouraging contact may not be helping parents the way we want it to. Our effort to get parents into the premie nursery was meant to counteract some of the grief and anxiety, to give parents a chance to work through it before taking the baby home.

We began to watch parents in our own nursery. We would suggest they do something with the baby and they would do it, but they did it with their eyes closed, or squinting, or with their faces all screwed up. Our timing wasn't right for them, obviously, and they were just performing for us.

Anneliese Korner: For many parents it's very important to be encouraged to be in touch with the baby, but I think we have to be careful not to expect this of everyone. We have to respect a parent's individual response to our encouragement.

Patricia Rausch: We felt that the opportunity to give tactile stimulation helped our parents along. At least it got them to the place where they could say, "Watch what the baby does when I do this."

Pat LaGruea has done some work on touching and parental grief in parents whose preterm infants die, Berry. She's found that grieving lasts considerably longer after the death if the parents have not had the opportunity to touch the baby. Sometimes the parents never come to terms with the fact that the baby has been born and has died. When there has been tactile contact, the parents show a less extended period of disorganization.

Allen Gottfried: A study based on interviews with parents whose infants had died showed exactly the same thing. The parents said they felt they had missed out on a very valuable experience if they had not been able to touch that baby and verify its existence.

Patricia Rausch: We are even encouraging parents to make contact with the baby following death, if they have not had that opportunity earlier. We encourage them to prepare the baby for the morgue, and to go through a very ritualistic scene. It's tremendously heart-wrenching, but it has proven to make the experience a beautiful one instead of the reverse, which we're all too familiar with.

Susan Rose: Returning to your idea that the encasing quality helps quiet babies, Pat, do you know whether swaddling reduces the incidence of apnea?

Patricia Rausch: I don't know. Swaddling a high-risk preterm, who has an I.V. and perhaps is on a ventilator, would be an interesting chore.

Kathryn Barnard: I'm not sure it would be wise to swaddle a preterm who is already at risk in terms of the musculature for breathing. They may do better with full range of motion.

Anneliese Korner: Ultrasound tapes of fetuses show that they are moving a great deal, and they move very similarly to the way preterms do. To restrict that movement for any length of time might not be good — which doesn't mean one shouldn't swaddle a premie when he's very agitated, just to calm him down.

Sandra Weiss: Conceptually, there seems to be a link between swaddling infants to calm them and what we do with neuropsychiatric patients who are demonstrating uncontrolled behavior that is threatening the safety of themselves or others. The procedure of wrapping these patients firmly in sheets calms them within minutes, as if serving to reduce the irritability of the nervous system and reorganize cognitive function. The potential effects of such generalized tactile experience, even through nonhuman contact, merit further research in infant, children, and adult groups.

THE MANY FACES OF TOUCH

Anneliese F. Korner, Ph.D.*

Touch is rarely, if ever, an isolated form of stimulation. The experience of being touched is commonly associated with proprioceptive, vestibular, and kinesthetic stimulation, and with visual and auditory experiences. Touch frequently has a temporal pattern or rhythm. It brings sensations of warmth or coolness, firmness or softness, containment, and texture. This admixture of different forms of stimulation makes it difficult to assess the effects of touch alone.

The problem is well illustrated by many intervention studies with preterm infants. Many studies purport to assess the effects of contact or handling on preterm infants, even though in most studies different forms of stimulation were provided simultaneously (e.g., Hasselmeyer, 1964; Powell, 1974; Rice, 1977). Other investigators deliberately set out to provide multimodal stimulation to preterm infants (e.g., Scarr-Salapatek & Williams, 1973). Such studies often seem to show beneficial effects — better weight gain and greater sensory responsiveness, for instance — but the benefits are not necessarily uniquely due to "handling," touch, or contact.

Soothing a Crying Baby

In our soothing studies with full-term infants (Korner & Thoman, 1970; 1972), Evelyn Thoman and I became keenly aware of how difficult it is to separate the effects of contact from those of other forms of stimulation. As we imitated various maternal ministrations, we found, not surprisingly, that one of the most effective interventions with crying newborns was to pick them up and hold them close to the shoulder. What we did not anticipate at all was that this intervention, in addition to soothing the infants, almost invariably made them bright-eyed and alert and caused them to scan their surroundings. In two studies, we produced visual alertness through this maneuver in 75 percent of all trials, although newborns show this state

*Preparation of this paper was assisted by Grant MH 36884-02 from the National Institute of Mental Health Center for Prevention Research, Division of Prevention and Special Mental Health Programs.

spontaneously very infrequently (Wolff, 1966). The reason we got excited about this was that we were predictably producing the state that many investigators believe is the one most conducive to the earliest forms of learning.

We were curious as to just what produced the soothing effect and the visual exploratory behavior. Was it mostly the body contact, which in this case involved cutaneous, tactile, and possibly olfactory stimulation as well as containment and warmth? Or was it mostly the vestibular-proprioceptive stimulation and the activation of the anti-gravity reflexes? Although these two forms of stimulation can never be completely separated, we attempted to assess their relative efficacy in an experimental study.

Our subjects were 40 normal, crying newborns, whom we lifted, held, or talked to in various ways. Their responses clearly indicated that interventions which included vestibular-proprioceptive stimulation evoked more alertness than did contact. Lifting the crying infant to the shoulder (vestibular-proprioceptive stimulation *and* contact) produced the strongest alertness effect. When the investigator embraced but did not lift or move the infant (contact alone), it produced no more alerting than would have occurred by chance. Very similar results were seen regarding the soothing effects of the interventions.

These findings made us realize that when mothers pick up their crying babies, they not only soothe them but provide them with a variety of visual experiences. I was also struck by the fact that in the literature, body contact has been stressed as an important form of stimulation for early development, while vestibular-proprioceptive stimulation — a by-product of almost any body contact between mother and child — has been largely overlooked.

Swaddled Rats

In a later study (Thoman & Korner, 1971), we investigated the effects of contact and vestibular-proprioceptive stimulation on the development of newborn rats. The pups in one experimental group were swaddled snugly for ten minutes per day during the first two weeks of life. A second group received the same treatment but was slowly rotated on a noiseless drum while swaddled. A third group, the controls, was reared under standard laboratory conditions.

This study showed that contact had some developmental effects, but they were much more pronounced when vestibular-proprioceptive stimulation was added. The swaddled-and-rotated group had the highest average weight at weaning age, and their eyes opened earliest. At 20 days, this group and the swaddled-only group showed significantly more exploratory behavior on a visual cliff test than did controls.

Considering the evidence from our studies, I began to feel increasingly that it might be beneficial to provide compensatory vestibular-proprioceptive stimulation to preterm infants. These infants experience a great deal of this type of stimulation prenatally but are largely deprived of it when growing to term in incubators. Mason's work (1968, 1979) points to the fundamental importance of movement stimulation for normal early development. Like Harlow, Mason reared isolated infant monkeys with surrogate mothers. But while Harlow produced highly abnormal monkeys that engaged in self-mutilation, rocking, and other "autistic" behaviors, Mason offset the most severe deficits by providing isolation-reared monkeys with *swinging* surrogate mothers. Mason also found that providing movement stimulation to young monkeys produced more visual exploratory behavior.

Water Beds for Preterm Infants

The gentlest way I could think of to provide compensatory vestibular-proprioceptive stimulation was through water-bed flotation. My goal was not to accelerate the development of preterm infants but to create conditions that might facilitate natural brain maturation and enhance normal functioning.

In addition to ordinary (though infant-size) water beds, which move only in response to movement by the infant or caregiver, we used water beds that oscillated, some continuously and others intermittently. The oscillations were very gentle, almost imperceptible to an observer. They followed a head-to-foot direction and had the temporal pattern of a maternal biological rhythm. For the continuously oscillating water beds, we chose a slightly irregular rhythm that corresponded to that of average maternal resting respirations in the third trimester of pregnancy. For the intermittent oscillations, we chose the rhythm of the basic rest-activity cycle as described by Kleitman (1969).

Apnea Reduction

Our first study (Korner et al., 1975), was designed to test whether placing infants on water beds for days at a time was a safe procedure. We found that it was. In addition, we obtained a totally unanticipated finding: The infants in the oscillating water-bed group had significantly fewer apneas than others, as indicated by the apnea alarm (see Figure 14).

We attempted to replicate this study with eight infants preselected for apnea of prematurity (Korner et al., 1978). Again the incidence of apnea declined significantly while the infants were on the oscillating water beds. Though all types of apnea were reduced, the most consistent reduction was in apneas long enough to trip the alarms. The most severe types of apnea, as defined by their association with a slowing of the heart rate to below 80 beats per minute, also were sharply reduced, at least in seven of the eight babies.

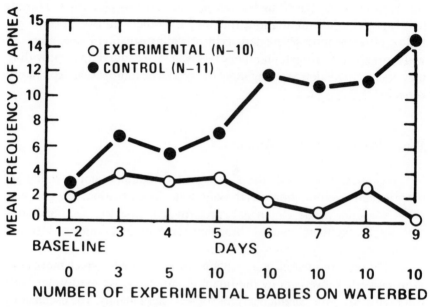

Figure 14. Results from an early study yielded the unexpected finding that infants on an oscillating water bed (experimental group) experienced fewer episodes of apnea than infants on ordinary mattresses (control group).

The eighth infant ran completely counter to the general trend. It later came to appear that the diagnosis of apnea of prematurity had been incorrect. We learned from this baby that highly unstable infants who are being weaned from ventilators or have major cardiopulmonary or neurologic complications are not apt to respond to water beds with apnea reduction. This treatment approach may be limited to infants with uncomplicated apnea of prematurity.

Behavioral Effects of Water Beds

We next began to investigate systematically what we had originally set out to study, namely, the effects of water beds on the behavioral responses of preterm infants. To date we have conducted two behavioral sleep and motility studies (Edelman, Kraemer, & Korner, 1982; Korner, Ruppel, & Rho, 1982). The subjects in one study were 12 healthy preterm infants; those in the other were 17 preterm infants being treated with theophylline, which causes wakefulness and restlessness. In both studies, infants showed a significant increase in sustained quiet sleep and a significant decrease in irritability while on the oscillating water bed. In addition, their movements were smoother and less jerky.

We also did a study that investigated the effects of water-bed flotation on neurobehavioral development (Korner, Forrest, & Schneider, 1983). The results showed that the infants raised on water beds performed significantly better in attending to and pursuing visual and auditory stimuli. They spent more time in a visually alert, inactive state than did control infants. They also showed more mature spontaneous motor behavior and fewer signs of irritability and hypertonicity. Though highly preliminary, this study suggests that compensatory vestibular-proprioceptive stimulation as provided by water beds may enhance the neurobehavioral development of preterm infants.

Intervention Studies Using Touch Alone

In conclusion, I would like to review three studies that used touch in relatively pure form as an intervention with preterm infants. In a study of six apneic infants, Kattwinkel and colleagues (1975) found that rubbing the infants' extremities produced a significant decrease in the frequency of apnea, both during and shortly after the period of stimulation. In another study (Schaeffer, 1982), a nurse provided touch to 13 mechanically ventilated preterm infants by placing her hands on their heads and abdomens. Over time, the experimental subjects had significantly higher hematocrit levels and required less oxygen than infants in a control group.

A final and very promising study using contact in relatively pure form is that of Scott and Richards (1979). Six infants served as their own controls on and off lambswool pads alternating with cotton sheets for several days. Lambswool pads not only provide softness but texture and, according to some New Zealand manufacturers, warmth when it is cold and coolness when it is warm. On the days when the infants were nursed on lambswool pads, they gained an extra ten grams and they moved significantly less.

One of the fascinating aspects of this study is how quickly its findings on a few babies have been integrated into preterm infant care. Whenever one goes into an intensive care nursery these days, one finds infants on lambswool or acrylic pads. There is a lesson to be learned from this. Ultimately, interventions that make a lot of common sense, that are not likely to do harm but are apt to do some good, and that can be implemented simply and inexpensively will be the ones that will find the most rapid and widespread acceptance in neonatal care.

DISCUSSION

T. Berry Brazelton: Anneliese, what comes to me out of your work is the beautiful layering of the effects you've examined. There is the improvement in state behaviors, and state is such an important control system in the baby. Increasing the baby's capacity to maintain an alert state is one of the most significant things you've done, as well as cutting off apnea at the bottom.

State organization really reflects the interaction of all the infant's sensory-motor and neurological systems. It cements them together, so to speak. I think what you've done with water beds is teach infants about utilizing inner state controls, which gives them a chance to build on that — to accept and learn from cognitive and social cues. When I first watched you working with the water beds and saw those babies you put on the beds settle down and begin to learn to manage state for themselves, and to become more effective as they gained mastery over state and motor responses in the process, it was really a breakthrough in my thinking.

Allen Gottfried: What do you think the variable facilitating the development of babies on water beds is? Do you think it's the soft touch or the almost imperceptible motion?

Anneliese Korner: Well, obviously I have placed my bets on vestibular stimulation. We are currently doing a sleep and motility study in which we compare the effects of the incubator mattress, a plain water bed, a continuously oscillating water bed, and an intermittently oscillating water bed. If the plain water bed has the same effect as the oscillating water bed, then the beneficial variable must be something about the soft fluid support system. We will also try to find out whether intermittent stimulation is much more effective than continuous stimulation, as some animal researchers have suggested. If this is the case, we will do another study to find out whether it is the intermittency or the maternal biological rhythm that has the effect.

Stephen Suomi: Why does it have to be one or the other? Are we making artificial distinctions?

Allen Gottfried: Yes and no. Ecologically, it makes no difference: Stimulation of different types is confounded in nature. Scientifically, however, I think it is important to trace developmental effects to specific sources if possible.

Anneliese Korner: Perhaps I should mention that our medical personnel usually request water beds because of the soft contact they provide rather than for the potential benefits of vestibular-proprioceptive stimulation. They request them for tiny preterms in order to preserve these babies' fragile skin and for infants with disseminated herpes or other severe skin diseases. They also request them for infants who are recovering from abdominal surgery and cannot be turned over, and for infants with conditions such as spina bifida in which pressure points on the skin and skeletal structure are to be avoided. Most often of all, they request them because the beds seem to improve the shape of the oblong, flat heads so commonly seen in preterm infants.

T. Berry Brazelton: Our nurses ask for water beds for a particular kind of baby: The infant who gets severely out of control very quickly. On a water bed, these babies begin to get contingent feedback, which is strongly reinforcing for state control and for other control systems.

Patricia Rausch: Anneliese, can you tell me how much a water bed costs?

Anneliese Korner: Not yet. However, Browne Technology from Santa Barbara will soon produce these water beds and then they will become available for other investigators and for general use.

Peter Gorski: In the past, perhaps because the state of water bed manufacturing has been so diverse, I have sometimes recommended that babies be removed from water beds, and they have had less apnea off the beds. Their movements improved, too.

T. Berry Brazelton: What kinds of babies were those?

Peter Gorski: The same babies you described: Babies who were having disjointed movements and were unable to inhibit their responses. I think the particular mattresses we were using gave a wave effect to the babies that enhanced their disorganization.

Anneliese Korner: We have never seen this with our types of water beds, probably because they cradle the baby slightly. All our controlled studies to date have shown that disjointed, tremulous movements are decreased on the water bed. However, very unstable babies may be adversely affected by the water bed or the oscillations with respect to apnea. It is primarily the fairly stable infants, the growing premies who still are showing some immaturity in terms of apnea, who are helped.

TOUCH AS AN ORGANIZER FOR LEARNING AND DEVELOPMENT

Allen W. Gottfried, Ph.D.

If we ask the question when does behavior begin, we find that prenatal behavior is rooted in the fetus' reaction to the stimulation of touch. According to Davenport Hooker's classic studies (1952), until seven and one-half weeks gestational age the human embryo shows no evidence of reflex activity. No area of the skin is sensitive to tactile stimulation. Over the next seven weeks, almost the entire surface of the body becomes sensitive to touch, beginning with the lips and ending with the feet and legs. (The top and back of the head remain insensitive until birth.)

Spontaneous movement, which Hooker described as a "vestibular righting response" apparently caused by a disturbance of head-body relations, first occurred at nine and one-half weeks. The first evidence of proprioceptive responsiveness appeared at the same time. Hooker described this as flexion at the wrist, elbow, and shoulder caused by passive extension of the fingers.

Thus, responses to somesthetic stimulation are the first human behaviors to develop, followed approximately two weeks later by responses to vestibular and proprioceptive stimulation. Touch has been given particular developmental significance. One may put forth the question, why? The answer may reside in a general embryological principle: "The earlier a function develops, the more fundamental it is likely to be" (Montagu, 1971, p. 3; Carmichael, 1954). Hence, an extensive amount of research has been conducted demonstrating that touch plays an important part in development. A number of investigators have claimed that early tactile contact influences growth rates, adaptability, learning, activity level, exploratory behavior, attachment, sociability, ability to withstand stress, and immunological development in many young mammals. However, it is not entirely clear whether these outcomes are due to cutaneous, vestibular, or social communicative factors, because the three generally operate simultaneously.

Preterms and Handling

A number of investigators have also examined the effects of touch stimulation on infants, especially premature newborns. In the past decade we have witnessed a surge of experimental intervention programs for at-risk newborns (see Cornell and Gottfried, 1976; Gottfried, 1981; Gottfried, 1984b). Most researchers have focused on tactile-vestibular stimulation. The studies described by Rose, Rausch, and Korner earlier in Part III provide fine examples. A review of intervention programs employing tactile-vestibular stimulation indicates that most data show positive effects. Although again it is difficult to discern whether the developmental changes are due to tactile or vestibular stimulation, it is clear that stimulation associated with touch regulates behavior and development.

However, the data presented by Lucey and Gorski et al. reveal that touching or handling premature infants can have a negative effect. Lucey reported a relationship between handling and transient hypoxemia, and Gorski reported that touching infants during convalescent care was associated with bradycardia. Perhaps there is "bad or unpleasant" handling, as when infants are manipulated for medical or nursing purposes, and "good or pleasant" handling, as when infants receive tender-loving-care types of touching or rocking. Perhaps the important thing is not just the type of handling but when it occurs. For example, sick infants may respond negatively whereas medically stable or healthy infants respond positively.

The five other papers in this section provide data on the consequences of handling or vestibular stimulation on premature infants. However, there is a paucity of data on the quality and quantity of the tactile contact normally experienced by premature infants in special care units. I would like to summarize some data from my research program addressing this issue (Gottfried et al., 1981; Gottfried, 1984a).

Special Care Units: An Observational Study

My colleagues and I have conducted continuous 24-hour recordings of the contacts between caregivers and premature infants in intensive and convalescent care units during a typical day. The data reveal that infants in special care units do not lack contact with persons. On the average, infants in the neonatal intensive care unit (NICU) received 70 contacts per day, with one infant receiving as many as 106. Infants in the neonatal convalescent care unit (NCCU) received 42 contacts per day with an upper limit of 55. Most contacts were only a few minutes long. They occurred two or three times per hour and added to daily totals of two and one-half hours in the NICU and 3.3 hours in the NCCU. There was no regularity or schedule involved.

Although virtually all contacts involved touching or handling, most of the handling may be appropriately described as nonsocial. It was administered for the purpose of giving medical or nursing care and seldom included social touching or rocking. Only 3 percent of the infants' contacts were with family members. The low occurrence of rocking in the NICU is understandable and recommended. However, the lack of social handling of infants in the NCCU is surprising in view of the large body of data suggesting that vestibular stimulation enhances development in young premature infants.

We also assessed caregivers' responses to infants' cries during contacts. Infants cried in approximately 21 percent of the contacts, but the caregivers attempted to soothe the infants on fewer than half those occasions. When they did try, it was usually by talking to the infant and seldom by social touching. The tendency not to attempt to soothe crying infants is interesting in view of Speidel's suggestion (1978) that crying may be the mediating factor in hypoxemia. The lack of responsiveness to infants' cries may also serve to delay the development of contingencies between infants' behavior and social environmental reactions.

Another series of analyses were conducted to determine the extent to which sensory experiences received by infants were coordinated during contacts. An example of coordinated experiences would be handling and talking to the infant while the infant can see one's face. The overall results showed relatively low percentages of coordinated sensory experiences for the NCCU and NICU infants. Although the effect of dissociated sensory experiences is unknown, this finding is significant in view of evidence showing a deficit in the ability of premature infants up to one year of age to integrate tactual and visual sensory information (Gottfried, Rose, & Bridger, 1977; Rose, Gottfried, & Bridger, 1978).

In summary, these observational findings show that premature infants in special care units receive a considerable amount of handling per day, but that it is primarily the result of medical and nursing care (the type of handling likely to be associated with transient hypoxemia and bradycardia as indicated by Lucey and Gorski). Social touching and rocking occur infrequently (the type of handling more comparable to the stimulation described by Rose, Rausch, and Korner). There was no regularity to the occurrence of these handling experiences. Social touching was infrequently used to soothe crying infants. Furthermore, integrated sensory experiences involving handling were fairly few. These data indicate that the nature of the tactile environment of infants in special care units may not be conducive to optimal development.

Tactile Perception and Cognitive Development

What does touch tell us about cognition? An interesting description of the cognitive aspects of touch in blind children is by Fraiberg (1977):

> Between five and eight months of age we have examples for
> all children in which the blind baby's hands explore the mother's
> or father's face, the fingers tracing features with familiarity and
> giving the viewer a sense that he was anticipating what he would
> find. The film record gives strong evidence that these exploring
> hands are discriminating and that the information from the
> fingers brings recognition as well as nonrecognition (pp.
> 107-108).

Manual activities are the eyes of blind infants, and these infants seem to recognize things by touch at an early age.

Can sighted infants recognize the shapes of objects by touch? In an experimental study of tactile recognition memory (Gottfried & Rose, 1980), one-year-old infants were given the opportunity to examine a group of identical objects in normal light. Then the lights were turned off, and the infants were presented with a tray containing the familiar objects and some novel objects. (Their behavior in the dark was videotaped by infrared recording.) The babies spent more time manipulating and mouthing the novel objects, and transferred them from hand to hand more often, than they did the familiar objects, showing tactile recognition memory.

Montagu (1971) called touch the "mother of the senses." It is the first sensory system to develop, and touch, or the vestibular and proprioceptive stimulation associated with touch, does play a significant role in mammalian development. However, the stimulation associated with touch can have a positive or negative effect. We need to look more critically at the components, correlates, and consequences of touch. In addition, we need to examine not only the mother of the senses but the family of senses, at least at the behavioral level, and to continue to explore the cognitive context in which sensory development takes place.

DISCUSSION

T. Berry Brazelton: One thing that comes to me out of your work, Allen, is that touch versus proprioceptive versus vestibular may not be the way to look at it. Touch as an organizer might be a lot better concept.

Allen Gottfried: Our main reason for investigating intersensory stimulation was our earlier finding that premies showed deficits in tactile-visual cross-modal skills. We suspect that the environment of special care units is not facilitating the development of intersensory skills. The environment we provide for these babies, in my opinion, is very abnormal.

In some of his articles, Jerry Lucey has called the intensive care nursery an alien environment, and I think this is true. The noise level, for instance, is not only painful for the staff but probably unpleasant for the infants as well.

Judith Smith: What was the noise level in the nurseries, Allen? Can you give us a decibel level of something we're familiar with?

Allen Gottfried: We found peak levels like those in a factory, or near a large engine, or in light traffic. These peak levels lasted as long as a couple of hours sometimes, and the noise level was high the rest of the day as well. The radio was on most of the time (as in many work environments); people talked; machinery ran; phones and alarms rang. We took recordings inside operating incubators and found that the sound level in there was a little higher. Although the incubator provides temperature control, it does not in any way shelter the infant from light or sound.

Patricia Rausch: Many people who work in nurseries are aware of the noise problem, as you know. In our nursery in Orlando, we've put tape recorders in the isolettes and found that, with a great deal of effort, we can keep it almost completely silent inside.

Allen Gottfried: Some nurseries are changing. For example, Sheridan just reported a recent survey showing that 47 percent of nurseries now try to simulate day-night rhythms of light and dark.

Marie-Thérèse Connell: Do you have any information on noise in nurseries in other countries?

Jerold Lucey: Most of the German and Swiss intensive care nurseries I've seen are much quieter than ours. English intensive care nurseries tend to be exactly like ours — noisy. The Swedish are in between. They also have a great many healthy babies, as you know. Sweden has only about half the premature rate that we do in the United States, 4 percent compared to our 8 percent.

Marian Diamond: I'm intrigued by Selma Fraiberg's observation that blind infants opened their mouths while they explored with their hands. The part of the brain that is associated with proprioception is just across the central gyrus from the motor area for oral function, so if you're groping for proprioceptive function, perhaps opening the mouth is not surprising.

T. Berry Brazelton: We had a couple of blind babies that we followed, and we noticed that in the two months before they started to walk they did a lot of posturing. They would hold their arms and legs wide apart and open their mouths, and we couldn't figure it out. Then when they started to walk, they never ran into anything. The radar started functioning before they got to the point of utilizing it, which was fascinating.

Arnold Scheibel: Thinking back over the last few papers, it seems to me that what many researchers are looking for is a common factor or substrate that would, in a sense, bring meaning to the curious effects of touch and sound and other early stimulation — curious because the effects are both positive and negative. I would like to draw your attention to some characteristics of the brain stem, particularly the reticular core, which is an assemblage of cell families that runs from the spinal cord into the base of the brain. Many of these cell groups have been chemically characterized, and some of them are rich in familiar neurotransmitters such as epinephrine, dopamine, and acetylcholine.

An interesting thing about the reticular core is that it has no direct contact with the extremities of the body. Information from the extremities is in a sense received second-hand, via fibers from brain-ascending tracts that we call collaterals. In addition, the reticular core contains a number of cell groups that are responsible and only responsible for respiration. These cells are located very near the input fibers that carry auditory information. It is quite possible, then, that in the immature organism any kind of auditory stimulation might temporarily overwhelm the activity of these respiratory cell groups.

Another interesting characteristic of the reticular formation is that its dendrites lose their spines between the newborn period and the age of three or four months. Our theory is that this is an aspect of maturation of the reticular core, and that until the spines disappear the cells may be multimodal in the sense that they can be loaded with many different kinds of information. Later, only certain kinds of inputs are effective. A group at Ohio State has examined the brain stems of sudden-infant-death syndrome (SIDS) babies and found that their reticular dendrites remained loaded with spines, so immaturity of the reticular core may be related to SIDS. I mention this to underscore the possible importance of the reticular core, not only as a substrate intellectually speaking but as a possible pathway for therapeutic interventions.

In the premie, the reticular formation is structurally fairly mature but chemically quite immature. Furthermore, the links to cortex through the thalamus are extremely immature. A 28- to 30-week-old premie is essentially a brain stem preparing links to cortex.

Peter Gorski: A clinical continuation of that very helpful information: We should not assume that what is normal behavior toward a full-term baby is also appropriate for an infant who is neurologically at risk. However, neither should we assume that environmental conditions that are shocking to *our* eyes and ears are necessarily bad for babies. Intuitively I think they probably are, but we have to discover that still. Our interventions, it seems to me, should be based on developmental outcomes and on a knowledge of how specific infants respond to our efforts.

T. Berry Brazelton: If our interventions were more appropriate to the ability of the baby to incorporate them as experience, either positive or negative, they might be more effective. We set up a violation of expectancy. Going back to Bill Greenough's terms, we fail to provide the experience-expectant interactions that the baby's nervous system is programmed to accept. Judging from the work that we've been doing with expectancy, this can be a very costly thing for a preterm infant.

Allen Gottfried: Just a few years ago, we really had no knowledge about the environment of these newborns. In the last two or three years, we've collected a considerable body of evidence on the environment, both physical and social. The findings are consistent, and the information gained already forms a foundation for much more sophisticated interventions to come. Our understanding of infant responses and the neurology underlying them is expanding at a similarly rapid rate, and we hope future intervention programs will be based on findings in all these areas.

Developmental Perspectives

PART V
TOUCH IN CHILDHOOD AND ADOLESCENCE

Touch communicates information and feelings not only during infancy but throughout life. In the first of three papers on touch during childhood and adolescence, Paul Satz and colleagues report findings from a longitudinal study relating children's ability to identify the finger(s) touched by an examiner to their early reading skills. This study, as Allen Gottfried commented, focuses on the same question as some of the infant research in Part IV: What does the hand tell the mind? Sandra Weiss' study of parental touch and the child's body image at eight to ten years also shows the cognitive importance of touch. In addition, it links qualities of parental touch to self-esteem variables.

The final paper in the section relates touch to a demographic variable: the incidence of pregnancy among young adolescents, particularly those under the age of fifteen. In "Touching and Adolescent Sexuality," Elizabeth McAnarney presents research and clinical evidence suggesting that young adolescents may use sex primarily to obtain nonsexual touch, or cuddling, which parents offer in very limited amounts after their children reach puberty.

FINGER LOCALIZATION AND READING ACHIEVEMENT

Paul Satz, Ph.D.
and colleagues*

This paper focuses on an aspect of touch that has long been of interest to behavioral neurologists — namely, finger sense and related disturbances of the body scheme. Spillane (1942), an early investigator in this area, wrote as follows:

> The term "body scheme" was introduced by Head and Holmes (1911) to signify the concept which a person develops of his own body. The body "scheme," "image" or "pattern" means the picture of the body which is formed in the mind....The sensory cortex becomes a storehouse of sensory experience: it receives impressions, stores them and judges new ones in the light of its experience. A standard is formed against which incoming impressions are modified and subsequent conduct determined. In the formation and maintenance of this plastic body image the importance of optical and postural impressions is therefore to be expected (p. 42).

Clinical and Developmental Studies

Gerstmann (1940) must be credited for his efforts to link a pattern of seemingly diverse disturbances in body scheme to a specific area in the left sensory cortex: the left angular gyrus. The pattern of behavioral deficits he defined, called the Gerstmann syndrome, included impairments in finger recognition (finger agnosia), left-right disorientation, writing (dysgraphia), and calculation (dyscalculia). Unfortunately, clinical studies in the past two decades have largely failed to support this assembly of symptoms as a naturally occurring pattern of deficits and have raised serious questions concerning the focal lesion presumed to underlie the syndrome (Benton,

*J. M. Fletcher, R. Morris, and H. G. Taylor

1961; Heimburger, DeMeyer, & Reitan, 1964; Poeck & Orgass, 1966).

Despite the empirical evidence against the Gerstmann syndrome, its elements (finger agnosia, left-right disorientation, dysgraphia, and dyscalculia) represent cognitive operations that are known to be altered by focal or generalized lesions in the left cerebral hemisphere of adults, though not in syndromatic fashion. These deficits, simply or in combination with many other cognitive operations, have also long been reported to occur in children with specific reading and learning handicaps without demonstrable brain injury (Benton, 1979; Satz et al., 1978; Lefford, Birch, & Green, 1974; Kinsbourne, 1968). One of the more interesting though puzzling deficits consistently found in this literature is finger agnosia.

A major problem in many of these clinical reports is that finger agnosia and other terms are loosely defined. Gerstmann defined finger agnosia as an inability to name or recognize one's own fingers or those of the examiner. As Benton (1979) notes, this definition is unfortunate because it "implies the existence of a unitary 'finger sense' or faculty of finger recognition when in fact it is only a collective term for different types of defective performance" (p. 86), such as a naming difficulty, an aphasia, a visuospatial defect, or a sequencing problem. Regrettably, many clinicians continue to treat finger agnosia as a unitary concept.

In contrast to clinical studies, developmental psychologists have approached the study of finger localization on a more empirical basis. Particular efforts have been made to define the specific stimulus characteristics and response requirements of the various finger localization tasks, to determine the different cognitive operations involved, and to investigate how performance on these tasks varies with chronological and mental age. Some of the landmark studies were conducted by Lefford, Birch, and Green (1974), Wake (1957), and Benton (1959).

Together, developmental studies suggest that the construct of finger sense involves a number of different task operations and cognitive processes that are probably tied to specific stages in development. Although these studies have managed to strip away much of the surplus meaning associated with finger agnosia, their methods have not entailed rigorous quantitative and sampling procedures.

A Longitudinal Study

The following study was conducted by the present authors as part of the Florida Longitudinal Project (Satz et al., in press). It represents an attempt to examine some of the cognitive and developmental aspects of finger localization in a longitudinal-prospective sample of kindergarten children who, in later grades (two and five), became average readers or poor readers. This design thus afforded a rare opportunity to use both a predictive and concurrent validation approach to examine the association between finger recognition and reading achievement. The predictive validation approach allowed us to evaluate an earlier hunch of Herbert Birch that finger recognition, because of its cognitive and developmental characteristics, might be of potential value in the early identification of children at risk for later school failure (Lefford et al., 1974). The concurrent validation approach allowed us to reexamine the putative association between finger recognition and reading achievement from a developmental perspective, using specific measures of finger recognition rather than a composite measure as in other studies. Finally, the use of factor analytic methods permitted a more objective assessment of the cognitive operations presumed to underlie performance on finger localization tasks.

Our subjects were 678 white male kindergartners in Alachua County, Florida. They were given a battery of developmental tests upon entering kindergarten. At the end of their third year of school (grade two), the kindergarten battery was readministered and measures of reading ability were obtained. These reading measures were used to identify 80 disabled readers: children whose reading scores fell more than one standard deviation below the mean for the total sample. Eighty nondisabled readers, matched for age with the disabled readers, were selected from those whose scores were no more than .4 standard deviation below the mean for the sample. This selection process yielded a disabled group functioning about two years behind on our reading measures and a nondisabled group with reading abilities slightly in advance of grade standard. At the end of the sixth year of school (grade five) the developmental test battery was given a third time and the children's reading ability was assessed again.

In addition to the measures just described, four finger recognition tasks were given in kindergarten, grade two, and grade five. In Task 1, the child held his hand palm up and the investigator briefly touched one of the child's fingers with the end of a paper clip while a card shielded it from view. Then the shield was removed and the child was asked to point to the finger that had been touched. Five trials were provided for each hand. In Task 2, the conditions were the same as in Task 1 except that, rather than pointing to his own finger, the child pointed to a finger on a diagram of the hands. Again, five trials were provided for each hand. Tasks 3 and 4 were preceded by a training phase in which the child's fingers were verbally labeled by the examiner from one (thumb) to five (little finger). After the child had mastered the numbering system, his fingers were touched behind the shield as in Tasks 1 and 2. One finger on one hand was stimulated on each trial of Task 3, and two fingers, one on each hand, were simultaneously stimulated on each trial of Task 4. In both tasks, the child was required to call out the number of the finger(s) stimulated.

Each task placed different cognitive demands on the child. Task 1 was the simplest, requiring only sensory discrimination of the finger stimulated. In Task 2, the child had to discriminate the finger and point to a pictorial representation of the hand. This latter act had been hypothesized to require an internal representation of the body schema (Benton, 1979). Task 3 added a verbal coding dimension to Task 1, and Task 4 required both verbal coding and a more complex sensory discrimination. Based on previous research, subjects were expected to meet these different task demands at different developmental rates.

Development of Finger Recognition Skills

With respect to the control group of average readers, a clear developmental pattern was evident on Tasks 2, 3, and 4. Task 1 showed no such trend because all the average readers had mastered it when tested at the start of kindergarten. The disabled readers also showed a clear developmental pattern on Tasks 2, 3, and 4. Their initial performance (kindergarten) was much lower than that of the control group, which produced a robust group-by-grade interaction, especially on Tasks 3 and 4. Both reading groups eventually attained mastery on all tasks, but significant delays occurred in the children who during kindergarten were destined to become disabled readers, especially on the more complex Tasks 3 and 4 (see Figure 15). These initial delays, in fact, helped identify developmental precursors of reading difficulty. In this framework, our results confirmed the earlier hypothesis of Birch and his colleagues.

To explore associations between performances on individual finger recognition tasks and other developmental measures, Tasks 2, 3, and 4 were subjected to factor analysis involving other Year 1 battery data. First, the factor structure of the test battery was analyzed independently of the finger recognition tasks. The results showed that the measures loaded on three different factors: perceptual-motor (Factor 1), verbal-conceptual (Factor 2), and verbal-cultural (Factor 3). Other factor analyses of these measures have consistently revealed the same three-factor structure.

Individual finger recognition tasks were added separately to determine where these tasks loaded. Task 2 loaded on a new fourth factor labeled somatosensory differentiation. Task 3 loaded on Factor 3 (verbal-cultural). In contrast, Task 4 loaded on Factor 1 (perceptual-motor). Since Task 3 required learning a verbal code, it was not surprising that it loaded on the verbal-cultural factor. Although Task 4 also required learning a verbal code, the simultaneous as opposed to successive stimulation of fingers imposed greater demands on sensorimotor-perceptual skills, resulting in the loading on the perceptual-motor factor.

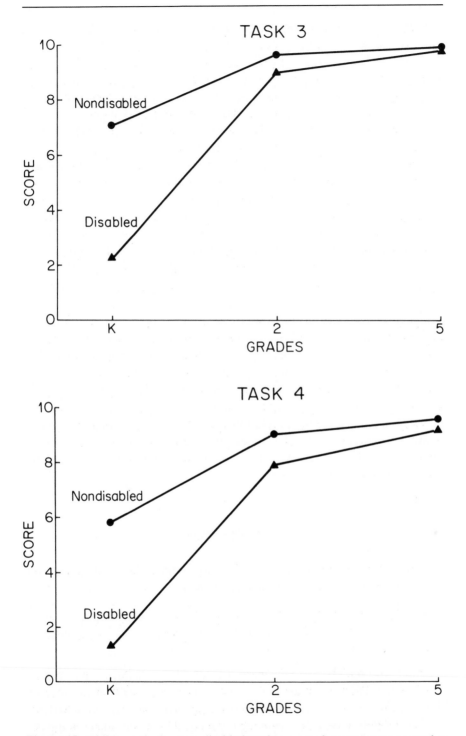

Figure 15. Children who became disabled readers were slower to master complex finger recognition tasks than children who became average readers.

Finger recognition performances significantly differentiated between the two reading groups at all three testings. Using techniques described by Huberty (1975), we determined that for kindergartners about 39 percent of the variance in later reading achievement could be accounted for by finger recognition skills. However, only 12 percent and 4 percent of the variance in reading achievement could be accounted for in grades two and five, respectively. This shows that the overall relationship between finger recognition tasks and reading achievement diminished over time.

In addition to verifying the predictive and concurrent validity of the finger recognition tasks for discriminating between the two reading groups, our analysis showed that the most uniquely neuropsychological task (Task 2) discriminated less well between reading groups than Tasks 3 and 4, which were related to other developmental variables. The sensitivity of Task 3 as a discriminator diminished with age. Task 4 remained related to reading achievement across all three probes, accounting entirely for the weak relationship between finger recognition and reading achievement in grade five.

In summary, our results shed additional light on the complex developmental and cognitive parameters of finger localization tasks, especially as they relate to reading achievement. The predictive validation analyses confirmed Birch's hypothesis that components of finger recognition skill might have value in the early identification of children at risk for school failure. The concurrent validation analyses demonstrated the effects of developmental change in the relationship between finger localization and reading. Finally, factor analysis yielded a useful objective framework for interpreting the cognitive and developmental operations associated with finger localization and reading.

DISCUSSION

T. Berry Brazelton: Why were all your subjects boys? Because you expected a higher rate of learning problems?

Paul Satz: Yes. The rates of reading failure are four to one in favor of boys, and we wanted to increase our chances of having a substantial number of index cases in later years.

Michael Merzenich: Do you learn anything by considering the degree of the error, Paul? In other words, were there a significant number of children who made more than, say, a one-digit error on your more difficult finger recognition tasks, or were the errors usually to the adjacent digits?

Paul Satz: I don't know. We treated that as a qualitative aspect of performance.

Michael Merzenich: It's a very interesting question whether it's a qualitative error, an error of kind, or whether it's just a matter of delayed development. Although I shouldn't really try to relate our work to yours, a kind of tunnel vision that I have is that as mappings of skin surfaces are developed, the associations that can be made from them relate to the qualities of the mappings generally.

Paul Satz: I could tell you as a clinician where most of the errors occur. Most of them are when stimulation is in the middle areas. With the first and fifth fingers, there are fewer errors.

Michael Merzenich: Map-to-map associations are really important, especially when maps are changing as a function of experience. There has to be a correction of associations as maps change, and the quality of the associations that can occur relates to the quality of the mappings. That may be largely where these problems lie. If I have a poor sense of or map of my hand, it may relate to all sorts of things.

T. Berry Brazelton: I had a 14-year-old girl who had learned to cope with her problems but had a difficult time. When I said to her during a routine checkup, "You've really gotten over all this and you really had to work at it," she started weeping. She said, "You know how hard it's been." I think these children need to know that we know how hard it's been.

Paul Satz: There's some evidence that females with reading disabilities, though very few, suffer more. In two Canadian follow-up studies, the females had more emotional scars 20 years later. In general, though, I think it's a myth that learning disabilities leave terrible scars during adolescence and adulthood. It's also a myth that children always outgrow these disabilities.

T. Berry Brazelton: We are now picking up newborns who are hypersensitive and whom we expect to be hyperactive and to have attentional disorders later. A mother told me the other day that her child had been identified as learning disabled at three years of age. When he was a small baby, this child was having trouble processing information, and the mother says she told me so. I replied that he'd outgrow it, so I missed my chance. By now, this child has an in-built expectation to fail. It's very subtle, but it's there. If we could predict these problems earlier, we could back the children up by not letting that expectation to fail get built in so early.

Paul, do you have any information on prematures or SGAs in your sample?

Paul Satz: No. However, a number of people around the country have been using my test as an outcome measure in studies of high-risk pregnancies and preterm infants. Researchers are using these measures as preliminary criteria when at-risk infants reach five years of age instead of waiting until they're eight or ten to see what happens.

Peter Gorski: Jane Hunt in San Francisco, along with other investigators, now has data on school-aged children who were born prematurely. Even though the children may score well on IQ tests, they are experiencing school failure at a phenomenal rate — 50 percent or higher. Tests of perceptual-motor difficulties seem to pick up school-failure children much better than language tests do at ages five and six.

Susan Rose: As I understand it, the deficits in IQ are not as marked as the deficits in perceptual-motor performance.

T. Berry Brazelton: We need to have a better developmental line on these babies. Perhaps if we gave them more time at school, or taught them differently, we might have better outcomes.

Paul Satz: I looked at four longitudinal studies on preterm birth and cognitive development. Although there are too little data to be sure, infants who were selected as at risk at birth seem to look all right at four years of age. At age seven, something starts showing up which changes at eleven and becomes something else. There are stages, and what we need are prospective studies to examine them.

PARENTAL TOUCH AND THE CHILD'S BODY IMAGE

Sandra J. Weiss, R.N., D.N.Sc.

The theoretical relationship that has been postulated between body image and the organization and functioning of the personality provides substantial rationale for better understanding factors that influence development of the body image. A person's entire sense of self, though not limited to sensations generated by the body, appears to originate in body awareness, body functions, and body activities (Wapner, 1965; Witkin et al., 1962). Both sentiment for the body and the cognitive model of the body have been identified as primary dimensions in an individual's overall system of standards for interpreting the world (Gorman, 1969; Fisher & Cleveland, 1968; Peto, 1972).

Tactile Experience and Body Perception

Evolution of the body image appears to start as an organism first interacts with other objects in the environment. It is postulated that the sensory experience of touch does much to aid the process of separating the "me" from the "not me" and encouraging a greater awareness of one's own body. Schilder (1950) maintained that every touch provokes a mental image of the spot touched, with these images being necessary for localization of the body parts and functions.

Intrauterine tactile experiences may provide the rudimentary foundations for perception of boundaries between one's own body and that of another. By birth, infants possess a fairly well-developed faculty within their central nervous system for registering and associating sensory impressions received through contact with other human beings. There is increasing evidence that the sensory pathways subserving cutaneous sensation are the first to complete myelinization and maturation in the infant, followed by the vestibular, auditory, and visual senses (e.g., Gottlieb, 1971).

These earlier developing functions may give an organism a base for higher order operations, determining many initial "cell assemblages" or "cognitive maps" (e.g., Merzenich & Kaas, 1980). A cell assemblage or map may be described as a cortical representation that is formed through frequently repeated sensory stimulations and neuromuscular excitations of the body. In this way, each separate tactile experience becomes related to the next and is ordered cognitively. The implications of such a process are that initially developed cortical representations may affect the core experiences and resulting meanings that an individual comes to understand.

In most work examining the effects of tactile stimulation, touch has been viewed as a homogeneous, consistent phenomenon that usually has positive effects. But tactile experience is not that simple. As an organ, the skin is highly complex and versatile, with an immense range of operations and a wide repertoire of responses. It is capable of discriminating among stimuli, with the form or quality of touch from the stimulus decidedly affecting the resulting perception. Thus, the therapeutic meaning or value of a touch would seem clearly dependent on its qualitative nature.

Qualities of Touch

Diverse qualities of touch may be viewed as symbols in a language of touch, just as word symbols create a verbal and written language. A tactile quality is a visible modifier of a tactile interaction that signifies something less visible or less tangible and gives touch its meaning.

Four major tactile qualities emerge from a review of neurophysiologic and sociopsychologic literature: duration, location, intensity, and sensation.

1. The *duration* of a touch is its temporal length. Physiological literature indicates that longer durations seem to allow the body time to experience the sensory stimulation, which encourages awareness of one's body as separate from its surroundings.
2 . The *location* of touch sounds straightforward but is actually a complex quality best measured on three dimensions: threshold, extent, and centripetality. *Threshold* refers to the degree of innervation in different parts of the body. Highly innervated body areas, such as the face and hands, yield bright, discrete, sharply localized sense impressions. *Extent* indicates the degree to which many parts of a person's body are touched rather than only a few. More extensive touching is said to be associated with accurate body perception and high self-regard (Jourard, 1966; Morris, 1967). *Centripetality* refers to the degree to which the trunk of the body is touched rather than the limbs. Both Jourard (1966) and Rubin (1963) maintain that trunk and limb contact between persons may carry strikingly different meanings.
3 . *Intensity* can be weak, moderate, or strong and is judged by amount of indentation of the skin. Touch of moderate intensity has been described in the literature as having the most therapeutic potential (e.g., Geldard, 1972).
4 . *Sensation* defines touch as comfortable or uncomfortable. Touching which is pleasurable rather than painful is thought to enhance perception of the body part touched (e.g., Tyler, 1972).

A Study on Parental Touch

In an attempt to better understand these diverse qualities of touch and their relation to body image, we undertook a study to examine qualities of parental touch and their correlation with body concept and body sentiment in children. This area of study seemed particularly important since ongoing tactile interaction with the mother and father may play a critical role in children's perceptions of their bodies as meaningful objects.

Our sample consisted of 40 white, middle-class families with children eight, nine, or ten years of age. Children this age were chosen specifically because of (1) their cognitive ability for accurate discrimination regarding their bodies, and (2) their retention of a primary bond to the nuclear family.

The families volunteered to participate in the study, which was described in a flyer as concerning nonverbal communication in normal, healthy families.

Upon arrival at the playroom in our laboratory, each child was given two tests: the Draw-a-Person test and the Body Sentiment Index. The Draw-a-Person test was scored for accuracy of body concept using Witkin's Sophistication of Body Concept Scale (Witkin et al., 1962). The Body Sentiment Index utilized a diagram of the body in the form of a puzzle. The child sorted the parts of the body into those he or she liked and those he or she disliked. A body sentiment score was calculated on the basis of the percentage of body parts identified as liked (Weiss, 1975).

Next, parents and child took part in a 15-minute nonverbal activity. The mother and father were asked to serve as guides and teachers as the child learned about the environment of the playroom, while communicating only through touch. Family members were told not to speak, and the children were blindfolded. The resulting behavior was videotaped, and judges who were trained to use a pretested measurement system scored the tapes of parental touch for indicators of duration, location, intensity, and sensation.

When we employed statistical tests to examine the data, we found that three qualities of parental touch were significantly correlated with children's body image. Strong intensity and contact with a large extent of the child's body were related to a sophisticated body concept, while strong intensity and discomfort sensation were related to positive body concept. The finding related to discomfort sensation becomes less puzzling when one notes that the children in our study rarely if ever experienced discomfort severe enough to be painful, and that the qualities of strong intensity and discomfort were consistently correlated. For example, the judges generally rated squeezing, grabbing, and pulling the child as high in intensity and uncomfortable in sensation. These findings would indicate that, in general, the qualities of touch associated with a sophisticated body concept and positive body sentiment were of a somewhat vehement, instrumental, or dynamic nature. It suggests that a substantive level of tactile arousal may be necessary for adequate cognitive and affective awareness of the body to occur.

Sex Differences

Breaking the data down to examine differences between mothers and fathers and sons and daughters produced some interesting results. Looking first at sophistication of body concept, we found that parental touch had little relationship to body concept in girls, with only extent of body parts touched and contact with the trunk of the girl's body being significant. However, many qualities of touch were related to body concept in boys.

As seen in Table 3, all of fathers' touching that was related to an accurate body concept in boys seemed to be highly stimulating to the sensory system, whereas mothers' touching varied in its characteristics. For example, shorter duration and weaker intensity of mothers' touch were related to a healthy body concept but so was their more stimulating use of highly innervated body areas. In general, touch from the father had a stronger predictive relationship to body concept in both boys and girls than did touch from the mother, that is, the data indicated more significant relationships to fathers' touch.

Table 3. Spearman Correlations between Tactile Qualities Used by Mothers[a] or Fathers and the Body Concept of Boys[b] or Girls

	Body Concept					
	Girls			Boys		
Tactile Qualities	**Form**	**Sex & Identity**	**Detail**	**Form**	**Sex & Identity**	**Detail**
Mothers						
Duration	-.13	-.30	-.27	-.45*	-.56**	-.51**
Intensity	.06	.14	.09	-.21	-.45*	.06
Sensation	.03	.20	.23	-.41*	-.15	-.44*
Location						
Threshold	.27	.06	.09	.52**	.29	.58***
Extent	.40*	.08	.15	-.21	-.20	-.34
Centripetality	.19	.20	-.04	-.21	-.37	-.33
Fathers						
Duration	-.18	-.21	-.26	.31	.27	.41*
Intensity	.11	.17	.07	.55**	.72****	.46*
Sensation	-.13	.15	.06	.58***	.68****	.49*
Location						
Threshold	-.32	-.01	-.19	-.40	-.29	-.30
Extent	.66****	.31	.31	.43*	.34	.27
Centripetality	.55**	.19	.18	.14	.16	.16

[a] n = 40 mothers; 40 fathers
[b] n = 20 boys; 20 girls
* p < .05
** p < .01
*** p < .005
**** p < .001

Note: All correlations are based on tactile scores of a continuous nature, with higher correlations indicating relationships to qualities of touch which are more conducive to CNS arousal (e.g., stronger intensity, longer duration, more discomfort sensation, contact with areas of higher innervation).

Turning to the children's scores on body sentiment, we found that scores on only two parental touch qualities predicted positive body sentiment in girls, mother's use of strong intensity and discomfort sensation. In contrast, many qualities of touch were correlated with body sentiment in boys (see Table 4). For paternal touch, these qualities were again primarily those of a highly stimulating nature, such as long duration, strong intensity, and contact with many body parts. Mothers' touch seemed to play the same varied role with body sentiment as it did with body concept. While mothers' touching of highly innervated areas of their sons' bodies was related to positive body sentiment, other qualities of their touching tended to reduce sensory stimulation, such as contact with fewer body parts.

Table 4. Correlations between Qualities of Touch Used by Mothers and Fathers and the Body Sentiment of Boys and Girls

Tactile Qualities	Body Sentiment	
	Girls	**Boys**
Mothers		
Duration	.20	−.30
Intensity	.56**	−.33
Sensation	.44*	−.22
Location		
Threshold	−.33	.61***
Extent	−.21	−.39*
Centripetality	.04	−.48*
Fathers		
Duration	−.12	.70****
Intensity	.10	.62***
Sensation	.28	.63***
Location		
Threshold	.06	−.64****
Extent	.08	.60***
Centripetality	−.07	.20

* $p < .05$
** $p < .01$
*** $p < .005$
**** $p < .001$

This could indicate that a healthy body image in children has some relationship to a more consistently instrumental, arousing nature of paternal touch, while it is related to maternal touch which functions to modulate or manage the degree of sensory arousal. This interpretation is in synchrony with the classic division of parental roles described by many family researchers (e.g., Parsons, 1964). In their frame of reference, one of a mother's primary functions in the family is tension management; thus, her use of touching to sometimes arouse and other times reduce stimulation would work to balance the child's sensory input.

Emerging data from primate research described earlier in this book support this conception. Infant primates seem to use maternal contact as a primary mechanism for modulating and reducing their level of arousal. Studies have shown that physical contact with the mother reduces or eliminates certain behavioral and endocrine responses of the infant to arousal-inducing stimuli (Levine, 1983; Vogt & Levine, 1980).

Because of differences in the relation of maternal and paternal touch to body image, we looked for differences in the pattern of touching by mothers and fathers. Here we examined the frequency (quantity) of touch as well as the four tactile qualities to see if parents showed differences in their actual use. The only significant differences were in frequency and extent. Mothers touched the child significantly more often than fathers, and they touched a larger percentage of the child's total body. Otherwise, the nature of touch used by mothers and fathers was similar. It is interesting to note that frequency of fathers' touch did prove to be a significant correlate of a healthy body concept and sentiment although frequency of maternal touch showed no relationship at all. These findings could indicate that children habituate over time to the touch of the primary caregiver, which in these families was the mother. The separation-individuation process that follows symbiosis in the womb may enhance the potential for habituation.

One might argue that the strong relationships shown between body image and father's touching could indicate that their touching has a more influential effect on the child. The father's role in child-rearing has only begun to receive substantial attention, and it is rapidly changing as well. The results of this study also raise questions as to the particular importance of touch to boys since various qualities of touch were more significantly predictive of boys' body image than girls'. Much research is still needed to examine the varying effects of maternal and paternal touch, particularly in relation to differences in development of body image for boys and girls.

It must be recognized that the size and character of our sample limits the generalizability of these findings, and that the touching behavior of parents in our laboratory situation may differ from touching under natural conditions at home. Despite these limitations, the study demonstrates a clear need for further research on parental touch and body image development. Different age groups and cultural groups should be studied in different settings, with the ultimate (and admittedly distant) goal of identifying the most therapeutic uses of touch with children.

DISCUSSION

T. Berry Brazelton: You've given us an elegant methodology, Sandra, and a beautiful way of looking at sex differences. A mother makes her contribution and a father makes his to the total body image of the child. It would be important if we could examine these contributions in more detail, particularly for single-parent families. We need to know how to back up single parents in ways that we can't right now.

Sandra Weiss: Gender differences in regard to touch are an exciting area for continued investigation. Research to date suggests that the two most consistent predictors of tactile differences are age and sex. I recommend that all investigators examine gender distinctions as part of their ongoing touch research.

William Greenough: These differences seem to be critical in modalities other than touch as well.

Seymour Levine: There are many gender differences in sensory processing—a tremendous difference in taste thresholds, for instance.

William Greenough: Do you think the contrived situation of being observed in the laboratory affected parents' behavior? As you know, people sometimes do things differently when the TV cameras are running.

Sandra Weiss: There's little evidence available right now to help us resolve the question of how laboratory behavior differs from "natural" behavior outside the laboratory. However, many methodologists in the field of nonverbal behavior are of the opinion that the pressure of observation provokes the emergence of existing patterns of behavior rather than foreign behavior.

T. Berry Brazelton: Sandra, your data on gender differences in parental touching of infants are similar to our data on parents and small infants. Mothers and fathers touch their infants in different ways, and by the age of six weeks the infant has clearly different expectations concerning each parent. The original differences may have to do with sex-typed behavior, but that in turn creates an expectancy in the infant or child that lends itself to the creation of body image.

Sandra Weiss: You're reminding me of a point Steve Suomi made earlier. He said that male monkeys assumed a distinct role in infant development in that they spontaneously reinforced different behaviors in female and male infants. For example, young female monkeys weren't allowed to play in a rough-and-tumble fashion, whereas such play was encouraged for young males. That fascinates me, because it suggests potential biological underpinnings for human sex-role stereotypes.

William Greenough: The biological influence is definitely present. The appearance of rough-and-tumble play in humans, in nonhuman primates, and even in rodents is governed largely by whether they were exposed to testosterone during a sensitive period (prenatal or postnatal, depending on the species). If they were exposed, they will exhibit more rough-and-tumble play.

T. Berry Brazelton: Dr. Spock was the first person to point out to me that there are subtle motoric and attentional differences between boy and girl babies at birth. For instance, they seem to look at you differently. Using just these little things that he'd observed, Spock could pick out girls and boys in the nursery with about 80 percent accuracy. Many parents are probably aware of these subtle differences, too, and of course that's going to confirm sex stereotyping.

Seymour Levine: You're into a marvelously interesting area. Those of us who study hormones are very aware of a whole variety of sex differences in response systems. For example, when a distressed squirrel monkey infant signals, the males don't respond. The females respond, both hormonally and behaviorally, whether they're mothers or not. They respond because they're females. There is a very profound set of sex differences in terms of responsivity.

TOUCHING AND ADOLESCENT SEXUALITY

Elizabeth R. McAnarney, M.D.

Adolescent pregnancy is considered a major health problem in the United States. Approximately one million young people less than 20 years of age become pregnant annually, of whom approximately 560,000 bear live children. Fifteen percent of pregnant women under age 15, compared with

6.5 percent of women between 20 and 29, have babies who weigh less than 2,500 grams.

Prevention of pregnancy is the ideal. One preventive strategy is to encourage the use of contraception; another is to encourage adolescents, particularly those under the age of 15, to delay the initiation of coitus. The purpose of this paper is to examine the question of whether coitus during early adolescence (10-14 years of age) represents the use of sexual behavior for nonsexual purposes and whether early adolescents who engage in coitus prematurely are seeking closeness and cuddling from another human being rather than sexual pleasure.

An Adolescent Dilemma

As children grow older, physical contact (by parents) becomes more restrained, and by adolescence is completely terminated (Montagu, 1971, p. 147).

If there is a diminution in tactual sensitivity and experiences in middle childhood, the so-called latency period, it abruptly ceases at puberty, when the pubertal boy and girl usually become avid for tactual contacts, seeking to touch and be touched (Frank, 1957, p. 233).

In examining these two quotations, one notes the potential for a major dilemma for adolescents. Their parents touch them less than they did during infancy and childhood, yet adolescents' need for touching has increased. The adolescent's basic need may be to be in close physical proximity to another human being, that is, to be touched or cuddled. Adolescents may use their newly acquired genital capability and coitus to meet this basic need.

Parental touching of children decreases as the child matures so that by adolescence, in most American families, touching between adolescents and their parents is minimal. Other factors affect touching behaviors between children and their parents, such as socioeconomic status, the child's sex, and race. As is true of other developmental phenomena, the age of the child is only one sociodemographic characteristic of importance, but the major one for this paper.

Figure 16 is a schematic representation of touching by the age of the child and the persons who are most likely to touch the child. These data are based partly on empirical data but mostly on clinical observation and clinical history. Data on the vertical axis represent an approximation of a quantitative measure of touching which is hypothesized, and thus are not exact.

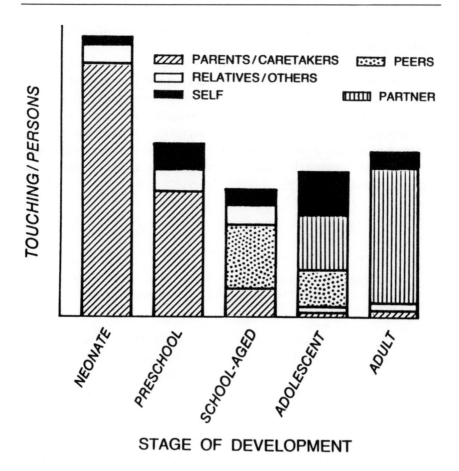

Figure 16. The older the child, the less touching by parents. During adolescence, a sexual partner becomes an important source of touching.

During infancy, parents (or caretakers) are the individuals who cuddle and touch the child, and the amount of touching by adults is maximal during this stage. Preschool children are ambulatory and can move physically away from their parents. Thus, the amount of touching between parent and child decreases. School-age children receive less touching from their parents than preschoolers but are more likely to engage in peer touching and self-touching.

Adolescents (12-18) receive still less parental touching and also touch their peers less than younger children. Willis and Reeves (1976) reported on a study of 1,028 junior high school students in the Kansas City area. Touching for black-black and white-black children was about half as much as had been observed in younger children. The junior high students were more likely to touch shoulder to shoulder or elbow to elbow in what appeared to be almost inadvertent contacts. Aggressive touching among junior high students was reflected in the use of fists by females and play fighting among males. Willis, Reeves, and Buchanan (1976) replicated their study of junior high students with 1,154 pairs of Kansas City high school students. The probability of touching was almost identical to that observed in the junior high population.

There are few quantitative observations of adolescents' interaction with heterosexual peers. Adolescents begin to move gradually away from parental and like-sexed peer touching to heterosexual peer touching (for the majority of adolescents), which may result in coitus.

Physical Versus Psychological Intimacy

> The young adult, emerging from the search for and the insistence
> on identity, is eager and willing to lose his identity with that
> of others: He is ready for intimacy (Erikson, 1950, p. 263).

Following puberty, adolescents are physically capable of adult genital behavior. They can perform coitus, and they begin to experience adult sexual urges. Most males reach a peak of sexual drive before 20 years of age; females experience increasing sexual responsiveness until the 30s which then levels off until they are 50 or older. The peak physiologic sex drive of male adolescents often occurs before they are psychologically capable of truly intimate sexual behaviors.

Indeed, an examination of psychoanalytic and psychosocial theory suggests that psychological growth and development during adolescence may not permit truly intimate sexual behavior. According to psychoanalytic theory (Freud, 1949), sexual impulses reemerge at adolescence, marking the onset of the genital stage. The adolescent begins to recognize that the opposite-sex parent cannot be the adult love object. In addition, the incest taboo prohibits the adolescent and the opposite-sex parent from becoming emotionally or physically too close. The combination of the emotional distancing that occurs when the young person surrenders the opposite-sex parent as a love object and the incest taboo may be the major theoretical reasons that adolescents and their parents do not engage in touching. Independence from the parents emotionally and physically is a major task of adolescence.

Psychosocial theory (Erikson, 1950; 1960) focuses on the definition of identity during adolescence. Initially, the "who am I?" is directed toward the definition of the physical self, or "who am I in this changing physical body?" This usually occurs between ages 10 and 14. The next step is the global question of "who am I as a person, the same or different from others around me?" This usually occurs at 15 to 16 years of age. The final step is "who shall I be in the future as a sexual being, as a vocational being, and as an integrated member of society?" This usually occurs between 17 and 21.

The psychosocial stage that follows adolescence, in young adulthood, is intimacy. Most young adolescents are not capable of true psychological intimacy. They are often egocentric and unable to separate their own needs from those of others. Their inability to think of others ahead of self is a bar to intimate sexual behavior, in which one must relate to another's needs as well as one's own.

The powerful effects of adult physical sexual capacity in psychologically immature adolescents whose parents and like-sexed peers are unlikely to touch them much sets the stage for the use of sexuality for nonsexual purposes. Under such circumstances, the purpose of coitus may be to be touched and closely held by another person.

As Montagu (1971) has stated, "Touching may take the form of caressing, cuddling, holding, stroking, or patting with the fingers to the whole hand, or vary from simple body contact to the massive tactile stimulation involved in sexual intercourse" (p. 290).

The Use of Sexuality for Nonsexual Purposes

> Being held or cuddled may reduce anxiety, promote relaxation and a feeling of security, and provide a distinctive type of gratification. Since women are usually held or cuddled before or after coitus, they can use sex as a means of obtaining this type of body contact (Hollender, Luborsky, & Scaramella, 1969, p. 188).

There are no empirical data known to this author about the use of sexuality for nonsexual purposes by adolescents. However, two studies from the adult literature have identified subgroups of women who engaged in coitus because of their need to be close to another human being and to be held or cuddled. Hollender and his colleagues studied 39 patients being treated for relatively acute psychiatric disorders, the most common of which was neurotic depression. All the women were or had been married, and more than half (53 percent) said they had used sex to persuade a mate to hold them. A response by one of these adults was: "I want somebody just to hold me. . .And it just seems to me...one thing goes with another. If I do go to bed with someone...they would hold me for a little while anyhow."

A second study (Malmquist, Kiresuk, & Spano, 1966) reported on 20 women who had three or more illegitimate pregnancies. The sexual life of these women began early: 13 of the 20 reported initiation of coitus before 12 years of age. Sexual pleasure was reportedly quite restricted. Eight of the 20 women said they were aware at a conscious level that coital activity was the price to be paid for being cuddled. Very young adolescents who engage in coitus may be similar to these adults encountered by Malmquist, Hollender, and colleagues.

Hollender (1970) described factors that might influence the wish to be held (the interpretation is slightly modified):

1. Depression. A depressed person may seek closeness at one point and withdraw from contact at other times. Some depressed individuals desire physical closeness to another person; others do not.
2. Anxiety. Some people feel less anxious and more secure when they are being cuddled. That is, the boundaries of an embrace may provide structure and security for a person who is experiencing lack of structure and insecurity.
3. Anger. Hollender reports that anger was more likely to make people draw away from body contact than move toward it. Some people are drawn together by anger, however, especially when making up after an angry interaction.
4. Misuse of self. This factor applies particularly to individuals whose validation of self and self-worth are based upon the demonstration of affection by another.

Hollender further suggests that some women think the wish to be held is childish. The use of adult sexuality as a means to being held and cuddled may make the wish to be held "adult" and therefore more acceptable.

Even though the adult literature focuses primarily on females and their use of sexuality for nonsexual purposes, it is also possible that males use their sexuality for nonsexual purposes, perhaps especially in early adolescence. This remains to be seen.

Do early adolescents who engage in early coitus have needs similar to those of adult women who have openly stated that they have used coitus to fulfill a need to be touched, held, and cuddled? Would substitution of parental touch of these early adolescents decrease the incidence of premature coitus? These questions are worthy of serious consideration in our effort to understand why very young adolescents engage in coitus and often suffer the consequences of unplanned pregnancies and sexually transmitted diseases.

DISCUSSION

T. Berry Brazelton: Elizabeth, I like the way you've presented the concept of the changing meaning of touch over time. Touch as a substitute for intimacy is another idea I like.

Louise Biggar: I used to work with teen-agers as a foster care worker, and I was amazed to find that the girls did not like sex. Sexual pleasure was not what they were using it for.

Elizabeth McAnarney: We've asked our pregnant adolescents about their early sexual experiences, and we've found, too, that by and large they are not pleasurable. The girls often say things were done in a very hurried way, and they are not exactly sure why it all happened. There's a lot of ambivalence on the part of both males and females.

Judith Smith: Have you looked at homosexual behavior in adolescents?

Elizabeth McAnarney: We recognize clinically that some homosexual experience is common during early adolescence — exploratory touching, often. This phase might best be called a period of undifferentiated sexuality. We haven't investigated homosexuality as an estabished pattern at later ages, partly because it is beyond our capability to predict what a young person's choices will be down the line.

William Greenough: Is it a problem getting accurate information from adolescents about their sexual experiences?

Elizabeth McAnarney: Yes, but as you get to know them, they're easy to work with. They're quite egocentric, and if you give them some attention they become more open and often give you very good data.

T. Berry Brazelton: Do they let you touch them?

Elizabeth McAnarney: Yes. Even if a young person is referred in for depression and suicidal tendencies, we always start with the physical examination. It seems to communicate our concern to the young person, to show that we want to look at everything totally. Even adolescents you've been told are very hostile and angry usually relax if you start talking with them and perform a physical examination. The awareness that their symptoms are being taken seriously seems to increase their sense of self-worth.

I will tell you though, Berry, that I find it easier to work with adolescents as I get older. Touch is less likely to be misinterpreted as a sexual message from someone of my age and stage. There's a sort of an incest taboo in clinical settings as well as in the family, I think.

Seymour Levine: Elizabeth, I wonder about your assumption that the parents and adolescents in virtually all families observe the incest taboo. As the issue of incest has begun to emerge more publicly, the incidence of reported cases has risen a lot, and I suspect that these are only the tip of the iceberg. For every rape reported, many others occur that are not reported. Don't you think this is also true of incest?

Elizabeth McAnarney: Yes, I do. In clinical work, we become concerned when a very young pregnant adolescent won't give a good history as to who the father is, for example. That happens quite frequently. When the youngster's eyes go directly toward the ground, you know you're getting into something that she doesn't want to talk about. Often these pregnancies can be traced to an incestuous relationship. There are good data on that.

Still, in the majority of families the taboo does hold. I think that most parents in the American culture feel a need to move away from their pubertal youngsters physically, and that this is related to the fact that coital activity between parent and child is seen as unacceptable by the culture.

T. Berry Brazelton: As we learn more about incest and it's made more and more of a public issue, I think parental touching is going to go down and not stay stable, unless we do something to counteract it.

This may seem irrelevant at first, but I'd like to mention a statistic that I've been using to talk to Congress. The national average for infant mortality is 12.8 per thousand. In Washington, D.C., it's 23.8, and if you break that down into black and white it becomes about 29 per thousand blacks and 8 per thousand whites. If you break the black group down further, you find that the two groups having babies who die in the first year are girls under 15 and women over 35, and girls under 15 are the larger group. The point I'm trying to make is that these young girls never get any sort of reaching out or touch from the medical community, and at one level or another all of us are paying the price. The example you're setting, Elizabeth, with your research and your fine clinical work, helps show us all some ways to get in there and begin to play a role.

Elizabeth McAnarney: Infant mortality and morbidity discourage us sometimes, but one advantage of having done something over time is that I see major gains in our thinking. There are now good data to show that prenatal intervention can reduce, at least, the incidence of prematurity in this age group.

Another encouraging thing is that, as Tiffany Field and others have shown, you can actually teach adolescents about development. Young women are quite interested in and involved with their babies. Although we would certainly like to reduce the adolescent birth rate, particularly during the early teens, it's heartening to know that young mothers have so much potential for becoming good parents.

Clinical Perspectives

PART VI
THERAPEUTIC TOUCH

Therapeutic touch is a new variation on an ancient theme: healing by the laying on of hands. In the first paper in Part VI, Marie-Thérèse Connell reviews the historical background and development of therapeutic touch, presents findings from early studies on its effects, and asks for additional, more rigorously designed research. Next, Judith Smith takes a hard look at the theory behind therapeutic touch and finds it wanting. She calls for a rational approach to the apparent mysteries of the technique, including careful scientific definition of such key concepts as therapeutic energy. Finally, in "Therapeutic Touch and Midwifery," Iris Wolfson shows herself to be an exemplary practitioner of this new/old healing art, as used with pregnant and laboring women and their families.

THERAPEUTIC TOUCH: THE STATE OF THE ART

Marie-Thérèse Connell, M.A., R.N.

Therapeutic touch evolved from several years of systematic observation by Kunz and Krieger (1965-1972) of a treatment in which a healthy person places the hands on or close to the body of an ill person for about 10 or 15 minutes, with a strong intent to help or heal that person. For centuries, this form of treatment has been referred to in the Western world as the laying on of hands. Kunz and Krieger were impressed with the healer's gentleness and focused intent to help, and they observed that the treatment often seemed to help the ill person feel more relaxed, comfortable, and energetic.

Krieger was particularly interested in this practice because of the centrality of touch to nursing practice. She thought the technique might be important for nurses and offer potential for nursing theory development. This paper will review the development of therapeutic touch, research investigating its effects, and its current scientific standing.

Rationale and Early Studies

Krieger faced the formidable problem of investigating a treatment which historical and contemporary observation suggested had some therapeutic value but which was frowned upon by orthodox science and could not be explained by the predominant scientific view. She began by reviewing a number of laboratory studies from the 1960s suggesting that touch coupled with the intent to help or heal had the potential to increase the growth rate and chlorophyll content of plants, hasten wound-healing in mice, and affect the activity of in-vitro enzyme systems. For a conceptual rationale, she turned to concepts from Eastern philosophy: that the human being is an open system, that there is an underlying interconnectedness between the human being and the environment, and that human health is an expression of an essential energy system called *prana*, the closest English translation of which is vitality. The healthy person has an abundance of this energy; the ill person's supply is inadequate for normal functioning.

Thus, Krieger (1973) wrote, "An interchange of vitality occurs when a healthy person purposefully touches an ill person with a strong intent to help or to heal" (p. 43). Because in the Eastern view it is assumed that prana is related to respiration and is intrinsic in what we would call oxygen, and because hemoglobin is concerned with transporting oxygen for cellular metabolism, Krieger reasoned that the hemoglobin value in the ill individual would be the most sensitive physiological index of this energy exchange.

Building on a pilot study, Krieger conducted a study with 43 subjects in the experimental group and 33 subjects in the control group, using a quasi-experimental before-after nonequivalent control group design. The subjects were people with chronic diseases residing at an in-patient community center concerned with investigating holistic approaches to healing. Krieger hypothesized that the mean hemoglobin value of the experimental group would be higher after treatment by the laying on of hands method than before, and that the mean hemoglobin value of the control group at comparable times would not differ. The hypothesis was confirmed at the .01 level of significance (Krieger, 1973). The finding has been repeated in another study that controlled for factors thought to influence hemoglobin values, such as smoking, yoga, and diet (Krieger, 1975). Though limited by their quasi-experimental design, these studies lend support to the view that this treatment has the potential to induce a therapeutic effect in ill individuals.

Based on these observations and under the direction of Kunz, Krieger developed the treatment she called therapeutic touch. She described the individual administering therapeutic touch as assuming a meditative state of consciousness and placing her hands on or close to the body of the person she intends to help. She then "passively 'listens' with her hands as she scans the body of the patient and gently attunes to his or her condition.... She places her hands over the areas of tension in the patient's body and redirects these energies" (Krieger, Peper, & Ancoli, 1979).

Krieger (1975) reasoned that therapeutic touch "is a natural potential in physically healthy persons who are strongly motivated to help ill people, and that this potential can be actualized." In other words, therapeutic touch can be taught and learned.

To confirm this, Krieger and Kunz taught therapeutic touch to a group of registered nurses. In a 1974 study, professional nurses administered the therapeutic touch treatments in a study of hemoglobin values similar to the one described above. Again, the values of the experimental group were significantly higher after treatment while those of the control group stayed the same.

Within the limits of the study design, this research supports the view that therapeutic touch can be learned and that it has the potential to have an intrinsic effect on the well-being of patients. Additional data suggest that therapeutic touch can decrease physiologic tension and promote a state of generalized relaxation in ill people (Krieger et al., 1979) and significantly decrease acute anxiety (Heidt, 1981).

Recent Research

In 1981, Quinn studied the effectiveness of therapeutic touch as it is usually done, without actual physical contact between practitioner and patient. She standardized a treatment called *noncontact therapeutic touch,* in which the practitioner's hands are held two to four inches from the patient's body, with a group of nurses with several years' experience using therapeutic touch. In a study in which acute anxiety, as measured on a questionnaire, was the dependent variable, these nurses used noncontact therapeutic touch with a group of patients hospitalized with cardiovascular disease. As a control, a second group of nurses who had no knowledge of therapeutic touch worked with another group of patients. They mimicked the physical actions of the nurses using noncontact therapeutic touch but did not include the meditative state of consciousness, intent to assist the patient, attuning to the condition of the patient, or understanding of an energy exchange between nurse and patient. The experimental group showed a significant decrease in anxiety after treatment, showing that physical contact is not necessary for therapeutic touch to be effective.

In current research, Krieger is investigating the use of therapeutic touch as an adjunct to prepared childbirth. My own doctoral research is an experimental study investigating the effect of therapeutic touch on the experience of acute pain.

The investigation of therapeutic touch is in its early stages. In the scientific sense little headway has been made in describing and explaining the nature of therapeutic touch or predicting its effects, and only a small amount of confidence can be placed in existing findings. As experimental research continues it is necessary that past studies be replicated and new ones planned using well-controlled designs. Among other things, all studies should include a double-blind technique or substitute, for example, a standard control group receiving a treatment of known effectiveness. It is only when experimental criteria like these are met that there is substantial basis for inferring a causal relationship between treatment by therapeutic touch and the results obtained.

A Paradox and an Enigma

Such issues raise the question of whether the experimental design is an appropriate methodology for investigating the effects of therapeutic touch. How can a humanistic treatment be examined using a methodology which is specifically designed to exclude the effect of human interaction? Obviously, therapeutic touch cannot be put into a capsule and administered blindly. The situation suggests a relationship between therapeutic touch and the placebo effect. If intent to help is an aspect of treatment both by therapeutic touch and by placebo, perhaps their effects can be traced to the same phenomenon.

In our attempts to discover a relationship between such hard-to-measure factors as a health professional's compassionate intent to help and a patient's experience of well-being, it seems wise not to rely on any single method of analysis or on statistical studies using aggregate data. We should approach the problem from a number of angles, using different kinds of data and different methodologies. Descriptive methodology could provide more basic information about the nature of therapeutic touch and the variables associated with it. The phenomenological approach could help identify aspects of the experience of therapeutic touch and their relative values and meanings. Ethnomethodology could help identify if and how aspects of the treatment are context-dependent.

Continued investigation of therapeutic touch is of particular concern to the nursing profession. In founding modern nursing, Nightingale (1859/1957) taught that nurses were to treat the individual as a whole and place the individual in the best environment for the natural healing process to take place. Of all health professionals, nurses spend the greatest amount of time with patients. It is often assumed that a nurses' presence and therapeutic intent facilitate the comfort of a person who is ill. Most nurses would agree that touch is an integral aspect of nursing practice.

In many ways therapeutic touch stands at the crossroads of contemporary consciousness. It is an enigma to modern science, yet its conceptual underpinnings stem from concepts addressed by the earliest Greek philosophers and by physicists at the forefront of the current scientific revolution. In some quarters it is controversial, yet it is one of the most popular subjects in nursing continuing education programs and in holistic health programs generally. It looks very simple, yet it is profoundly complex. It is an intuitive, subjective process, yet it must be subject to the scrutiny of scientific inquiry. It involves the intensely humanistic yet nonpersonal concern of one human being for another. I am pleased to have you join me in considering the state of the art and its possible future directions.

DISCUSSION

T. Berry Brazelton: I think nursing is ahead of most of the helping professions in that, for a long time, nurses have been trying to identify the forces behind caring and the transmission of caring. As Kathy Barnard explained to me while we were planning this conference, the kind of training we've had as physicians has really followed a pathological model. We've been trained to look for disease, for any kind of failure in the system, but we haven't been trained to look for strengths, for ways of energizing the system.

Marie-Thérèse, your exhortation to all of us to look at therapeutic touch seriously shows the opportunity for touch in health care. I really want to get on now to a field model of what you're doing. Intentionality on the part of the giver, and also intentionality or expectation on the part of the receiver, are critical ingredients. But therapeutic touch techniques should not be kept in the area of mysticism or good intent. They can be studied systematically, and they must be, in order for others to believe in the techniques and to utilize them.

Seymour Levine: In Krieger's initial studies evaluating therapeutic touch, why was hemoglobin chosen as a variable?

Marie-Thérèse Connell: Because one of the assumptions in the Eastern literature is that *prana* is associated with breathing, with what we would call oxygen. Also, some earlier studies looking at the laying on of hands had found an increase in chlorophyll in plants, and chlorophyll and hemoglobin are related. Does that clarify it?

Seymour Levine: It clarifies why Krieger looked at it, but not why it would be related in any way to the therapeutic facts.

Renée Weber: A standard yoga practice in India is to slow down breathing rates and deepen respiration. The rate of slow-down has been studied by Western medical teams, and I think it is correlated with other changes. Therefore, I think it was the easiest external indicator that Krieger could take.

Michael Merzenich: Would normal, healthy people presumably show the same hemoglobin response to therapeutic touch as people who are ill?

Marie-Thérèse Connell: That's an interesting question. You might find significant effects only with people who are ill or in a state of imbalance. If a person is healthy, you're assuming there's a state of balance and openness, so you might not see much effect.

Kathryn Barnard: An important issue for nursing right now is whether we should study how to comfort people who've become ill or study the comfort of people, regardless of their particular state. It's interesting to me that Krieger took patients regardless of condition. Their particular illness was not important to her.

Ruth McCorkle: Perhaps the kind of monitoring systems used in some of the newborn studies described earlier could also be used to assess therapeutic touch.

Jerold Lucey: That's a good idea, but it's expensive. What you really need, obviously, is some kind of "prana meter." Show me someone who radiates more of these pranas, and I'll show you someone who is good at therapeutic touch.

T. Berry Brazelton: A high score on a "prana meter" might be related to compassionate intent, Jerry. The intent to heal is a critical ingredient of therapeutic touch.

Michael Merzenich: Marie-Thérèse, you said at the end of your paper that therapeutic touch is enigmatic. To my mind, nothing that's been described is not potentially understandable, nor is it contrary to our understanding of the organization of touch or the way people represent personal space. Why do you call it an enigma?

Marie-Thérèse Connell: I think what is difficult to understand is the human stance from which therapeutic touch is done. Something is going on, promoting the effect, that we don't understand very well. The first step in therapeutic touch is called centering, and during centering a switch in consciousness occurs that is difficult to describe. It makes you see the patient as a new person, an amazing, unique human being, even if moments before you felt overworked and angry and burned out. We don't understand how this happens or why the process of taking on a meditative state of consciousness is so important, yet it seems to make a difference in helping people.

Seymour Levine: The studies you described in your paper didn't convince me it helps. At this point I don't care so much what the therapeutic action is; what I want to know is whether patients who receive therapeutic touch are better off in any real way. So far there really has not been a credible demonstration that the procedure works.

Paul Satz: The hope is there, but I think there's more hope than evidence right now.

Michael Merzenich: I think it can be understood exactly what the consequences of therapeutic touch are, and exactly what the therapist does to produce the positive impact. Our body surface, and the region immediately around us within reach of our limbs, represent our personal territory. This representation is not created out of nothing; it's created out of our experiences and our use of our limbs. When someone enters our territory, we either defend it or surrender to the intruder. When someone touches us or strokes us, the tendency to surrender is strong.

The importance of the meditative state may be that it requires the therapist to adopt a mental attitude that promotes the most natural kind of focus in terms of tactile contact. The closer touch comes to being what the person's nervous system wants to accept, the more therapeutic it is, presumably. In any event, it isn't magic; it's something that can be studied.

Cathleen Fanslow: I've been studying and practicing therapeutic touch since 1973, and I think I agree with you. These things are not such an enigma, because we see the results.

Marie-Thérèse Connell: I've been asked to help with some case study reporting at a hospital in the New York area where the nurses in the neonatal intensive care unit often use therapeutic touch with the babies. They don't touch the babies physically; they just use the technique, and it seems to promote relaxation and quieting.

Michael Merzenich: If a sense of extrapersonal space is a product of experience and development, as I've suggested, then it would be surprising if newborns had such a sense, beyond perhaps a crude awareness of contact or impending contact.

Marie-Thérèse Connell: My intuitive sense, from the small amount of time I spend with babies, is that they would be particularly skillful in this way.

Michael Merzenich: There is a difference between being able to detect the presence of something off the skin and having a sense of ownership of the field around you. The latter, I think it is largely believed, arises by your development of operations in the immediate area around you. Certainly you gain ownership of this space around you, and somewhere in your mind you have a highly defined construct of it. When it's invaded, there are reactions to it of a special kind, just as there are reactions to direct contact with the skin.

Marie Thérèse Connell: This is fascinating, because your perception of what is happening, using your model, is very different from my perception of what's happening using the field model. My intuitive suppositions are exactly the opposite of yours.

A CRITICAL APPRAISAL
OF THERAPEUTIC TOUCH

Judith A Smith, R.N., Ph.D

For some time now the technique known as therapeutic touch has received growing attention and use. Therapeutic touch has gained a wide following among nurses. During the past decade, attempts have been made to refine and elaborate its techniques and to develop theoretical justifications for its procedures. It should be noted at the outset that although various claims have been made concerning the effectiveness of this therapy, as far as I know therapeutic touch healers have not claimed that they can accomplish healings that medical science has not accomplished. For example, therapeutic touch practitioners do not claim to cure cancer. In its present state of development, the claim for therapeutic touch is that it facilitates healing. Its practitioners argue that where medicine may require prolonged treatment and medication, the therapeutic touch healing art accomplishes the same results quicker. This seems to be the extent of their claims.

The growing practice of this unorthodox medical art provokes some challenging questions. For example:

What precisely is this therapeutic touch?
What is known of its effectiveness?
What theoretical explanations of the procedure do its practitioners believe give it support?
How do traditional medical treatment and therapeutic touch differ?

Answers to these questions will require more than this brief paper, but we might for the present point to some implicit theoretical issues. The fact is that advocates of therapeutic touch have developed elaborate theoretical doctrines in an effort to explain how therapeutic touch works. In certain respects, the theories of the technique are as unorthodox as the techniques themselves. Of course, in an examination of this new healing art, one has to admit the possibility that while the art itself is effective, its theoretical support may be unsound.

What is Therapeutic Touch?

What exactly is the art of therapeutic touch? Therapeutic touch is said to be concerned with "fields" and "energy flow" in and around a patient's body. Whatever the nature of these fields and energies (and their nature is not made sufficiently clear), the healer is supposed to be sensitive to their presence and, to a certain degree, is supposed to be able to control and modify them (Boguslawski, 1980; Krieger, Peper, & Ancoli, 1979). In proximate healing, where the patient is in close proximity to the healer, this control and modification is achieved by movements and gestures of the healer's hands. The therapeutic touch procedure is employed in four stages:

Stage 1: A subjective procedure of the healer called *centering*
Stage 2: An appraisal of the patient's fields and energies called *assessment*
Stage 3: *Diagnosis*
Stage 4: *Treatment*

In the first stage, centering, the healer tries to develop a sense of deep internal stillness or quietness, along with an intent to heal. In the assessment stage, the healer's hands move several inches above the patient's body. During these movements, the healer becomes conscious of sensations like heat, cold, tingling, and pressure. In the diagnostic stage, the healer interprets these as revealing the condition of the patient. The diagnosis is formulated in terms of so-called energy needs, not in terms of pathophysiologic diagnostic criteria. During treatment, the healer holds her hands over those areas of the body allegedly needing energy and is supposed to transmit energy through her hands into the patient's body. In order to transmit energy, the healer visualizes light or color in her mind as flowing through her hands and into the patient's body. The entire process then is psychological or mental.

Efficacy of the Technique

Does therapeutic touch work? Dependable statistical techniques are available for testing the effectiveness of this healing practice. We can take three groups of people with a condition where a medication is needed, like acute bronchitis. The first group would get no treatment. The second group would get traditional medical treatment, and the third group would get therapeutic touch treatment. Then the recovery rates of the three groups could be compared. There have not been large-scale clinical trials to differentiate between self-limiting illnesses; those that may be affected by therapeutic touch; and those that are not affected at all by therapeutic touch. If one wanted to test its effectiveness, these are the kinds of studies one would do. The proponents of therapeutic touch should consider performing such statistical tests repeatedly with different ailments and in different parts of the world.

Unless there is statistical evidence indicating the effectiveness of therapeutic touch treatments, a skeptical attitude toward the practice should be adopted. As far as the literature indicates, no such tests of efficacy of the therapeutic touch healing art have been done. On what, then, does the confidence of practitioners rest? At least for the present, it rests partly on subjective reports and hearsay but not on scientific evidence. In view of this, is one compelled to conclude that the confidence of therapeutic touch practitioners rests on faith?

Theoretical Explanation for Therapeutic Touch

Although there is no proof of the efficacy of therapeutic touch, the advocates of this healing art have developed elaborate theories of how it works. According to one theory, therapeutic touch is a communication or transfer of energy from the healer to the patient (Boguslawski, 1979; Krieger, 1979). This energy transfer is viewed as occurring in different ways and can be described according to (1) the distance between the healer and the patient and (2) the source of the energy transfer. First, with regard to the distance between the healer and the patient, two kinds of energy transfer can be distinguished. One is over a short distance between the healer and patient; this is called proximate healing. The healer's hands are held several inches from the patient's body. The second type of energy transfer is over an indefinitely long distance where the patient may be thousands of miles from the healer.

Furthermore, in proximate healing, the energy has two possible sources. Either it is generated within the healer and transmitted to the patient, or it originates in the environment and is channeled through the healer to the patient.

Despite frequent reference to the sources of this therapeutic energy in the literature on therapeutic touch, there is no indication of how this difference in sources of energy is known. Nothing is said about experimental techniques for determining whether in any particular case the therapeutic energy is generated by the healer or is derived from the healer's environment. In the absence of such experimental determinations one is compelled to conclude that the distinction is altogether speculative.

Authoritative literature on therapeutic touch refers to an energy named *prana* that is characterized as a basic life energy. This is what is said to be transmitted during the healing act. It is allegedly different from other forms of energy and as yet unrecognized by modern science. It is said to be fundamental to animate matter and is viewed as a necessary condition for a state of health or well-being (Kunz & Peper, 1982; 1983). In healthy persons, it allegedly flows in currents up and down the body and can be replenished at will. Energy flows within the body, from the environment into the body, and from the body to the environment. In the sick, according to this theory, certain blocks can obstruct this free flow of energy. These blocks are said to be physical, emotional, or mental. Considering the fact that science distinguishes several types of energy, one can ask what type this might be. If it is different from other physical energies, what are the characteristic traits attributed to it? Does this energy in fact exist?

The notion of life energy, viewed as different from other forms of energy and peculiar to animate matter, introduces a kind of vitalism into the theory of therapeutic touch. The theory of vitalism holds that living organisms function by virtue of a life energy, that is, some nonmaterial mind or spirit as distinct from physicochemical phenomena. Life according to vitalism is a special creation — in the universe but not of it, so to speak. Thus, organisms possess qualities that defy analysis by the methods of science, that is, by the method of mechanistic analysis upon which much of modern science, including medicine, is based.

Defining Therapeutic Energy

The current literature on therapeutic touch employs theoretical concepts like prana, life energy, and energy field, but no adequate definitions of these concepts are provided. Their meaning can be clarified only by means of experimental or operational definitions. In an operational definition, the meaning of a concept is seen in the way it is tested or measured (Hempel, 1966). In contrast to this, an ordinary definition is verbal. It sets two expressions as equivalents. For example, the word *chair* means a seat, especially for one person, usually having four legs for support and a rest for the back. It often also has a rest for the arms. What this definition does is say that the meaning of the word *chair* is equivalent to the meaning of the foregoing expression. In an operational definition, on the other hand, a word is not defined by saying that it is equivalent to other words. It is defined by showing the experimental conditions under which the word is used. It usually takes the following form: (1) some experimental condition is set up at a certain place; (2) then if under these conditions and at that place one observes certain traits, one can apply in that context the term in question.

If the concept of therapeutic energy is to be clearly understood, the experimental conditions under which it manifests itself need to be stipulated. In the absence of operational definitions that meet specific criteria, key concepts in the doctrine of therapeutic touch have no reference to the real world. In other words, they are speculative.

Theories of therapeutic healing seem to use the term energy without specific association with established scientific usage. In modern physics, for example, the word is used in a specific way. Energy is characteristic of a body if it has the capacity to do work. Work is a force acting over a distance. The capacity to do this is called energy in the area of mechanics. A body can possess either kinetic or potential energy. That is, a body does work by virtue of its motion, as falling water and the winds do. Or it has the energy of position: potential energy. A coiled spring, with its temporarily stored energy, is an example of potential energy.

We can see that great care is needed when using the term *energy*. It is used in mechanics in a limited sense. The idea becomes more complicated, more refined, as we proceed from mechanics to thermodynamics to electromagnetism. When we speak of chemical energy, we don't have a force moving over a distance, as we do in mechanics. Chemical energy arises out of the capacity of atoms to evolve heat as they separate or combine. Chemical energy is the energy stored in the chemical makeup of material like food, oil, and dynamite.

But in all these contexts — mechanical, thermodynamic, electromagnetic, chemical — what we call energy can be subjected to certain procedural tests. In other words, the concept of energy employed in the various physical sciences is invariably associated with operational ways of testing and measuring the energy. For a clearer understanding of the theory of therapeutic touch, operational definitions of therapeutic energy and other central concepts are essential.

Distance Healing

In so-called distance healing, healer and patient may be miles apart. The healer makes use of a name or photograph, that is, some representative symbol of the patient. The symbol acts as a means to influence the patient, that is, to transfer energy to the patient. The healer by merely becoming conscious of the patient in some way can exert an influence on the distant patient's body.

Action-at-a-distance theories have not been acceptable to science because of their association with magic, voodoo, and telepathy. The belief that a person can be influenced through use of a representative symbol is common to both distance healing and voodoo. In voodoo, influence is exerted on a person at a distance by means of symbolic devices like gestures and dolls. But voodoo is viewed as a method of destroying, not healing. Instead of the intent to heal which exists during therapeutic touch, there is instead an intent to do harm.

Presumably, practitioners of therapeutic touch want to avoid an association with voodoo. Thus, it is important that the theory underlying therapeutic touch make suitable distinctions from these magical practices. In the physical sciences, there is an inverse relationship between distance and energy. In other words, energy attenuates with distance. The therapeutic energy allegedly does not attenuate with distance. What kind of energy could account for such a phenomenon? It is possible that such a form of energy exists, but its existence must be demonstrated by scientifically acceptable tests.

Alternative Theoretical Explanations

Other theories can account for therapeutic touch healing without any reference to energy exchange or field theory. For example, Jerome Frank in *Persuasion and Healing* (1961) argues convincingly that the key ingredient in psychological healing is what he calls a sound therapeutic relationship. According to Frank, the successful therapist combats a sense of demoralization in the patient and increases the patient's feeling of control over his or her own life, thus restoring self-confidence and hope in the patient. The successful therapist is able to convey genuine concern for the patient's welfare and an acceptance of the patient which is communicated as caring, warmth, empathy, and understanding.

Within this context, the expression of attitude becomes the important factor in healing. The significance for healing is what the healer communicates. The effective medium of transaction for the sick person is the expression of love, caring, and the deep desire to help. The healer is actively communicating feelings of concern, care, and love, and the patient responds with a confident hope. Presumably, in this view, the gestures and manipulations of the healer in therapeutic touch function as a way of communicating the healer's attitude.

Differences Between Medicine and Therapeutic Touch

A major difference between traditional medicine and the use of therapeutic touch in clinical practice arises from the lack of specific correspondence between the cause of disease or dysfunction in the patient and the procedures of therapeutic touch. Consider, for example, the treatment of pain by therapeutic touch. Regardless of the locus or cause of the pain, the procedure for relieving it is the same. The treatment thus appears in the light of a universal cure, a panacea.

This uniformity of treatment is alien to medical practice. If a patient has bronchitis, there is a specific procedure used to deal with it. There is also a specific treatment used for a person with a diagnosis of pericarditis. The medical treatment that cures the bronchitis does not cure the pericarditis.

In therapeutic touch, certain features of the treatment itself are also very curious and require explanation. For example, the theory on the one hand affirms that the healer imagines a certain color; on the other hand, it affirms that the color itself is transmitted into the patient's body, and on reaching the locus of the problem brings relief. How does an imagined color become the source of an actual color? One might analogously say that a healer might imagine the nourishment needed by an underweight infant and then from this imagined nourishment transmit the nourishment itself. Other questions arise once the theory is scrutinized. These questions are perhaps not unanswerable, but they have to be dealt with if we are to develop a sound theory of therapeutic touch healing.

The foregoing comments are not made in opposition to the practice of therapeutic touch. They are made to highlight certain questions, doubts, and the absence of proof regarding the effectiveness and the theoretical explanations of the procedure and to indicate directions for further thought and investigation.

DISCUSSION

T. Berry Brazelton: Judy, in asking for rigorous research on therapeutic touch I think you are really talking about increasing the confidence and improving the self-image of the nurses who practice it. I know that when the Brazelton Neonatal Assessment Scale was developed, nothing in it was new. The scale just pinned down the clinical or intuitive insights that we'd all been relying on for a long time. Putting it down on paper made it viable, and I think this is what you're asking of therapeutic touch: that it be made into a viable system rather than a religious or mystical one.

Judith Smith: Yes, it should be critically appraised. I tried in my paper to raise the questions that should be asked at this sort of conference.

T. Berry Brazelton: I think many of us would prefer a rational approach to a mystical one. One thing we've learned from studying attachment and mother-child relationships is that when you start to break things down, the mystery begins to clear.

Allen Gottfried: Eliminating this mystical quality is of the utmost importance if any progress is to be made on therapeutic touch, I think. Finding out how touch works may require a social learning theory framework, because a social transmission of information is going on that is crucially important. We haven't given much attention to that.

Seymour Levine: One of the things that has struck me throughout this conference has been the parameters of touch within the concept of a social system. We've tried to isolate touch from other essential processes, but we've been unable to separate it from its interaction with a social communicative system. Touch as social communication is something I wish we had more time to discuss.

Louise Biggar: I'd like to follow up on what Michael Merzenich said earlier about surrendering to someone in one's personal space. Being able to say to oneself, "Oh, there's an attachment figure in my space" is probably related to the relaxation that you get in a baby with its mother, and also to the good things that you get in response to therapeutic touch. Marty Reite tried to suggest this earlier.

Martin Reite: There are some striking parallels between the current therapeutic touch movement and the early days of the psychoanalytic movement. In both we have healing systems that are alleged to impact favorably upon certain functional disturbances. The psychoanalytic movement was concerned primarily with disturbances in behavior; therapeutic touch is concerned with disturbances that are more medical. Both movements have theoretical systems that are very dependent upon special ideas that are not part of everyday experience; both work from a position of special knowledge. Both make therapeutic claims based predominantly upon case reports from practitioners and not on controlled observations by others.

I think both systems are open to empirical investigation. Psychoanalysis has chosen not to partake of that, and as a result it has tended to languish. Therapeutic touch, if it is going to become anything other than a cult, will have to make the other choice. After empirical investigation has established that it does something, then you can worry about how it does it and begin looking at mutually exclusive testable hypotheses and trying to get at mechanisms. The first thing you need is evidence that it in fact does something.

Michael Merzenich: We should keep in mind that the technique has potential advantages beyond the medical. Psychosocial consequences may be just as important, maybe more so.

T. Berry Brazelton: The danger of mysticism and cultism is that it devalues what the process really seems to me to be. As you suggested in your paper, Judy, the interpersonal relationship between therapist and client may be critical to the positive outcome. It intrigues me that with therapeutic touch you use touch as a language, and in the process you're somehow freeing up the communication system between you and the patient.

I like your parallel with psychoanalysis, Marty. It did set itself up as mysticism of a kind, which really kept it out of the mainstream. I use it in my work with pediatricians and parents, though, and there's nothing mystical about that. We do need to understand the ingredients. There are plenty of behavioral ingredients, and plenty of ingredients that demand that the therapist understand himself. These aren't mystical, but they do take a kind of focus.

Kathryn Barnard: Ned Muller's work on how children develop shared meaning seems relevant here, because what is going on may be a social learning process, as Allen Gottfried said. When children play, they communicate intent to one another even without words. A similar transmission of intent may occur in therapeutic touch.

Michael Merzenich: Yes. Intent is communicated through nonverbal cues. There's no reason to believe such things are not understandable.

Renée Weber: I am very much in favor of scientific investigation of therapeutic touch and would in fact applaud the use of some of the very sophisticated techniques and hardware that we've seen displayed at this conference. However, Judy suggested in her paper that an operational definition of the energy involved in therapeutic touch is an essential early step in this research, which raises a philosophical issue. If you restrict your scientific methods too narrowly to operational definitions, especially where biological or psychological systems are concerned, you're going to rule out much that contemporary scientists accept in practice. Rigidly construed, operationalism says that the meaning of a statement is its method of clarification. This is not acceptable to philosophers of science or to scientists today. Modern physics makes use of a lot of non-sensible objects. If you require operational definitions, I don't know what you're going to do with black holes, the big bang theory, and self-consciousness, for instance.

In other words, operational definitions can be a preemptive kind of methodology. It may be too early to impose a precise definition on the energy involved in therapeutic touch. At the beginning, the best you can do is get some kind of working consensus so that you at least adopt a similar vocabulary. Then you allow data to pile up. Only much later do you interpret them and pin things down. This is what has happened, essentially, in the history of physics.

Marie-Thérèse Connell: I'm not sure that it's appropriate to do experimental studies of any sort. What you are looking at is individual and unique, a feeling that's going to help people, and experimental designs don't tell us what's unique. They tell us a general kind of thing that's common to everybody. What's going to be most therapeutic depends on the individual person, so I think a phenomenological approach is most appropriate.

Louise Biggar: As some of you know, my branch of science, psychology, suffers from what we call physics envy. It wants to skip the stage of natural description and jump right to cause and effect. Doing this, in my opinion, doesn't get us very far. If I were studying therapeutic touch, the first thing I would want to do is sit down with some videotapes and take a lot of looks at what is happening. I could not subscribe to the extra-energy idea or to action at a distance, but if I couldn't tell the difference between a nurse who was really doing therapeutic touch and a nurse who was merely imitating the moves, I'd turn in my ticket as an ethologist.

A second point I'd like to make about my field is that psychology really hasn't paid much attention to intention, and to our ability to perceive intentions in one another. The theory of evolution, as expanded by such people as G. C. Williams and Maynard Smith, allows us now to talk about individuals being equipped with a lot of knowledge of one another's behavioral strategies. Robert Trivers, in his introduction to Dawkins' *The Selfish Gene*, proposes that we are evolved to understand the intentions of conspecifics. In fact, we have become such good readers of each other that individuals do better if they are able to deceive other individuals. But because of the way we are wired it is hard to deceive another; one's emotions just spill out of one. Therefore, one might need to evolve self-deception, the better to deceive others. Unconscious processes of the sort described by Freud might enter the picture here.

I believe, as does anyone who does microanalysis, that human beings communicate much more rapidly than they speak, and much more rapidly than they realize. We are hyperalert to all kinds of little things without being aware of it. So long before we get touch, we're alert to someone's intention to touch us and to how they intend to touch us.

T. Berry Brazelton: Sensitive observations like yours, Louise, can begin to demystify therapeutic touch just as they've helped to demystify mother-infant attachment. When I first heard Mary Ainsworth present her work some 15 years ago, people literally laughed and got up and walked out — just like the audiences at Mozart's and Bach's concerts. But I stayed, and I thought, this is the first time I've ever heard anyone at the Society for Research in Child Development talk about anything but stimulus-response systems as if they were clearly and easily defined. Since then, an enormous amount of work has gone on, and we've begun to identify a lot of aspects of attachment and love that aren't mystical. Therapeutic touch needs the same sort of scrutiny.

THERAPEUTIC TOUCH
AND MIDWIFERY

Iris S. Wolfson, R.N., B.S., C.N.M.

Therapeutic touch has been described as the direction and transfer of energy to facilitate healing in another individual. The touch in therapeutic touch is only occasionally and incidentally touch in the narrow tactile sense of skin to skin. It is rather part of a wider spectrum of sensations and connections between two people and between them and the world outside themselves. The touch or communication is between energy fields, those immediately surrounding the physical body and those beyond.

The Philosophical Framework

The idea of energy transfer and direction derives from a philosophical framework most familiar to us through Eastern religious thought. Basically, this philosophy sees the world as interconnected, a universe not of separate and distinct substances, beings, and things that act and react in a mechanical manner but rather one of an indivisible substance that is in fact not substance at all. Because of its essence, which is motion, it is often labeled as energy. In acupuncture it is referred to as *chi* or life force; in Hinduism it is *prana,* translated as breath or vital force. In subatomic physics, solid matter cannot be found. The atom's particles yield up their particulateness to appear as energy, waves or rays in motion, the motion itself defining the so-called particle.

If we can accept the possibility that this is the universe as it exists beyond our categorizing brain, then life itself is part of the process of movement and flow, and health can be defined as the state of being in harmony with this flow. Disease or illness can be defined as blockage of the flow, a cutting off from the flow of universal energy. Acupuncture, for example, defines illness in just this way, as a blockage of *chi,* or life energy, at the body meridians.

A nearly perfect example of interconnection and transfer of energies is a pregnant woman and her unborn child. Here are two bodies which, for nine months and beyond, act as a unity, existing together, energies moving back and forth, indivisible. The mother and her child really are an inseparable, indivisible entity. The task of a successful pregnancy is to maintain the open system, the energy flow between mother and baby, and to keep these energies harmonious and balanced prenatally, through the labor and delivery, and into the postpartum time.

Therapeutic touch in midwifery deepens the inherent ties between mother and baby and within the family by adding a new dimension to their communication with one another. It is also an excellent tool for alleviating common discomforts and complications during the childbearing cycle.

The Practice of Therapeutic Touch

The practice of therapeutic touch includes four basic steps, as explained in the preceding paper: centering, assessment, diagnosis, and treatment. Centering, as its name implies, is an exercise aimed at finding a stable center in the swirl of everyday thought and energy. It allows one to become a channel or conduit for the direction of universal energy, rather than using one's own personal energies. Our individual energy is limited and can be draining to draw upon. It is crucial to remain aware of oneself as a channel rather than a source of energy, and centering is the primary skill needed for this awareness.

During assessment, we try to avail ourselves of all cues regarding a person's state, with a particular expansion of our intuitive senses. We move our hands through the energy field, searching for areas of disturbance, asymmetrical areas from one side of the body to the other, hot or cold areas, tingling sensations, and pressure. The practitioner's next task is to adjust the field imbalances that have been identified and to remove blockages, in order to open the energy field and make it more receptive. Krieger called the process of freeing congested or bound energies "unruffling the field," because the healer feels a sensation of pressure and overlapping layers of densities, like ruffles.

The final step is to channel energy into the patient's field. It is axiomatic to say that in an area of heat, the intent is to cool it; in an area of pressure, to relieve it; if one senses pulsation, to moderate it. This is accomplished by a process of experimentation and intuition, and also by using information about the qualities of energy itself. For example, each color of the light spectrum is a wavelength of energy and as such has been said to have its own unique properties and effects on the body. Blue is calming and pain-relieving, yellow stimulating, green balancing. Part of therapeutic touch involves developing skill at imaging the particular form of energy felt necessary and then projecting and directing it appropriately.

Therapeutic touch is based on the interrelatedness of all life. The use of therapeutic touch in the practice of midwifery is centered on the interconnection of a mother with her baby, and on other special connections within the family unit. In midwifery, therapeutic touch is used, first, as a therapy for the treatment of anxieties, discomforts, and complications related to pregnancy and birth. Second (and perhaps even more fundamentally), it is used as a teaching tool to foster interconnections within the family. In this context, therapeutic touch becomes part of a philosophy that the midwife attempts to impart to the family throughout the entire pregnancy and into the birth and postpartum time.

Prenatal Care

During the prenatal phase, therapeutic touch focuses on two central issues: the development of communication between the midwife and the family and within the family itself, and the development of positive attitudes toward the birthing experience. I believe that a positive attitude can prevent problems that often arise from a woman's fears and lack of confidence in her own ability to complete the labor and birth process. In order to foster positive attitudes and a belief in the body's integrity, I teach a centering and visualization exercise during prenatal classes that focuses on the normal and healthy functioning of the woman's body and an active and perfectly developing fetus. We project forward in time to the imaged experience of the normal events and physiological processes of labor and birth.

Visualizing the fetus as healthy and normal is further encouraged through abdominal palpation, which occurs during each prenatal visit. The touching connection to the baby gives the mother someone to focus her energies toward. The abstraction of the pregnancy begins to become a real baby, with legs, buttocks, and head. Palpation is also a very good way to introduce the father and other children to the baby as a real entity.

I have taught fathers therapeutic touch in childbirth classes and have found that when practiced it facilitates communication and deepens the father's involvement in the pregnancy. At some point, the father can usually distinguish the energy field of the baby from that of the mother. This new way of perceiving and experiencing both mother and baby strengthens the already-existing bonds.

Labor

During labor and delivery, it is crucial to remain aware of other aspects of birth beyond the merely physical. One must not lose sight of the total person. As an example, I had a woman in labor who continued to contract but was not dilating, and her blood pressure was rising dangerously. After therapeutic touch she began to cry and had an emotional release, expressing some previously unrecognized fears that she had suppressed. Following this release, her blood pressure dropped and her contractions became more effective, leading to a successful and uncomplicated delivery. Therapeutic touch can sometimes have this effect of facilitating the release of emotional blocks in unexpected or unforeseen areas. Throughout labor, one attempts to incorporate levels other than just the physical.

A woman in labor is especially open and susceptible to others' energy fields. Fearful or negative people should not be present at the birth. I have seen women's labors totally stop upon arrival at the hospital, where the surrounding environmental energy is felt by them as threatening or frightening. Because women are so vulnerable now, one must be very sensitive to what is said and to the feelings that are projected. It is now that the imagery developed during the prenatal time proves its usefulness: images of a cervix opening, softening, becoming elastic; images of a baby's head moving downward and slipping through the cervix and into the vagina.

Labor is essentially a rhythmic progression of uterine contractions leading to the birth of the baby. All efforts are focused on the smooth flow of this process. Pain and fear can slow down and even stop the progress of labor. Therapeutic touch is especially useful for alleviating the painful sensations of labor contractions and enhancing relaxation. I usually perform a total assessment in between contractions and work with the field according to my findings. Often the kidney and adrenal area has a "drawing" sensation, indicating the need for an input of energy here. It is also important to assure that there is a good flow of energy throughout the entire body down the legs and out through the feet. In general, I have found it most helpful to laboring women when I use a downward stroking gesture over the abdomen, in a very even and rhythmic manner.

It is important to establish a slow and steady rhythm of sending energy. I have been told on a number of occasions by people watching me perform therapeutic touch that the motions remind them of a dancer's. A smooth, graceful, and rhythmic movement can be very important in enhancing the comfort and relaxation of therapeutic touch recipients. In addition, downward stroking reminds the woman to keep her energy moving and centered low in her body, where it is most needed.

If the father has learned therapeutic touch and is interested, I encourage him to use it now. When the couple works well together, the father will have a natural attunement to the mother and can use therapeutic touch very effectively.

Delivery

When labor has progressed to the pushing stage, I have found the squatting position to best encourage a focus on release and descent. I use perineal massage with a slow and steady rhythm, always being sensitive to the mother's response and always between contractions so as not to interfere with the energy flow. As in much of the labor process, we try to find the mother's birth rhythms and work with them in order to amplify their energy.

Pushing is a phase that demands active participation from the woman to make the contractions efficient instead of a surrender to the forces of labor as in earlier stages. Pushing is unforced. Women are encouraged to go at their own pace, unhurried and in an atmosphere of calm and quiet. I watch the woman's body language carefully. Her shoulders, neck, mouth, and jaw should all be loose, indicating that tensions are not building up and that she is concentrating her energy low in her body.

At the moment of crowning, I encourage the mother to touch the baby's head. This physical connection helps the pelvis and vagina to relax and also helps the mother realize the reality of the baby and the imminence of birth. The woman is encouraged to open her mouth and relax her tongue, which also helps the vagina to be relaxed. Noise is encouraged with exhale pushing, as it keeps the throat open and loose. After the head and shoulders are delivered, I have the woman reach down and I guide and help her to deliver her baby directly onto her abdomen.

As soon as the baby is born, I encourage the mother and father to touch the child. They are perfect energy channels to help the baby get started. Skin contact with the mother is crucial. The energy fields of the mother and baby are closely bound, and it is best not to disturb this sensitive connection.

If the baby is having difficulty getting started, I project the color yellow through my hands and stimulate the baby physically by rubbing its spine and feet. I also have the mother touch and talk to her baby, as this is the energy the baby has been so deeply connected to and is most familiar with. Yellow is used again to help stimulate contractions and facilitate delivery of the placenta.

It is important to encourage some quiet time for the new family to continue with the bonding process. As we know, the mother and baby are in a state of heightened sensitivity and are particularly open to one another. They are also now especially vulnerable to outside influences, which should be kept to a minimum. In the immediate postpartum period, therapeutic touch is used to rebuild energy in the mother and to maintain a peaceful atmosphere.

If there is a point to be emphasized in this paper, it is that all life energy has a pattern and a rhythm, and that pregnancy and birth have their own particular rhythms and patterns. There are many factors, such as fear, pain, and anxiety, which can interfere with this rhythmic process. The object of therapeutic touch is to allow the process to develop unhindered. This is not to say that all pregnancies and births can be uneventful, but even with complications there is a logic and pattern that one can sense and work with.

For me, therapeutic touch has proved an invaluable tool in the pursuit of healthy and successful birthing experiences for the mother, the baby, and the family. It is hoped that continued scientific documentation and research will increase our understanding of therapeutic touch and make it more widely available in all settings.

DISCUSSION

Louise Biggar: As you were talking, Iris, I kept thinking about channeling energy through the self. What you said reminded me of Plato, who said that artists are not really powers in themselves but channels of energy. I also thought of the Bible, where Saint Paul says, "Not I move, but It moves in me."

What's the difference between a good artist and a bad artist, a good therapist and a bad therapist? What would be the difference between someone who is good at therapeutic touch and someone who is not? One difference might be a lack of ego. An artist who feels that something is flowing through her is a quite different artist from one who goes on an ego trip. The same may be true of psychiatrists, or nurses.

Peter Gorski: Like Louise, I was struck by the description of channeling energy through yourself, but unlike Louise, I didn't reference Plato or the Bible. What I thought of was that I chose the profession I did in part because the work is interpersonal. To me, the channeling that was described sounded almost like a defense against using yourself in the healing process. When I think about how a psychiatrist or even I myself work with families, it's to use my own personal reactions to the feelings that I perceive in somebody else to help me understand what they're feeling. So, when I hear about using myself as a conduit for universal energy and about having to depersonalize myself because if I don't I'll block the energy flow, I have a defensive reaction. To me, communication at a personal level is also communication at a therapeutic level. It's the best tool we have.

T. Berry Brazelton: That's an excellent point, Peter. Many people have been trying for a long time to understand the ingredients of a positive therapeutic relationship, and it seems to me that what both the last two papers have emphasized is the crucial nature of that relationship.

What you said to me, Iris, was that the communication systems that are available around labor and delivery are wide open, and I couldn't agree more. At that time they are open for enhancement, as well as for going awry. There are opportunities to use this open system not only for attachment but for the goal of attachment, which ultimately is an autonomous baby. Offering mothers and family members a chance to participate in the pregnancy and birth by using touch as a modality is another enlightening and very exciting idea. I hope you're going to study this further, and look at it systematically.

Clinical Perspectives

PART VII
TOUCH NEAR THE
END OF LIFE

The papers in Part VII show what touch can do to overcome the physical and social isolation of individuals near the end of the life cycle. In "Touch and the Acutely Ill," Ruth McCorkle and Margaret Hollenbach draw on both research and clinical experience. Although individual differences in people's responses to touch abound, these authors suggest that the social support and loving concern communicated through touch may have special value for patients in hospital settings. In a final essay by a gifted practitioner of therapeutic touch, Cathleen Fanslow offers a sensitive appraisal of the touch needs of the very old and dying.

TOUCH AND THE ACUTELY ILL

Ruth McCorkle, R.N., Ph.D.
and Margaret Hollenbach, Ph.D.

In nursing practice we usually assume that touching the patient is a good thing. We assume that touching expresses nurturing and that sick people need to feel nurtured as well as to feel they are receiving competent health care. Clinical experience almost continually reinforces this assumption. However, when we scientifically examine the usefulness of touching in patient care, this assumption becomes a question. How do we know that touching is a good thing — and when, how, and for whom it is most likely to be therapeutic?

Although no more than a handful of studies have been done on touch and the acutely ill, some findings from more general research on touch have interesting implications. We will begin by reviewing these findings. Next, we examine the effects of the hospital environment and the experience of illness on acutely ill patients. Finally, we describe a particular touch program used with cancer patients undergoing bone marrow transplantation.

Cultural and Social Differences

Mainstream, white, North American culture inhibits or at least restricts touching. A convincing demonstration of this has been provided by Sidney Jourard (1966). Jourard simply counted how many times one person touched another while engaged in conversation at a table in a coffee shop in four cities — San Juan, Puerto Rico; London; Paris; and Gainesville, Florida. The score was San Juan 180, Paris 110, London 0, and Gainesville 2. Jourard also discovered that unmarried Americans without a close friend of the opposite sex are hardly touched at all, even by family members, except occasionally on hands, forearms, shoulders, and head.

In short, in this culture extensive touching is confined to sex partners. But this is not a universal human norm; cross-cultural comparison reveals wide variation in the amount, kinds, and contexts of touching allowed in normal daily life. Our society varies too, from family to family and along ethnic and class lines. In some contexts, touch conveys a message about social status. Higher status people touch or initiate touch toward lower status persons, and not the reverse (Henley, 1973; Juni & Brannon, 1981).

Women are touched more than men, and in many social contexts they respond more positively to touch than men, who are apparently more likely to interpret touch in terms of dominance, dependence, or intrusion than as simple contact or nurturing (Sussman & Rosenfeld, 1978). In some contexts both sexes respond more positively to touch when it comes from a person of the opposite sex, even when the touch is unmistakably nonerotic (Alagna et al., 1979).

Whitcher and Fisher (1979) explored sex differences in interpreting touch in the natural environment of the hospital. The experimental situation was a brief presentation by a nurse of information about surgery to preoperative patients, during which the nurse gently touched the patient's hand and then forearm. Female patients who had been touched were less anxious about the surgery, and anticipated less unpleasantness in hospitalization. Male patients were more anxious when they had been touched. "The findings on a variety of measures," the researchers concluded, "suggested that in this context, touch led to positive effects primarily for females" (pp. 93-94).

This conclusion may relate to Jourard's suggestion that a willingness to be touched is a personality trait. "Presumably there are people who freely exchange touches with others, and another population which sharply restricts the points of physical contact" (1966, p. 228). In our culture, men are more likely to be in the latter group and women in the former.

Caregivers' Perceptions of Touching

Touching as a therapeutic event is not so simple as a mechanical procedure or a drug, because it is, above all, an act of communication. As in all embodied communication, the message being sent is not necessarily the same as the message received. While the studies just reviewed concentrated on how receivers interpret touch, other investigators have explored caregivers' perceptions of touching. For example, Aguilera (1967) found that, although touching increased verbal interaction between psychiatric nurses and patients, the nurses felt more comfortable about touching schizophrenic patients than depressive patients, and more comfortable touching younger than older patients.

A reluctance or hesitance about touching the elderly was also found by Tobiason (1981), who asked nursing students to choose words describing the sensations of touching newborn babies and elderly patients. She found that the students used more positive words about newborns than about the elderly, with contrasts such as "warm" versus "dry," and that they became even more positive about the babies after actually touching them, but not about the elderly. Similarly, Barnett (1972) found that nurses touched acutely ill patients significantly less often than those in fair or good condition. She speculated that the nurses' own fear of death and illness might affect their motivation toward touching.

Very Ill Patients: Does Touch Help?

Regardless of possible negative interpretations of touching by male patients or distaste on the side of the healthy physician or nurse, what of the evidence that touching does indeed have positive effects for the acutely ill patient?

First, there is ample evidence that touching has a physiological effect — even when the patient is unconscious. Lynch et al. (1974) found significant heart rate changes during pulse taking or handholding of curarized patients in a shock-trauma unit. Knable (1981) found changes in blood pressure, heart rate, and respiratory rate in acutely ill patients whose hands had been held by nurses for up to three minutes. (How to interpret these changes was another matter.)

McCorkle (1974) hypothesized that a nurse's touching seriously ill patients while talking with them in the hospital setting would produce more positive responses than a similar interaction without touching. In both cases (talk with and without touch) the nurse tried to convey to the individuals that she cared about them and that they were not alone at a time when their outlook or prognosis was very poor. Sixty patients, age 20 to 64 years, were randomly assigned to two groups. The nurse asked the patients how they felt, what had been happening to them, and what they were thinking about as they lay in bed. As the nurse talked, she touched 30 of the patients on the wrist, increasing pressure with each question. The other 30 patients served as untouched controls.

After the interaction, an assistant stayed behind to get the patient's opinion about whether the nurse had been interested in him or her and how she showed it. Counting smiling, laughing, crying, and nodding as positive responses, blank looks and raised eyebrows as neutral, and yawns, sighs, frowns, moans, and shaking the head as negative, McCorkle determined that more patients in the experimental group had shown positive facial expressions and the controls, more negative ones. In addition, those who had been touched lay still (neutral) more often and turned away (negative) less often than the controls. On balance, it may be more realistic to expect a seriously ill person to be less negative than more positive when touched.

The Hospital Environment

For the acutely ill, the nature of the hospital setting does much to determine responses to touch. Norman Cousins observed in *Anatomy of An Illness* (1979) that a hospital is no place for a person who is seriously ill. As a patient he felt that hospital routine regularly took precedence over the human aspects of care, negatively affecting his own recovery. There is increasing concern among health professionals that environment plays a significant role in the etiology of disease, in adaptation to illness, and in recovery.

An adequate social support system is an environmental factor that is thought to reduce susceptibility to disease (Cassel, 1976), and a number of studies have produced reasonably convincing evidence implicating lack of social support in disease genesis (McFarlane et al., 1980). Hospitalization changes the quality and quantity of the support a patient receives from his or her social system, generally not for the better.

In addition, hospitalization is known to have the potential for being very invasive of a patient's personal space (Geden & Begeman, 1981). Patients, from the viewpoint of hospital staff, are not assigned territories. Instead, they are temporary occupants of specified areas in the hospital to which all authorized personnel appropriately have access. Psychologically, of course, ill people bring their own personal space with them to the hospital, but their concept of that space can be drastically altered during hospitalization. For example, Tolor and Donnon (1969) found that the longer patients are hospitalized, the smaller their personal space preference.

Health care professionals appear to have no reluctance about intruding into a patient's personal space. The ill person must stay in bed and permit a host of strangers to observe, move, and monitor his or her body and disease. Nowhere is this intrusion greater than in critical care units such as coronary care units, burn units, and trauma centers. Patients in these units are continuously monitored. They quickly learn they have little or no control over their physical environment, not even over the inside of their bodies.

The Nature of Illness

As a young medical student, Selye (1956) observed that physicians tend to concentrate on a patient's specific disease without giving any attention to what he called "the syndrome of being sick." Today we find it useful to distinguish between this syndrome, which is illness, and an abnormality in the structure and function of the body, which is disease (see Fabrega, 1979; Eisenberg, 1979). Traditionally, physicians have diagnosed and treated diseases, but patients universally suffer illnesses.

Illness is a stressful event for most people, especially if it occurs suddenly and threatens the future. During the acute phase of an illness, the person temporarily withdraws from adult responsibility and is dependent upon others for care. In this situation, the patient has a tendency to reach backward in time for modes of communication that had some success during earlier periods of stress. The use of touch and physical closeness may be the most important way to communicate to acutely ill persons that they are important as human beings and that their recovery is related to their desire to improve.

Yet patients in critical care units are seldom touched in nontechnical ways — and not even the inside of the body is treated as personal space. Some important questions need to be answered. Under what conditions do patients' needs for human contact take precedence over their needs for mechanical care and their own personal space? Should specific structured touching interventions be developed for patients in critical care environments? If so, what effects would such interventions have on recovery?

A Structured Touch Program

For the last several years, the senior author has been a consultant to the nursing staff at the Fred Hutchinson Cancer Comprehensive Research Center in Seattle. Both adults and children are treated at the center for bone marrow transplantation, which is a procedure to replace diseased marrow cells with the bone marrow stem cells from a normal, healthy donor. The great danger in bone marrow transplantation is that the patient will die from infection if the transplant is not successful, and extraordinary measures are taken to prevent infection. As consultant, McCorkle recommended structured touching experiences between nurse and patient to mitigate the stressful effects of the unusual conditions of treatment.

Patients are assigned to either a laminar flow room or a private hospital room. In the laminar flow room all materials brought into the room must be sterilized and both staff and family members must wear protective clothing. There is no skin-to-skin contact with the patient for 35 to 40 days. In all, a successful transplant takes at least 100 days.

These patients, who come from all over the world and from various cultural backgrounds, have a 50 percent chance of survival. They experience multiple procedures that are painful and exhausting. At times they are extremely fatigued and have little energy to interact with others, especially if the transplanted bone marrow is not accepted and the patient progressively dies. Often these patients feel confused, alone, and isolated. They want human contact but retreat when someone touches them because their memories are filled with only the pain and not the pleasure associated with touching.

We have found that structured experiences in which the nurse very gradually establishes a relationship with the patient may enhance the patient's quality of living during the transplant process. The formula used may differ between men and women, adults and children. An example of an experience for a man 43 years old and a nurse who is 26 years old would be:

Days 1 and 2: Nurse remains about five feet from patient during interaction.

Day 3: Nurse moves within three feet to interact.

Day 4: Nurse moves within one foot of patient.

Day 5: Nurse interacts with patient using touch in some systematic and nonprocedural way (such as hand-holding).

It is recommended that only one or two nurses participate in this structured experience, and that they be nurses who have limited responsibility for the procedural aspects of care.

Clinically we have observed that these steps are especially important in establishing a relationship with children and helping them tolerate the invasive procedures. The outcomes observed have been improved self-concept, less depression, and a shorter overall hospital stay. Clearly, these recommended experiences need to be formalized into protocols that are pilot-tested and revised.

Research is needed to determine if touching acutely ill patients in noninvasive ways over time will affect their sense of who they are and eventually their recovery. Although recent studies show a clear shift in emphasis from disease to the human beings in whom the disease exists, the knowledge we have gained about human beings and their responses is minimal in relation to what is needed.

DISCUSSION

Seymour Levine: The importance of a strong social support system has been demonstrated repeatedly, in animal studies as well as human studies. We have some marvelous data showing that if you subject animals in a social group to environmental stress, they do not show a physiological response. They do show a response when they're alone. Other recent work indicates that people who are very high on a loneliness scale, for example, show more immunological incompetence. There are also data relating social support or the lack of it to complications of pregnancy, and to the behavior of combat personnel during the Vietnam war. It's a very profound variable.

Jerold Lucey: Ruth, do the people who come to the hospital for bone marrow transplants know what they're getting into? How do you warn them about what it means to get a transplant?

Ruth McCorkle: That's one of the most devastating things about it. Most people come from a distance. Their referring physician is the one who has prepared them, and I'm not sure that person knows what is really going to happen. There's a point of no return, too. Their community has raised all this money for them, and they almost feel they'll betray people if they don't go through with it.

Elizabeth McAnarney: Is there a television set in the laminar flow room?

Ruth McCorkle: Yes. As a matter of fact, one of the biggest and most important things that has happened to these patients is video games. The amount of physical touching that goes on between family members and patients sitting on the bed together playing video games is a most rewarding thing to see.

William Greenough: One of the issues that your work raises, Ruth, which should be empirically decided, is whether touch is "magic" in some way or whether it's not particularly special, as long as you communicate concern. The wave of this meeting seems to be that touch is special, but it may not be.

T. Berry Brazelton: I don't think we can ignore in the medical professions the need to use symbolic modalities like touch to convey the fact that we are going to take over what control we can and try to help. Even if we can't save somebody, we certainly can do that.

However, touch is not the only modality that can be used. We've been looking at immunological failures in children at Boston Children's Hospital, and we've been trying to reach these children in other ways, too — through eye contact, for instance. At first, when they've been isolated for a long time, the children give us a defensive smile, sort of a grimace. Later, when they are really smiling and accepting interpersonal communication via visual, auditory, and other modalities, then we think we're on the right wavelength with them.

Susan Rose: I agree that we should question the idea that touch has unique effects. Certainly in all the work that we've done with preterm infants, if we find deficits in responses to tactile stimuli, we also find deficits in responses to visual stimuli and in the ability to integrate information from various sense systems.

William Greenough: There is probably nothing "magic" and possibly nothing very special about cutaneous activation per se. The important consideration from the clinical perspective is to find the optimal conditions for treating patients, ranging from premature infants to older patients and those likely to die. Touch may be of value in many cases, but so may anything that mitigates the inhospitable environment of the hospital. Many types of intervention have potential value.

Anneliese Korner: In many hospitals, particularly university hospitals, if you come up with a good, common-sense, and humane proposition and you ask for permission to implement it, the answer usually is: Show me the evidence that it does any good. One can play the game and look for evidence in order to get it done, but there is something very wrong with this attitude.

From a humanistic point of view, it should not be necessary to have to do research on touch to prove its effectiveness. It seems amply clear that touch gives comfort to patients, and that is reason enough to provide it.

Kathryn Barnard: In American institutions, particularly hospitals, it's important to show that you've accomplished things. A humanistic approach runs counter to being efficient. One of the reasons we need supporting data is so that the medical and nursing staff can take time to be human.

Paul Satz: I might prefer just to do what seems right, but I think we have to be somewhat hard-nosed about it. An experimental design that can't demonstrate an effect is a poor experimental design, unless nothing is happening. I have to disagree with the implication that humanism is incompatible with science.

Ruth McCorkle: I think there can be a combination of the two. We just haven't looked at all the right variables. In other words, there are certain types of patients for whom one thing is good and others for whom another thing is good. We need to define subgroups of patients, using individual factors of personality and temperament — human qualities. But that doesn't mean these factors can't be part of an experimental design. In fact, I think they have to be if we're to make any valid generalizations.

T. Berry Brazelton: In our work with immunological patients, we found that when we and the staff became convinced we could reach these children, the whole ambience of the floor changed. I guess you could call it a Hawthorne effect, but it was very powerful.

Elizabeth McAnarney: There's a tremendous contrast between the environment of our adolescent in-patient unit and the environment of the adult unit. In our unit, patients who are not critically ill wear their own clothes, and they can have friends in any time they want. We have a room where no medical procedures are done, a teen canteen. The unit works very well. In the adult unit, the patients wear nightgowns all day and the window shades are sometimes pulled down. The atmosphere is oppressive, and illness behavior is reinforced.

But I don't think you need data to change this kind of thing. It's very obvious, and I think most hospitals will agree to change the routine if you make a serious effort to show them a better way. Research is helpful, of course, but it doesn't necessarily need to come first.

T. Berry Brazelton: Nurses seem to have fewer problems with burn-out if you give them some back-up for what they're doing and free up this humanism on their part. In our premie nursery, we got rid of burn-out almost completely by giving the nurses some intellectual back-up for what they would like to do anyway.

William Greenough: Another reason for collecting data is that if you don't, you may miss some very important things. For example, data could show that touch is a less important therapeutic intervention than we think. But the studies have to be done. You really have to investigate these things and see what works and what doesn't.

Kathryn Barnard: Well, we're trying to. In order to establish a better research base in nursing, we need financial support, and support from all of you. You must realize that as a scientific endeavor, nursing is very young. We've only been dealing in science for the last 50 years at most. So we haven't had as much experience as some of you here — but we're getting it.

Cathleen Fanslow: Although I am perhaps more a practitioner than a scientist, I would be happy for the marriage of the scientist and the practitioner. I would welcome it.

TOUCH AND THE ELDERLY

Cathleen A. Fanslow, M.A., R.N.

Aging in our American society is not as pleasant or respected as it is in parts of the world where the aged population is revered. For us here in the United States, it seems to be just something that happens to us, an unpleasant occurrence that heralds the sunset time of our lives. Indeed, we seem to view the aging process as a series of changes or losses over which we have no control. Thus, an elder is seen as a person changed and lessened by aging rather than still in the process of becoming.

A great deal of this Round Table has been geared to the touch needs of those at the beginning of life, and rightfully so. But it is equally important to address touch needs at the end of life. It has always fascinated me that two of the earliest sensory experiences in fetal development, touch and pain, are also the experiences that help us stay in contact with life until life ends.

Three Levels of Touch

The road to healthy and normal growth and development is marked by experiences that touch us and make us whole on many levels. The physical or tactile level plays a crucial role in defining our personal life world, our own body view. The psychological level helps us form a deeper internal self-image, so that we can participate in life and evolve from within. Emotional touches may be even more expansive and penetrating than either physical or psychological touches.

The need for touch on all these levels increases with age and wisdom. The empathetic physical touch, hand clasp, embrace, or hug assures elders that in fact they are in safe hands. The manner of the physical touch may become gentler, cognizant of thin skin and frail tissue, but the need for actual physical contact remains paramount with this population. With agitated and confused, withdrawn, and regressed patients, the need is especially clear. Physical touch seems to ground or quiet them so that others can relate to them differently.

Many elderly people require assistive devices to provide a safe, secure environment, such as walkers, wheelchairs, geri chairs, and raised side rails on the bed. These safety devices seem to become fences. They create barriers between us and the elderly, particularly the frail elderly. How difficult it is to touch the old people we have so carefully and carelessly fenced in. Surmounting the barriers means consciously directed, caring touches during transfer activities and reaching past the fences, particularly to those confined behind bed rails, the worst fences of all.

The internal self-image which is established and nurtured by psychological touch takes on even greater importance in the elderly, since the external self is changing and diminishing as the result of aging or illness. Psychological touch makes the difference between living out life and merely surviving for the elderly. Although physical touch is how we actually make contact with them, it is the caring, empathy, compassion, and acceptance of psychological touch that sustains the growth and development of their internal self-image.

Lastly, emotional touch is essential because it makes the aged feel more alive and connected with the world. By reason of illness as well as aging, the elderly often have impaired hearing, visual acuity, mobility, and vitality. These problems can make them feel helpless and vulnerable. The emotional component of touch can reach through the isolation and express love, trust, affection, and warmth.

The myriad meanings of touch have a special place in our interaction with the elderly. In so many ways, they have become the untouched, the forgotten. Touch has always been the special art of the nursing profession, its way of making its unique and special presence felt by those in need of comfort and care. One might say that the art of nursing is made manifest through the touch of the nurse as primary caregiver for the elderly.

Therapeutic Touch

Therapeutic touch has been called the imprimatur of nursing by its discoverer, Dolores Krieger (1975), and is gaining a well-deserved place in our modern-day health care system. It awards the art of touching its rightful place in the art of nursing.

The manner and application of therapeutic touch responds to elders' need for touch on all the levels I have described and in particular to their reduced energy levels. Decreased physical energy in the elderly is very apparent in the need for frequent rest periods, and in physical exhaustion after even mild physical exertion. Decreases in psychological and emotional energy are shown by an inability to maintain deep relationships or intense emotion for any length of time. The distractedness, withdrawal, and regression evident in this population are other indications of diminished energy reserves.

As explained in other papers, therapeutic touch is an energy exchange in which the caregiver, after becoming centered (quiet within), transfers energy through herself and makes it available to the person in need. With the help of this infusion of energy, the person restores his or her own inner balance and harmony.

A major component of therapeutic touch is intentionality, the intent to help or heal. The caregiver tries to imagine the person in need as whole and well, before and during therapeutic touch. Many of the negative effects of disease relate to the individual's self-image. Seeing the elderly as whole and well while channeling energy toward them helps meet their special self-image sustenance needs.

Compassion is a second essential component of therapeutic touch. It is a pure form of love, love without hooks, a love that gives freely to the one in need with no expectations of return. Compassion conveys to the other warmth, respect, and acceptance. It creates a climate of trust and greatly decreases the insecurity, fear, and anxiety that plague the aged.

Since therapeutic touch reaches the elderly person on all levels, it is an effective and holistic therapeutic tool. I know of no other type of treatment that is so integrative for the human person, and since elders in our society fear and are made to think that they are disintegrating, it has special application to this population.

Pilot Studies on Therapeutic Touch

I would like to share with you several pilot studies utilizing therapeutic touch as a primary modality with various groups of elderly people over a five-year period. The first study group included six patients between the ages of 70 and 80 years with advanced arterosclerotic heart disease. The only treatment in addition to medication was therapeutic touch. As a result of continuous, repetitive therapeutic touch treatments, ambulation and mobility were increased from baseline in all six patients to varying degrees. One elder was even transferred back to a more independent floor and reunited with his wife.

In the second year, due to degenerative disease processes, arterosclerotic heart disease, and congestive heart failure, three subjects in this sample became bedbound. Continued use of therapeutic touch with two of the patients, whose skin was in a very fragile condition, contributed to the prevention of decubitus ulcer formation. None occurred, even though the patients were bedridden for six months. The third subject in this group was transferred to another floor with no therapeutic touch practitioner available and developed decubitus ulcers after one month in bed. Upon this patient's return to the original unit, therapeutic touch treatments were resumed, and the decubitus ulcers were healed in three weeks.

The second study concerned four arthritic patients age 68 to 77. Three had long-standing osteoarthritis and one suffered from traumatic stress-related rheumatoid arthritis. Using therapeutic touch as the primary therapy for one year, the symptoms of pain, inflammation, and joint swelling associated with arthritis were decreased, and the improvement has been maintained for a year to date in all four patients.

Subjects in the third study were eight stroke veterans, five right hemiplegics and three left hemiplegics. All were white males age 68 to 72 who had completed a regular physical and occupational therapy program at a small private hospital. After six months of therapeutic touch, the most noticeable response was that spasticity of the affected upper extremity was markedly reduced and pain was drastically lessened. This phenomenon occurred more quickly and was more lasting in right hemiplegics than in left hemiplegics.

After several therapeutic touch treatments, all eight stroke veterans, even those with aphasia, began to indicate by word or gesture that they felt a sensation of flow, current of electricity, or movement in the affected extremity. This sensation coupled with a decrease in pain and spasticity has greatly lessened the fear and anxiety commonly seen with stroke victims.

What has greatly impressed me in using therapeutic touch with stroke patients has been the change in their own way of seeing and relating to themselves. The energy made available to them appears to facilitate a new harmony and balance within them and to obviate some of the disequilibrium and body distortion usually shown in post-stroke periods. The patients seem able to see themselves as two-sided again, which profoundly increases their sense of integrity and wholeness.

Touch and the Dying

My particular approach to the dying process and death transition of our elders utilizes therapeutic touch. When treating people near the end of the life continuum, I am drawn to place my hands on or near the heart, since this is the area of relationship and fear and requires life energy so that the dying can make amends and say good-bye, I'm sorry, or I love you before death occurs. As I hold my hands on or near the heart, I am consciously sending thoughts of peace, love, and wholeness, which makes energy available for patients to finish their business with those who will remain here and decreases pre-death anxiety. The elders feel a deep warmth penetrating the heart area and report a sense of peace and deep calm.

Other hand movements in the therapeutic touch interactions follow the human life flow from head to foot and from body center points out to the upper and lower extremities. These gentle, rhythmic movements give the elder a sense of total body calming and relief as well as of wholeness.

I have taught countless nurses and family members this technique as a primary modality to facilitate the pre-death separation phase and assist the dying person in the transition we call death. It also helps the family adjust to the reality of the imminent transition. The inner balance and harmony that is effected releases the dying to begin the last leg of their personal life journey, which must be embarked upon and finally accomplished essentially alone, as was our initial journey into life.

As family members and nurse practitioners realize that they can facilitate the dying person's separation through this unique, exquisitely human interaction, they are able to begin their own separation and deeper letting go, which is initiated by the sudden yet clear recognition of the reality of the impending death. Therapeutic touch is therefore effective in assisting not only the dying person but the family and the helper with the difficulties of holding on and letting go.

In conclusion, I would like to share with you what I feel are the most profound effects that I have experienced with therapeutic touch and the elderly. I have become convinced that therapeutic touch, more than any other helping modality, on a very deep level responds to the most basic needs of elders. First, it meets their need for actual, tangible, physical touch, which creates a sense of safety and security for them. Second, it meets psychological and affective needs, which enables them to see themselves as becoming, not being lessened. Lastly, but perhaps most importantly, the energy transfer integral to the therapeutic touch interaction decreases the fear, anxiety, and insecurity experienced by elders so that they begin to really live each day rather than just to exist. The functional and affective quality of their lives is greatly improved, and they regain balance and harmony during perhaps the most critical period of their lives.

From my work with the elderly, I have come to realize how much greater is the significance of touch for those at the end of life. Through the medium of therapeutic touch, the nurse's intentionality, desire to help, and compassion for the abandoned elder is actualized, expressed, and made manifest to and for those who are waiting and longing to be touched on so many levels.

DISCUSSION

Paul Satz: It's interesting that you got better results with right hemiplegics than with left in working with stroke patients. There is evidence now that right hemiplegics tend to go into rehabilitation feeling anguished, often aphasic, with comprehension impaired and unable to communicate. These people feel frustrated, and they suffer. Left hemiplegics come in with benign indifference to their problems, by and large. A year later we find that the right hemiplegics have made a great recovery and the left hemiplegics have not, by virtue of being somewhat neglectful of the diseased side or extremity.

Cathleen Fanslow: My observations fall right in line with what you're saying, Paul.

William Greenough: With the brain-injured, the way you treat the person has to vary somewhat depending on the injury. One form of therapy is not going to be good for all.

Paul Satz: Absolutely. For example, a person with left hemiplegia tends to deny or neglect what happens on the left side of space. If you don't under-stand this — if you approach these people from the left and perhaps try to lay hands on them — this could do them a disservice. It could make them very paranoid.

T. Berry Brazelton: Couldn't you pick up on that behaviorally?

Paul Satz: Probably not. They would smile at you. Even though they're devastated, they might seem unresponsive. There's a basic lack of affect.

T. Berry Brazelton: Cathy, at the beginning of this Round Table Renée Weber described three models for an approach to touch: the physical-sensory, which we are more or less stuck with in this culture; the psychological-humanistic, which hopefully we're reaching for; and the field model, which has been tough for some of us here to take. I'd like to thank you for showing us what clinical work based on the field model can do. The idea that safe-and-secure touches can overcome the barriers of age is a beautiful image for all of us.

Sandra Weiss: I'd like to add that I believe the multidisciplinary nature of this conference has been extremely valuable. The diversity of our perspectives will expand the ways that all of us conceptualize our work in the future. It should increase both the validity of our research efforts and the effectiveness of our therapeutic interventions.

Seymour Levine: This has been a very illuminating couple of days for me, in a whole variety of ways. One thing that's come out of it for me is a whole new appreciation of the nursing profession. I don't think I really had any notion of the nature of the different roles and how they can be defined.

Kathryn Barnard: I have a great deal of respect for the descriptive work you've done, Cathy. It's helped us become ready to move from a descriptive level to one that gives us more ability to infer general phenomena. The elderly and the dying have, until very recently, been abandoned by most of us in health care, so my hat is off to you. They need touch very badly.

Cathleen Fanslow: And the world needs it. The world needs it very, very much. What's come through to me here is that there's always a risk, but we have to act anyway. It's hard to give people the courage to try even though we don't know everything. But we must try — the more knowledgeably, the better, of course. We have to take the risk, and not to wait.

References and Suggested Readings

Ader, R., & Cohen, N. 1975. Behaviorally conditioned immunosuppression. *Psychosomatic Medicine* 37:333-340.

Aguilera, D. C. 1967. Relationship between physical contact and verbal interaction between nurses and patients. *Journal of Psychiatric Nursing* 5(1):5-21.

Ainsworth, M. D. S., Blehar, M. L., Waters, E., & Wall, S. 1978. *Patterns of attachment*. Hillsdale, N.J.: Erlbaum.

Alagna, F. J., Whitcher, S. J., Fisher, J. D., & Wices, E. A. 1979. Evaluative reaction to interpersonal touch in a counseling interview. *Journal of Counseling Psychology* 26:465-472.

Averill, J. R. 1968. Grief: Its nature and significance. *Psychological Bulletin* 70:721-748.

Barnett, K. E. 1972. The development of a theoretical construct of the concepts of touch as they relate to nursing. Final Report to U.S. Department of Health, Education and Welfare, Project No. O-G-027.

Bartrop, R. W., Lazarus, L., Luckhurst, E., Kiloh, L. G., & Penny, R. 1977. Depressed lymphoctye function after bereavement. *Lancet* 1:834-836.

Bateson, G., Jackson, D., Haley, J., & Weakland, J. 1956. Toward a theory of schizophrenia. *Behavioral Sciences* 1:251-264.

Benton, A. L. 1959. Right-left discrimination and finger localization: Development and pathology. New York: Hoeber-Harper.

Benton, A. L. 1961. The fiction of the "Gerstmann syndrome." *Journal of Neurology, Neurosurgery and Psychiatry* 24:176-181.

Benton, A. L. 1979. The neurophysiological significance of finger recognition. In M. Bortner (Ed.), *Cognitive Growth and Development*. New York: Brunner/Mazel.

Berkman, L. F., & Syme, S. L. 1979. Social networks, host resistance and mortality: A nine-year follow-up study of Alameda County residents. *American Journal of Epidemiology* 109:186-204.

Berkson, G. 1968. Development of abnormal stereotyped behaviors. *Developmental Psychobiology* 1:118-132.

Boguslawski, M. 1979. The use of therapeutic touch in nursing. *Journal of Continuing Education in Nursing* 10:9-15.

Boguslawski, M. 1980. Therapeutic touch: A facilitator of pain relief. *Topics in Clinical Nursing* 2:1.

Borelli, M., & Heidt, P. (Eds.). 1980. *Therapeutic touch: A book of readings*. New York: Springer.

Bowlby, J. 1953. Some pathological processes set in train by early mother-child separation. *Journal of Mental Science* 99:265-272.

Bowlby, J. 1960. Grief and mourning in infancy and early childhood. *Psychoanalytic Study of the Child* 15:9-52.

Bowlby, J. 1969. *Attachment and loss Vol. 1: Attachment.* London: Hogarth.

Bowlby, J. 1973. *Attachment and loss Vol. 2: Separation.* London: Hogarth.

Bowlby, J. 1980. *Attachment and loss Vol. 3: Loss.* London: Hogarth.

Buber, M. 1970. *I and thou.* R. G. Smith, tr. New York: Scribner.

Campbell, B. A., & Campbell, E. H. 1962. Retention and extinction of learned fear in infant and adult rats. *Journal of Comparative and Physiological Psychology* 55:1-8.

Campbell, B. A., & Spear, N. E. 1972. Ontogeny of memory. *Psychological Review* 79:215-236.

Carmichael, L. 1954. The onset and early development of behavior. In L. Carmichael (Ed.), *Manual of Child Psychology.* New York: Wiley.

Cassel, J. 1974. An epidemiological perspective of psychosocial factors in disease etiology. *American Journal of Public Health* 64:1040-1043.

Cassel, J. 1976. The contribution of the social environment to host resistance. *American Journal of Epidemiology* 104:107-123.

Chang, F.-L. F., & Greenough, W. T. 1982. Lateralized effects of monocular training on dendritic branching in adult split-brain rats. *Brain Research* 232:283-292.

Coleman, P. D., & Riesen, A. H. 1968. Environmental effects on cortical dendritic fields. I. Rearing in the dark. *Journal of Anatomy* 102:363-374.

Cornell, E. H., & Gottfried, A. W. 1976. Intervention with premature human infants. *Child Development* 47:32-39.

Cousins, N. 1979. *Anatomy of an illness as perceived by the patient.* New York: Norton.

Dellon, A. L. 1981. *Evaluation of sensibility and reduction of sensation in the hand.* Baltimore: Williams & Wilkins.

Diamond, M. C., Ingham, C. A., Johnson, R. E., Bennett, E. L., & Rosenzweig, M. R. 1976. Effects of environment on morphology of rat cerebral cortex and hippocampus. *Journal of Neurobiology* 7:75-86.

Diamond, M. C., Johnson, R. E., & Ingham, C. A. 1971. Brain plasticity induced by environment and pregnancy. *International Journal of Neuroscience* 2:171-178.

Diamond, M. C., Johnson, R. E., & Ingham, C. A. 1975. Morphological changes in the young, adult and aging rat cerebral cortex, hippocampus and diencephalon. *Behavioral Biology* 14:163-174.

Diamond, M. C., Johnson, R. E., Ingham, C. A., Rosenzweig, M. R., & Bennett, E. L. 1975. Effects of differential experience on neuronal nuclear and perikarya dimensions in the rat cerebral cortex. *Behavioral Biology* 15:107-111.

Diamond, M. C., Law, F., Rhodes, H., Lindner, B., Rosenzweig, M. R., Krech, D., & Bennett, E. L. 1966. Increases in cortical depth and glial numbers. *Journal of Comparative Neurology* 128:117-126.

Dreyfus-Brisac, C. 1970. Ontogeneses of sleep in human prematures after 32 weeks of conceptional age. *Developmental Psychobiology* 3:91-121.

Edelman, A. M., Kraemer, H. C., & Korner, A. F. 1982. Effects of compensatory movement stimulation on the sleep-wake behaviors of preterm infants. *Journal of the American Academy of Child Psychiatry* 6:555-559.

Edelman, G. M. 1982. Group selection as a basis for higher brain function. In F. B. Schmitt, & F. G. Worden (Eds.), *The Organization of the Cerebral Cortex*. Cambridge: MIT Press.

Edelman, G. M., & Finkel, L. 1984. Neuronal group selection in the cerebral cortex. In G. M. Edelman, W. M. Cowan, & W. E. Gall (Eds.), *Dynamic Aspects of Neocortical Function*. New York: Wiley.

Eisenberg, L. 1979. Disease and illness. *Culture, Medicine and Psychiatry* 1:9-23.

Epstein, G., Weitz, L., Roback, H., & McKee, E. 1975. Research on bereavement: A selective and critical review. *Comprehensive Psychiatry* 16:537-546.

Erickson, M. T. 1976. The relationship between psychological variables and specific complications of pregnancy, labor, and delivery. *Journal of Psychosomatic Research* 20:207-210.

Erikson, E. 1950. *Childhood and society.* New York: Norton.

Erikson, E. 1960. *Identity and the life cycle.* New York: International Universities Press.

Fabrega, H. 1979. The ethnography of illness. *Social Science and Medicine* 13:565-576.

Fanslow, C. 1981. Death: A natural facet of the life continuum. In D. Krieger (Ed.), *Foundations for Holistic Health Nursing Practices: The Renaissance Nurse*. Philadelphia: Lippincott.

Fanslow, C. 1983. Therapeutic touch: A healing modality throughout life. *Topics in Clinical Nursing* 7:72-79.

Feng, A. S., & Rogowski, B. A. 1980. Effects of monaural and binaural occlusion on the morphology of neurons in the medial superior olivary nucleus of the rat. *Brain Research* 189:530-534.

Field, T. In press. Attachment as psychobiological attunement: Being on the same wavelength. In M. Reite, & T. Field (Eds.), *The Psychobiology of Attachment.* New York: Academic Press.

Fisher, S., & Cleveland, S. F. 1968. *Body image and personality,* 2nd ed. New York: Dover.

Floeter, M. K., & Greenough, W. T. 1979. Cerebellar plasticity: Modification of Purkinje cell structure by differential rearing in monkeys. *Science* 206:227-229.

Fraiberg, S. 1977. *Insight from the blind.* New York: Basic Books.

Frank, J. D. 1961. *Persuasion and healing: A comparative study of psychotherapy.* Baltimore: The Johns Hopkins University Press.

Frank, L. K. 1957. Tactile communication. *Genetic Psychology Monographs* 56:209-257.

Freud, S. 1949. The development of the sexual function. In S. Freud (Ed.), *An Outline of Psychoanalysis.* New York: Norton.

Gaensbauer, T. J., & Harmon, R. J. 1982. Attachment behavior in abused/neglected and premature infants. In R. N. Emde, & R. J. Harmon (Eds.), *The Development of Attachment and Affiliative Systems.* New York: Plenum Press.

Geden, E., & Begeman, A. 1981. Personal space preferences of hospitalized adults. *Research in Nursing and Health* 4:237-241.

Geldard, F. 1972. *The human senses,* 2nd ed. New York: Wiley.

Gerstmann, J. 1940. Syndrome of finger agnosia, disorientation for right and left, agraphia and acalculia. *Archives of Neurology and Psychiatry* 44:398-408.

Gibson, J. J. 1962. Observations on active touch. *Psychological Review* 69:477-491.

Globus, A., Rosenzweig, M. R., Bennett, E. L., & Diamond, M. C. 1973. Effects of differential experience on dendritic spine counts. *Journal of Comparative and Physiological Psychology* 82:175-181.

Gorman, W. 1969. *Body image and the image of the brain.* St. Louis: Warren Green.

Gorski, P. A., Hole, W. T., Leonard, C. H., & Martin, J.A. 1983. Direct computer recording of premature infants and nursery care: Distress following two interventions. *Pediatrics* 72:198-202.

Gottfried, A. W. 1981. Environmental manipulations in the neonatal period and assessment of their effects. In V. L. Smeriglio (Ed.), *Newborns and Parents.* Hillsdale, N.J.: Erlbaum.

Gottfried, A. W. 1984a. Environment of newborn infants in special care units. In A. W. Gottfried, & J. L. Gaiter (Eds.), *Infant Stress Under*

Intensive Care: Environmental Neonatology. Baltimore: University Park Press.

Gottfried, A. W. 1984b. Environmental neonatology: Implications for intervention. In A. W. Gottfried, & J. L. Gaiter (Eds.), *Infant Stress Under Intensive Care: Environmental Neonatology.* Baltimore: University Park Press.

Gottfried, A. W., & Rose, S. A. 1980. Tactile recognition memory in infants. *Child Development* 51:69-74.

Gottfried, A. W., Rose, S. A., & Bridger, W. H. 1977. Cross-modal transfer in human infants. *Child Development* 48:118-123.

Gottfried, A. W., Wallace-Lande, P., Sherman-Brown, S., King, J., Coen, C., & Hodgman, J. 1981. Physical and social environment of newborn infants in special care units. *Science* 214:673-675.

Gottlieb, G. 1971. Ontogenesis of sensory function in birds and mammals. In E. Tobach, L. R. Aronson, & E. Shaw (Eds.), *The Biopsychology of Development.* New York: Academic Press.

Goy, R. W., Wallen, K., & Goldfoot, D. A. 1974. Social factors affecting the development of mounting behavior in male rhesus monkeys. In W. Montagna, & W. Sadler (Eds.), *Reproductive Behavior.* New York: Plenum Press.

Green, E. J., Greenough, W. T., & Schlumpf, B. E. 1983. The effects of complex or isolated environments on cortical dendrites of middle-aged rats. *Brain Research* 264:233-240.

Gunnar, M. R., Gonzalez, C. A., Goodlin, B. L., & Levine, S. 1981. Behavioral and pituitary-adrenal responses during a prolonged separation period in infant rhesus macaques. *Psychoneuroendocrinology* 6:65-75.

Haber, W. B. 1958. Reactions to loss of limb: Physiological and psychological aspects. *Annals of the New York Academy of Science* 74:14-24.

Hansen, E. W. 1966. The development of maternal and infant behavior in the rhesus monkey. *Behaviour* 27:107-149.

Harlow, H. F. 1958. The nature of love. *American Psychologist* 13:673-685.

Harlow, H. F. 1962a. Development of the second and third affectional systems in macaque monkeys. In T. T. Tourlentes, S. L. Pollack, & H. E. Himwich (Eds.), *Research Approaches to Psychiatric Problems.* New York: Grune & Stratton.

Harlow, H. F. 1962b. The heterosexual affectional system in monkeys. *American Psychologist* 17:1-9.

Harlow, H. F. 1969. Age-mate or peer affectional system. In D. Lehrman, R. Hinde, & E. Shaw (Eds.), *Advances in the Study of Behavior* Vol.

2. New York: Academic Press.

Harlow, H. F. 1975. Love and aggression. Kittay Scientific Foundation Annual Award Address, New York, New York.

Harlow, H. F., & Harlow, M. K. 1962. The effects of rearing conditions on behavior. *Bulletin of the Menninger Clinic* 26:213-224.

Harlow, H. F., & Harlow, M. K. 1965. The affectional systems. In A. M. Schrier, H. F. Harlow, & F. Stollnitz (Eds.), *Behavior of Nonhuman Primates* Vol. 2. New York: Academic Press.

Harlow, H. F., Harlow, M. K., & Suomi, S. J. 1971. From thought to therapy. *American Scientist* 59:538-549.

Hasselmeyer, E. G. 1964. The premature neonate's response to handling. *American Nurses Association* 11:15-24.

Head, H., & Holmes, G. 1911. *Brain* 34:102.

Heidt, P. 1981. Effects of therapeutic touch on anxiety level of hospitalized patients. *Nursing Research* 1:32-37.

Heimburger, R. F., DeMeyer, W., & Reitan, R. M. 1964. Implications of Gerstmann's syndrome. *Journal of Neurology, Neurosurgery and Psychiatry* 27:52-57.

Hempel, C. G. 1966. *Philosophy of natural science.* Englewood Cliffs, N.J.: Prentice-Hall.

Henley, N.M. 1973. Status and sex: Some touching observations. *Bulletin of the Psychoanalytic Society* 2:91-93.

Hennessy, J. W., & Levine, S. 1979. Stress, arousal, and the pituitary-adrenal system: A psychoendocrine hypothesis. In J. M. Sprague, & A. N. Epstein (Eds.), *Progress in Psychobiology and Physiological Psychology* Vol. 8. New York: Academic Press.

Hennessy, M. B., Heybach, J. P., Vernikos, J., & Levine, S. 1979a. Plasma corticosterone concentrations sensitively reflect levels of stimulus intensity in the rat. *Physiology and Behavior* 22:821-825.

Hennessy, M. B., Kaplan, J. N., Mendoza, S. P., Lowe, E. L., & Levine, S. 1979b. Separation distress and attachment in surrogate-reared squirrel monkeys. *Physiology and Behavior* 23:1017-1023.

Hennessy, M. B., & Levine, S. 1977. Effects of various habituation procedures on pituitary-adrenal responsiveness in the mouse. *Physiology and Behavior* 18:799-802.

Hesse, M. B. 1965. *Forces and fields.* Totowa, N.J.: Littlefield, Adams.

Hinde, R. A. 1966. *Animal behavior.* New York: McGraw-Hill.

Hinde, R.A., & Spencer-Booth, Y. 1967. The behaviour of socially living rhesus monkeys in their first two and a half years. *Animal Behaviour* 15:169-196.

Hinde, R. A., & White, L. 1974. Dynamics of a relationship: Rhesus mother-infant ventro-ventro contact. *Journal of Comparative and Physiological Psychology* 86:8-23.

Hollender, M. 1970. The need or wish to be held. *Archives of General Psychiatry* 22:445-453.

Hollender, M., Luborsky, L., & Scaramella, T. 1969. Body contact and sexual enticement. *Archives of General Psychiatry* 20:188-191.

Hooker, D. 1952. *The prenatal origins of behavior.* Lawrence, Kansas: The University of Kansas Press.

Hoover, D., & Diamond, M.C. 1969. The effects of handling on the morphology of the cerebral cortex in preweaned rats. Unpublished data.

Hubel, D. H., Wiesel, T. N., & LeVay, S. 1977. Plasticity of ocular dominance columns in monkey striate cortex. *Proceedings of the Royal Society* 32:477-522.

Huberty, C. J. 1975. Discriminate analysis. *Review of Educational Research* 45:543-598.

Huch, R., Huch, A., & Lubbers, D. 1981. *Transcutaneous PO₂.* New York: Thieme-Stratton.

Ivy, G. O., & Killackey, H. P. 1981. The ontogeny of the distribution of collosal projection neurons in the rat parietal cortex. *Journal of Comparative Neurology* 195:367-389.

Jacobs, S., & Ostfeld, A. 1977. An epidemiological review of the mortality of bereavement. *Psychosomatic Medicine* 39:344-357.

Jourard, S. M. 1966. An exploratory study of body-accessibility. *British Journal of Social and Clinical Psychology* 5:221-231.

Jowett, B., tr. 1937. *The dialogues of Plato.* New York: Random House.

Juni, S., & Brannon, R. 1981. Interpersonal touching as a function of status and sex. *Journal of Social Psychology* 114:135-136.

Juraska, J. M., Greenough, W. T., Elliott, C., Mack, K. J., & Berkowitz, R. 1980. Plasticity in adult rat visual cortex: An examination of several cell populations after differential rearing. *Behavioral and Neural Biology* 29:157-167.

Kaplan, J., & Russell, M. 1974. Olfactory recognition in the infant squirrel monkey. *Developmental Psychobiology* 7:15-19.

Kasamatsu, T., & Pettigrew, J. D. 1976. Depletion of brain catecholamines: Failure of ocular dominance shift after monocular occlusion in kittens. *Science* 194:206-208.

Kattwinkel, J., Nearman, H. S., Fanaroff, A. A., Katona, P. G., & Klaus, M. H. 1975. Apnea of prematurity: Comparative therapeutic effects of cutaneous stimulation and nasal continuous positive airway pressure. *Journal of Pediatrics* 86:588-592.

Kaufman, I. C., & Rosenblum, L. A. 1969. The waning of the mother-infant bond in two species of macaques. In B. Foss (Ed.), *Determinants of Infant Behavior* Vol. IV. London: Methuen.

Kennedy, J. M. 1978. Haptics. In E. R. Carterette, & M. P. Friedman (Eds.), *Handbook of Perception Vol. VIII: Perceptual Coding.* New York: Academic Press.

Kenshalo, Sr., D. R. 1978. Biophysics and psychophysics of feeling. In E. R. Carterette, & M. P. Friedman (Eds.), *Handbook of Perception Vol. VI B: Feeling and Hurting.* New York: Academic Press.

Killackey, H. P., & Belford, G. R. 1979. The formation of afferent patterns in the somatosensory cortex of the neonatal rat. *Journal of Comparative Neurology* 183:285-304.

Kinsbourne, M. 1968. Developmental Gerstmann syndrome. *Pediatric Clinics of North America* 15:771-778.

Klaus, M. H., & Kennell, J. H. 1976. *Maternal-infant bonding.* St. Louis: Mosby.

Klaus, M. H., & Kennell, J. H. 1982. *Parent-infant bonding,* 2nd ed. St. Louis: Mosby.

Kleitman, N. 1969. Basic rest-activity cycle in relation to sleep and wakefulness. In A. Kales (Ed.), *Sleep Physiology and Pathology: A Symposium.* Philadelphia: Lippincott.

Knable, J. 1981. Handholding: One means of transcending barriers of communication. *Heart and Lung* 10:1106-1110.

Korner, A. F., Forrest, T., & Schneider, P. 1983. Effects of vestibular-proprioceptive stimulation on the neurobehavioral development of preterm infants: A pilot study. *Neuropediatrics* 14:170-175.

Korner, A. F., Guilleminault, C., Van den Hoed, J., & Baldwin, R.C. 1978. Reduction of sleep apnea and bradycardia in preterm infants on oscillating water beds: A controlled polygraphic study. *Pediatrics* 4:528-533.

Korner, A. F., Kraemer, H. C., Haffner, M. E., & Cosper, L. M. 1975. The effects of water bed flotation on premature infants: A pilot study. *Pediatrics* 56:361-367.

Korner, A. F., Ruppel, E. M., & Rho, J.M. 1982. Effects of water beds on the sleep and motility of theophylline-treated preterm infants. *Pediatrics* 70:864-869.

Korner, A. F., & Thoman, E. B. 1970. Visual alertness in neonates as evoked by maternal care. *Journal of Experimental Child Psychology* 10:67-78.

Korner, A. F., & Thoman, E. B. 1972. The relative efficacy of contact and vestibular stimulation in soothing neonates. *Child Development* 43:443-453.

Krieger, D. 1973. The relationship of touch with intent to help or to heal to subjects' in-vivo hemoglobin values: A study in personalized interactions. *Proceedings of the Ninth American Nurses' Association Nursing Research Conference.* New York: American Nurses' Association.

Krieger, D. 1975. Therapeutic touch: The imprimatur of nursing. *American Journal of Nursing* 5:784-787.

Krieger, D. 1979. *The therapeutic touch.* Englewood Cliffs, N.J.: Prentice-Hall.

Krieger, D., Peper, E., & Ancoli, S. 1979. Searching for evidence of physiological change. *American Journal of Nursing* 4:660-662.

Kulka, A. C., Fry, S. T., & Goldstein, F. J. 1960. Kinesthetic needs in infancy. *American Journal of Orthopsychiatry* 30:562.

Kunz, D., & Krieger, D. 1965-1972. *The Pumpkin Hollow Foundation.* Craryville, N.Y.: The Theosophical Society in America.

Kunz, D., & Peper, E. 1982. *Fields and their clinical implications.* Wheaton: The Theosophical Research Institute Monograph.

Kunz, D., & Peper, E. 1982. Fields and their clinical implications, Part I. *American Theosophist* 70:395-401.

Kunz, D., & Peper, E. 1983. Fields and their clinical implications, Part II. *American Theosophist* 71:3-4, 19-20.

Larson, J. R., & Greenough, W. T. 1981. Effects of handedness training on dendritic branching of neurons in forelimb area of rat motor cortex. *Society for Neuroscience Abstract* 7:65.

Laudenslager, M. L., Reite, M., & Harbeck, R. 1982. Suppressed immune response in infant monkeys associated with maternal separation. *Behavioral and Neural Biology* 36:40-48.

Lawson, K., Daum, C., & Turkewitz, G. 1977. Environmental characteristics of a neonatal intensive care unit. *Child Development* 48:1633-1639.

Lefford, A., Birch, H. G., & Green, G. 1974. The perceptual and cognitive bases for finger localization and selective finger movement in preschool children. *Child Development* 45:335-343.

LeVay, S., Wiesel, T. N., & Hubel, D. H. 1980. The development of ocular dominance columns in normal and visually deprived monkeys. *Journal of Comparative Neurology* 191:1-51.

Levine, S. 1983. A psychobiological approach to the ontogeny of coping. In N. Garmezy, & M. Rutter (Eds.), *Stress, Coping and Development in Children.* New York: McGraw-Hill.

Levine, S., Coe, C. L., Smotherman, W. P., & Kaplan, J. N. 1978. Prolonged cortisol elevation in the infant squirrel monkey after reunion with mother. *Physiology and Behavior* 20:7-10.

Levine, S., Weinberg, J., & Brett, L. P. 1979. Inhibition of pituitary-adrenal activity as a consequence of consummatory behavior. *Psychoneuroendocrinology* 4:275-286.

Lindemann, E. 1944. Symptomatology and management of acute grief. *American Journal of Psychiatry* 24:141-148.

Long, J. G., Lucey, J. F., & Philip, A. G. S. 1980. Noise and hypoxemia in the intensive care nursery. *Pediatrics* 65:143.

Long, J. G., Philip, A. G. S., & Lucey, J. F. 1980. Excessive handling as a cause of hypoxemia. *Pediatrics* 65:203.

Lucey, J. F. 1981. Clinical uses of transcutaneous monitoring. *Advances in Pediatrics* 28:27.

Lynch, J. J., Flaherty, L., Emrich, C., et al. 1974. Effects of human contact on the heart activity of curarized patients in a shock-trauma unit. *American Heart Journal* 88:160-169.

Macrae, J. 1979. Therapeutic touch in practice. *American Journal of Nursing* 4:664-665.

Malkasian, D., & Diamond, M. C. 1971. The effect of environmental manipulation on the morphology of the neonatal rat brain. *International Journal of Neuroscience* 2:161-170.

Malmquist, C., Kiresuk, T., & Spano, R. 1966. Personality characteristics of women with repeated illegitimacies: Descriptive aspects. *American Journal of Orthopsychiatry* 36:476-484.

Martin, R. J., Herrell, N., Rubin, D., & Fanaroff, A. 1979. Effect of supine and prone positions on arterial oxygen tension in the preterm infant. *Pediatrics* 63:528-531.

Mason, W. A. 1968. Early social deprivation in the nonhuman primates: Implications for human behavior. In D. C. Glass (Ed.), *Environmental Influences*. New York: Rockefeller University Press and Russell Sage Foundation.

Mason, W. A. 1970. Motivational factors in psychosocial development. *Nebraska Symposium on Motivation* 18:35-67.

Mason, W. A. 1979. Wanting and knowing: A biological perspective on maternal deprivation. In E. B. Thoman (Ed.), *Origins of the Infant's Social Responsiveness*. Hillsdale, N.J.: Erlbaum.

Mazis, G. A. 1971. Touch and vision: Rethinking with Merleau-Ponty and Sartre on the caress. *Psychology Today* 23:321-328.

McCorkle, R. 1974. The effects of touch on seriously ill patients. *Nursing Research* 23:125-132.

McFarlane, A., Norman, G., Streinei, D., Roy R., & Scott, D. 1980. A longitudinal study of the influence of the psychosocial environment on health status: A preliminary report. *Journal of Health and Social Behavior* 21:124-133.

McNichols, T. 1975. Some effects of different programs of enrichment on the development of premature infants in the hospital nursery. Unpublished doctoral dissertation, Purdue University.

Mendoza, S. P., Smotherman, W. P., Miner, M. T., Kaplan, J., & Levine S. 1978. Pituitary-adrenal response to separation in mother and infant squirrel monkeys. *Developmental Psychobiology* 11:169-175.

Merzenich, M. M., & Kaas, J. H. 1980. Principles of organization of sensory-perceptual systems in mammals. In J. M. Sprague, & A. N. Epstein (Eds.), *Progress in Psychobiology and Physiological Psychology* Vol. 9, New York: Academic Press.

Merzenich, M. M., Kaas, J. H., Wall, J. T., Sur, M., Nelson, R. J., & Felleman, D. J. 1983. Progression of change following median nerve section in the cortical representation of the hand in the Areas 3b and 1 in adult owl and squirrel monkeys. *Neuroscience* 10:639-665.

Merzenich, M. M., Nelson, R. J., Stryker, M. P., Cynader, M., Schoppman, A., & Zook, J.M. In press. Somatosensory cortical map changes following digit amputation in adult monkeys. *Journal of Comparative Neurology.*

Miller, N. E. 1978. Biofeedback and visceral learning. *Annual Review of Psychology* 24:373-404.

Miller, N. E. 1981. An overview of behavioral medicine: Opportunities and dangers. In S. M. Weiss, J. A. Herd, & B. H. Fox (Eds.), *Perspectives on Behavioral Medicine.* New York: Academic Press.

Mineka, S., & Suomi, S. J. 1978. Social separation in monkeys. *Psychological Bulletin* 85:1376-1400.

Mirmiran, M., & Uylings, H. B. M. 1983. The environmental enrichment effect upon cortical growth is neutralized by concomitant pharmacological suppression of active sleep in female rats. *Brain Research* 261:331-334.

Mitchell, G. D. 1970. Abnormal behavior in primates. In L. A. Rosenblum (Ed.), *Primate Behavior.* New York: Academic Press.

Montagu, A. 1971. *Touching: The human significance of the skin.* New York: Columbia University Press.

Morris, D. 1967. *The naked ape.* New York: Dell.

Nagy, Z. M., & Murphy, J. M. 1974. Learning and retention of a discriminated escape response in infant mice. *Developmental Psychobiology* 7:185-192.

Newton, Niles. 1977. The effect of fear and disturbance on labor. *21st Century Obstetrics Now* 1:61-71.

Nightingale, F. 1859/1957. *Notes on nursing: What it is, and what it is not.* Philadelphia: Lippincott.

Nyman, A. J. 1967. Problem solving in rats as a function of experience at different ages. *Journal of Genetic Psychology* 110:31-39.

Ouseley, S. G. J. 1976. *The science of color healing.* Essex, England: L. N. Fowler.

Panksepp, J., Siviy, S. M., & Normansell, L. A. In press. Brain opioids and social emotions. In M. Reite, & T. Field (Eds.), *The Psychobiology of Attachment.* New York: Academic Press.

Parkes, C. M. 1972. *Bereavement.* New York: International University Press.

Parsons, T. 1964. *Social structure and personality.* London: Free Press.

Peabody, J. L., Gregory, G. A., Willis, M. M., et al. 1979. Failure of conventional monitoring to detect apnea resulting in hypoxemia. *Birth Defects* 15:275.

Peterson, G. H. 1981. *Birthing normally: A personal growth approach to childbirth.* Berkeley, California: Mindbody.

Peto, A. 1972. Body image and depression. *International Journal of Psychoanalysis* 53(2):259-263.

Piaget, J. 1980. *Adaptation and intelligence: Organic selection and phenocopy.* S. Eames, tr. Chicago: University of Chicago Press.

Poeck, K., & Orgass, B. 1966. Gerstmann's syndrome and aphasia. *Cortex* 2:421-437.

Powell, L. F. 1974. The effect of extra stimulation and maternal involvement on the development of low-birth-weight infants and on maternal behavior. *Child Development* 45:106-113.

Prescott, J. W. 1970. Early somatosensory deprivation as an ontogenetic process in the abnormal development of brain and behavior. In E. Goldsmith, & J. Morr-Jankowski (Eds.), *Medical Primatology.* Basel, Switzerland: Karger.

Quinn, J. 1981. An investigation of the effects of therapeutic touch done without physical contact on state anxiety of hospitalized cardiovascular patients. Unpublished doctoral dissertation, New York University.

Reite, M., & Capitanio, J. P. In press. On the nature of social separation and social attachment. In M. Reite, & T. Field (Eds.), *The Psychobiology of Attachment.* New York: Academic Press.

Reite, M., Harbeck, R., & Hoffman, A. 1981. Altered cellular immune response following peer separation. *Life Sciences* 29:1133-1136.

Reite, M., Pauley, J. D., Kaufman, I. C., Stynes, A. J., & Marker, V. 1974. Normal physiological patterns and physiological-behavioral correlations in unrestrained monkey infants. *Physiology and Behavior* 12:1021-1033.

Reite, M., & Short, R. 1983. Maternal separation studies: Rationale and methodological considerations. In K. Miczek (Ed.), *Ethopharmacology: Primate Models of Neuropsychiatric Disorders*. New York: Alan R. Liss.

Reite, M., Short, R., Kaufman, I. C., Stynes, A. J., & Pauley, J.D. 1978. Heart rate and body temperature in separated monkey infants. *Biological Psychiatry* 13:91-105.

Rice, R. 1977. Neurophysiologic development in premature infants following stimulation. *Developmental Psychology* 13:69-76.

Robertson, J. 1953. Some responses of young children to loss of maternal care. *Nursing Times* 49:382-386.

Rose, S. A., Gottfried, A. W., & Bridger, W. H. 1978. Cross-modal transfer in infants: Relationship to prematurity and socioeconomic background. *Developmental Psychology* 14:643-652.

Rose, S. A., Gottfried, A. W., & Bridger, W. H. 1979. Effects of haptic cues on visual recognition memory in full-term and preterm infants. *Infant Behavior and Development* 2:55-67.

Rose, S. A., Gottfried, A. W., & Bridger, W. H. 1983. Infants' cross-modal transfer from solid objects to their graphic representations. *Child Development* 54:686-694.

Rose, S. A., Schmidt, K., & Bridger, W. H. 1976. Cardiac and behavioral responsivity to tactile stimulation in premature and full-term infants. *Developmental Psychology* 12:311-320.

Rose, S. A., Schmidt, K., Riese, M. L., & Bridger, W. H. 1980. Effects of prematurity and early intervention on responsivity to tactual stimuli: A comparison of preterm and full-term infants. *Child Development* 51:416-425.

Rosenzweig, M. R., Bennett, E., Diamond, M., Wu, S. Y., Slagle, R., & Saffran, E. 1969. Influence of environmental complexity and visual stimulation on development of occipital cortex in the rat. *Brain Research* 14:427-445.

Rothblat, L. A., & Schwartz, M. L. 1979. The effect of monocular deprivation on dendritic spines in visual cortex of young and adult albino rats; evidence for a sensitive period. *Brain Research* 161:156-161.

Rubin, R. 1963. Maternal touch. *Nursing Outlook* 2:828-831.

Ruppenthal, G. C., Arling, G. L., Harlow, H. F., Sackett, G. P., & Suomi, S. J. 1976. A 10-year perspective of motherless mother monkey behavior. *Journal of Abnormal Psychology* 85:341-349.

Sackett, G. P. 1968. Abnormal behavior in laboratory reared rhesus monkeys. In M. Fox (Ed.), *Abnormal Behavior in Animals*. Philadelphia: Saunders.

Sackett, G. P., Holm, R., & Ruppenthal, G. C. 1976. Social isolation rearing: Species differences in behavior of macaque monkeys. *Developmental Psychobiology* 10:283-288.

Sackett, G. P., Ruppenthal, G. C., Fahrenbruch, C., Holm, R.A., & Greenough, W. T. 1981. Social isolation rearing effects in monkeys vary with genotype. *Developmental Psychobiology* 17:313-318.

Satz, P., Fletcher, J. M., Morris, R., & Taylor, H. G. In press. A developmental study of finger localization and reading achievement. In K. C. Brown (Ed.), *Touch*. Boston: Lippincott-Ballinger.

Satz, P., Taylor, H. G., Friel, J., & Fletcher, J. M. 1978. Some developmental and predictive precursors of reading disability. In D. Pearl, & A. L. Benton (Eds.), *Dyslexia: An Appraisal of Current Knowledge*. New York: Oxford University Press.

Scarr-Salapatek, S., & Williams, M. L. 1973. The effects of early stimulation on low-birthweight infants. *Child Development* 44:94-101.

Schaeffer, J. S. 1982. The effects of gentle human touch on mechanically ventilated very-short-gestation infants. *Maternal-Child Nursing Journal, Monograph 12*, 11(4).

Schilder, P. 1950. *Image and appearance of the human body*. New York: International Universities Press.

Schleifer, S. J., Keller, S. E., Camerino, M., Thornton, J. C., & Stein, M. 1983. Suppression of lymphocyte stimulation following bereavement. *Journal of the American Medical Association* 250:374-377.

Scott, S., & Richards, M. 1979. Nursing low-birthweight babies on lambswool. *Lancet* 1:1028.

Seay, B. M., Alexander, B. K., & Harlow, H. F. 1964. Maternal behavior of socially deprived rhesus monkeys. *Journal of Abnormal and Social Psychology* 69:345-354.

Seay, B. M., Hansen, E. W., & Harlow, H. F. 1962. Mother-infant separation in monkeys. *Journal of Child Psychology and Psychiatry* 3:123-132.

Seay, B. M., & Harlow, H. F. 1965. Maternal separation in the rhesus monkey. *Journal of Nervous and Mental Diseases* 140:434-441.

Seiler, C., Cullen, J. S., Zimmerman, J., & Reite, M. 1979. Cardiac arrhythmias in infant pigtail monkeys following maternal separation. *Psychophysiology* 16:130-135.

Selye, H. 1956. *Stress of life*. New York: McGraw-Hill.

Sherman, S. M., & Spear, P. D. 1982. Organization of visual pathways in normal and visually deprived cats. *Physiological Review* 62:738-855.

Siqueland, E. R. 1973. Biological and experiential determinants of exploration in infancy. In L. Stone, H. Smith, & C. Murphy (Eds.), *The Competent Infant*. New York: Basic Books.

Sotelo, C., & Palay, S. L. 1971. Altered axons and axon terminals in the lateral vestibular nucleus of the rat. Possible example of axonal remodeling. *Laboratory Investigation* 25:653-671.

Sparrow, S., & Satz, P. 1970. Dyslexia, laterality and neuropsychological development. In D. J. Bakker, & P. Satz (Eds.), *Specific Reading Disability*. Rotterdam, The Netherlands: Rotterdam University Press.

Speidel, B. D. 1978. Adverse effects of routine procedures on preterm infants. *Lancet* 1:864-865.

Spencer-Booth, Y., & Hinde, R. 1971. Effects of brief separations from mothers during infancy on behavior of rhesus monkeys 6-24 months later. *Journal of Child Psychology and Psychiatry and Allied Disciplines* 12:157-172.

Spillane, J. 1942. Disturbances of the body scheme. *Lancet* 2:42-44.

Spitz, R. A. 1946. Anaclitic depression. *Psychoanalytic Study of the Child* 2:313-342.

Steklis, H., & Kling, A. In press. Neurobiology of affiliative behavior in nonhuman primates. In M. Reite, & T. Field (Eds.), *The Psychobiology of Attachment*. New York: Academic Press.

Suomi, S. J. 1979a. Peers, play, and primary prevention in primates. In M. Kent, & J. Rolf (Eds.), *Primary Prevention of Psychopathology* Vol. 3. Hanover, N.H.: Press of New England.

Suomi, S. J. 1979b. Differential development of various social relationships by rhesus monkey infants. In M. Lewis, & L. A. Rosenblum (Eds.), *Genesis of Behavior Vol. 2.: The Child and Its Family*. New York: Plenum Press.

Suomi, S. J. 1983. Social development in rhesus monkeys: Consideration of individual differences. In A. Oliverio, & M. Zappella (Eds.), *The Behavior of Human Infants*. New York: Plenum Press.

Suomi, S. J., Collins, M. L., Harlow, H. F., & Ruppenthal, G. C. 1976. Effects of maternal and peer separations on young monkeys. *Journal of Child Psychology and Psychiatry* 17:101-112.

Suomi, S. J., & Harlow, H. F. 1975. The role and reason of peer friendships in rhesus monkeys. In M. Lewis, & L. A. Rosenblum (Eds.), *Friendship and Peer Relations*. New York: Wiley.

Sussman, N. M., & Rosenfeld, H. M. 1978. Touch, justification and sex: Influences on the aversiveness of spatial violations. *Journal of Social Psychology* 106:215-225.

Thoman, E. B., & Korner, A. F. 1971. Effects of vestibular stimulation on the behavior and development of infant rats. *Developmental Psychology* 5:92.

Tobiason, S. J. 1981. Touching is for everyone. *American Journal of Nursing* 81(4):728-730.

Tolor, A., & Donnon, M. S. 1969. Psychological distance as a function of length of hospitalization. *Psychological Reports* 25:851-855.

Turkewitz, G., & Kenny, P. A. 1982. Limitations on input as a basis for neural organization and perceptual development; a preliminary theoretical statement. *Developmental Psychobiology* 15:357-368.

Tyler, N. 1972. A stereognostic test for screening tactile sensation. *American Journal of Occupational Therapy* 26:256-260.

Uylings, H. B. M., Kuypers, K., & Veltman, W. A. M. 1978. Environmental influences on the neocortex in later life. In M. A. Corner et al. (Eds.), *Maturation of the Nervous System, Progress in Brain Research* Vol. 48. Amsterdam: Elsevier/North Holland.

Van der Loos, H., & Woolsey, T. A. 1973. Somatosensory cortex: Structural alterations following early injury to sense organs. *Science* 179:395-398.

Vogt, J., & Levine, S. 1980. Response of mother and infant squirrel monkeys to separation and disturbance. *Physiology and Behavior* 24:829-832.

Wake, F. R. 1957. Finger localization scores in defective children. Paper presented at meeting of Canadian Psychological Association, Ontario, June 1957.

Wapner, S. 1965. *The body percept.* New York: Random House.

Weber, R. 1981. Philosophical foundations and frameworks for healing. In M. Borelli, & P. Heidt (Eds.), *Therapeutic Touch: A Book of Readings.* New York: Springer.

Weber, R. 1982. The enfolding-unfolding universe: A conversation with David Bohm. In K. Wilber (Ed.), *The Holographic Paradigm and Other Paradoxes.* Boulder: Shambhala.

Weiss, S. 1975. *Familial tactile correlates of body image in children.* Unpublished doctoral dissertation, University of California, San Francisco.

Weiss, S. 1978. The language of touch: A resource to body image. *Issues in Mental Health Nursing* 1:17-29.

Weiss, S. 1979. The language of touch. *Nursing Research* 28:76-80.

Whitcher, S. J., & Fisher, J. D. 1979. Multidimensional reaction to therapeutic touch in a hospital setting. *Journal of Personality and Social Psychology* 36:87-96.

White, B. L., & Castle, P. W. 1964. Visual exploratory behavior following postnatal handling of human infants. *Perceptual and Motor Skills* 18:497-502.

Willis, F. N., & Reeves, D. L. 1976. Touch interactions in junior high school students in relation to sex and race. *Developmental Psychology* 12:91-92.

Willis, F. N., Reeves, D. L., & Buchanan, D. R. 1976. Interpersonal touch in high school relative to sex and race. *Perceptual and Motor Skills* 43:843-847.

Witkin, H. et al. 1962. *Psychological differentiation.* New York: Wiley.

Witkin, H., & Dyk, R. B. 1974. *Psychological differentiation.* Hillsdale, N.J.: Erlbaum.

Wolff, P. 1966. The causes, controls, and organization of behavior in the neonate. *Psychological Issues, Monograph 17,* 5(1).

Woolsey, T. A., & Wann, J. R. 1976. Areal change in mouse cortical barrels following vibrissal damage at different postnatal ages. *Journal of Comparative Neurology* 170:53-66.

Zarzecki, P., & Wiggin, D. M. 1982. Convergence of sensory inputs upon projection neurons of somatosensory cortex. *Experimental Brain Research* 48:28-42.